Instructor's Resource Manual

Chemistry
Concepts
and Connections

Instructor's Resource Manual

Charles H. Corwin

American River College

Chemistry
Concepts
and Connections

Prentice Hall
Englewood Cliffs, New Jersey 07632

© 1994 by **PRENTICE-HALL, INC.**
A Simon & Schuster Company
Englewood Cliffs, N.J. 07632

10 9 8 7 6 5 4 3 2 1

ISBN 0-13-481961-6
Printed in the United States of America

Contents

Preface   **vii**

Demonstration Resources   **ix**

Media Resources   **xi**

Overview Contents with Detailed Objectives   *Objectives* **1–25**

1	A Mathematical Foundation	1
2	Measurement	2
3	Matter and Energy	3
4	Atomic Theory and Structure	5
5	The Periodic Table	6
6	Naming Chemical Compounds	7
7	Chemical Formula Calculations	8
8	Writing Chemical Equations	9
9	Chemical Equation Calculations	11
10	Modern Atomic Theory	11
11	Chemical Bonding	12
12	The Gaseous State	13
13	Liquids, Solids, and Water	15
14	Solutions	16
15	Acids and Bases	17
16	Chemical Equilibrium	19
17	Oxidation and Reduction	21
18	Advanced Chemical Calculations	22
19	Nuclear Chemistry	23
20	Organic Chemistry	24

Solutions to the Even Exercises   *Solutions* **1–162**

Sample Final Examination   *Final Exam* **1–20**
    Answers to Final Examination

Preface

To the Professor

Over the last 20 years, I have taught introductory chemistry to thousands of students using various technologies and methodologies. These methods have included chemical demonstrations, computer-assisted-instruction (CAI), self-paced learning (PSI), and media presentations including slide, transparency, film, audiotape, and videotape.

It is my experience that each of these supplemental aids have a relatively short "half-life" and must be constantly revised and updated in order to continue to have a strong impact in the classroom. To this end, there is a fresh set of four-color transparencies available as part of the ancillary package. In addition, there is the *New York Times* Contemporary View Program and the ABC News/PH Video Library. Also note the list of current resources for demonstrations and media listed in this Instructor's Resource Manual (IRM).

In terms of a guiding principle, I have achieved the best results when I carefully organize an entire course so that for each topic there is a lecture aid that makes the material more interesting by adding another dimension. That is, I try to provide one or more demos, films, videotapes, or interactive computer programs for each topic within a chapter. A second guiding principle is that each topic should be supported in laboratory by a corresponding experiment. For example, when discussing atomic structure in lecture, I would simultaneously have students perform the experiment *Electron Energy Levels* found in the supplementary laboratory manual.

Flexible Coverage

This text is designed to support the objectives of different courses and the preferences of different professors. In my conversations and communications with other professors, I have become quite aware of the potentially polarizing issues regarding topic sequences for bonding, nomenclature, gas laws, and solutions. Although it is neither advisable nor desirable to try to accommodate every preference, there are many subtle ways of designing a chapter so as to better support a broader range of preferences. As a result of extensive class-testing of different chapter configurations, it is possible to cover selected chapters out of sequence; for example,

- Emphasis on *Chemical Calculations:*
  Chapters 1, 2, 3, 4, 5, 6, 7, 12, 8, 9, 11, 13, 14, 15, 16, and 18.
- Emphasis on *Chemical Reactions:*
  Chapters 3, 1, 2, 4, 5, 6, 7, 8, 9, 11, 12, 13, 14, 15, 16, and 17.
- Emphasis on *Atomic and Molecular Structure:*
  Chapters 1, 2, 3, 4, 5, 10, 11, 6, 7, 8, 9, 12, 13, 14, 15, and 19.

In those courses where time allows for only a very brief treatment, the following sequence is recommended: Chapters 1, 2, 3, 4, 5, 6, 7, 8, 9, 11, 12, 14, 15, and 16. Moreover, the last sections in selected chapters (e.g., Sections 2.11, 5.11, 6.10, 6.11, 9.7, 9.8, 11.9, 12.10, 12.11, 14.10, 14.11, 15.9, 15.10, 15.11) may be deleted without loss of continuity.

Supplements

The text *CHEMISTRY: Concepts and Connections* has an extensive support system for the professor and the following ancillaries are available upon adoption:

- Instructor's Resource Manual
- Test Item File
- 3.5" IBM Test Manager DOS
- 5.25" IBM Test Manager DOS
- Mac Test Manager
- 150 Four-color Transparencies
- "How to Study Chemistry" Booklet
- *New York Times* Contemporary View Program
- ABC News/PH Video Library

Acknowledgments

The peer reviewers along with the colleagues that class-tested the material provided many valuable comments that gave shape and balance to the entire textbook package. Considerate and thoughtful comments were received from each of the individuals listed in the text acknowledgments.

Charles H. Corwin
Department of Chemistry
American River College
Sacramento, CA 95841

Demonstration Resources

Scientific Calculator for Overhead Projector

This is an excellent aid (4 in. by 8 in.) for introducing the handheld calculator to a class of introductory students. The calculator demonstrates basic arithmetic operations using AOS as well as exponential notation. Numerical digits and functions project clearly and this overhead scientific calculator is appropriate for large classrooms. (~$70.00)

Available from: Micro Mole Scientific
1312 North 15th Street
Pasco, WA 99301
(509) 545-4904

Reference Sources for Chemical Demonstrations

- *Chemical Demonstrations — A Sourcebook for Teachers*
Lee R. Summerlin & James L. Ealy, Jr.,
Volume 1 and Volume 2, $21.95 each, $36.95 per set.
- *Chemical Activities — Teacher Edition*
Christie L. Borgford & Lee R. Summerlin

Available from: American Chemical Society
1155 16th Street, N.W.
Washington, D.C. 20036
(800) 227-5558

- *Chemical Demonstrations — A Handbook for Teachers of Chemistry*
Bassam Z. Shakhashiri, Volumes 1 – 4, University of Wisconsin Press.

Plant Tours and Chemistry Teacher Resources

- *CMA — Education Resource Guide*

Contact: Manager, Education Services
2501 M Street, N.W.
Washington, D.C. 20037
(202) 887-1223

Media
Resources

Videotapes

- *World of Chemistry*
  Series Host: Roald Hoffmann
  The series consists of 26 half-hour programs on 13 cassettes including Measurement,
  The Atom, The Periodic Table, and The Mole. "Ingenious, beautiful, exciting."
  $29.95 per 2 program cassette or $350.00 for the entire series.

  Available from: Corporation for Public Broadcasting
  ....1 (800) LEARNER

- *The Mechanical Universe and Beyond*
  Series Host: David Goodstein
  The series consists of 52 half-hour programs on videocassette. This series is more physics
  than chemistry and only selected programs are appropriate. "Alive, breathing, relevant."
  Parts 1 and 2 for $350.00 each, or $650.00 for the entire series.

  Available from: Intellimation
  ....The Annenberg/CPB Project
  .............................P.O. Box 1922
  ....Santa Barbara, CA 93116-1922
  ....1 (800) LEARNER

- *Close-Up on Chemistry: Chemical Demonstrations*
  This 70 minute videotape program includes Barking Dogs, Aladdin's Lamp, Instant Fire,
  The Ammonia Fountain, The Lemonade Reaction, and others.
  $89.95 including teacher's manual. (Catalog No. V-5000)

- *Starting with Safety: An Introduction for the Academic Chemistry Laboratory*
  This 35 minute videotape program includes the use of a Bunsen burner, safety equipment,
  use of thermometers, glass tubing, centrifuges, and avoiding accidents.
  $79.95 including teacher's manual. (Catalog No. V-5100)

  Available from: American Chemical Society
  ....Distribution Office #565
  .............................P.O. Box 57136
  ....West End Station
  ....Washington, D.C. 20037
  ....(800) 227–5558

Instructor's Resource Manual

Chemistry
Concepts
and Connections

Overview Contents
with Detailed Objectives

CHAPTER 1 A Mathematical Foundation

1.1   Uncertainty in Measurement
- To identify the following measuring instruments: metric ruler, graduated cylinder, pipet, and buret.
- To understand that no measurement is exact because all instruments have uncertainty.

1.2   Significant Digits
- To identify the number of significant digits in a given measurement.

1.3   Rounding Off Nonsignificant Digits
- To round off a given measurement to a stated number of significant digits.

1.4   Adding and Subtracting Measurements
- To add and subtract measurements and round off the answer to the proper number of significant digits.

1.5   Multiplying and Dividing Measurements
- To multiply and divide measurements and round off the answer to the proper number of significant digits.

1.6   Exponential Numbers
- To become generally familiar with the concept of exponents and specifically with powers of 10.
- To express a value both as a power of 10 and as an ordinary number.

1.7   Scientific Notation
- To express any number in scientific notation.

1.8   Calculators and Significant Digits
- To use a calculator to multiply and divide ordinary and exponential numbers.
- To express a value obtained from a calculator to the proper number of significant digits.

1.9   Unit Conversion Factors
- To write a unit equation based upon an equivalent relationship.
- To write the two unit conversion factors related to a unit equation.

1.10   Problem Solving by Unit Analysis
- To state and apply the three steps in the unit analysis method of problem solving.

1.11   Percentage
- To apply the concept of percentage.

CHAPTER 2 Measurement

2.1   The Metric System
- To understand the logic and simplicity of the metric system.
- To know the three basic units and symbols of the metric system.
- To write symbols for multiples and fractions of basic units.

2.2   Metric Unit Conversion Factors
- To write equivalent relationships between a basic unit and units having the following metric prefixes: kilo, deci, centi, milli, micro, and nano.
- To write two unit conversion factors derived from an equivalent metric relationship.

2.3   Metric Problems by Unit Analysis
- To review the three steps in the unit analysis method of problem solving.

2.4   Metric–Metric Unit Conversions
- To convert a given metric measurement to another metric unit having a different prefix.

2.5   Metric–English Unit Conversions
- To state the metric equivalent of an inch, pound, and quart.
- To perform metric–English unit conversions.

2.6 Volume by Calculation
- To perform calculations that relate volume to length, width, and thickness of a rectangular solid.
- To convert a given volume measurement to cubic centimeters, milliliters, or cubic inches.

2.7 Volume by Displacement
- To understand the laboratory technique of volume by displacement.

2.8 Density
- To understand the concept of density and state the value for the density of water: 1.00 g/mL.
- To write the unit conversion factors related to a given density.
- To perform calculations that relate density, mass, and volume.

2.9 Temperature
- To state the values for the freezing point and boiling point of water on the Fahrenheit, Celsius, and Kelvin scales.
- To express any temperature measurement using Fahrenheit degrees, Celsius degrees, or Kelvin units.

2.10 Heat and Specific Heat
- To describe the difference between heat and temperature.
- To understand the concept of specific heat and state the value for the specific heat of water: 1.00 cal/g·°C.
- To calculate an unknown quantity for a heat change given any three of the following: heat gain or loss, mass of substance, specific heat of substance, temperature change of substance.

2.11 The International System of Measurement (SI)
- To become familiar with the base units and prefixes of the International System of Units (SI).
- To state the seven base units and symbols of SI.
- To perform conversions between SI units and other measuring units.

CHAPTER 3 Matter and Energy

3.1 Physical States of Matter
- To describe the three physical states of matter in terms of the motion of particles.

3.2 Physical State and Energy
- To understand the relationship of physical state and the amount of attraction between individual particles.
- To relate the temperature of a gas to the kinetic energy and velocity of its molecules.

3.3   Classification of Matter
- To classify a sample of matter as an element, compound, or mixture.

3.4   Names and Symbols of the Elements
- To identify a few of the most abundant elements in the earth's crust, oceans, and atmosphere.
- To state the names and symbols of several common elements.

3.5   Metals, Nonmetals, and Semimetals
- To distinguish between the properties of metallic and nonmetallic elements.
- To predict whether an element is a metal, a nonmetal, or a semimetal using the periodic table.
- To predict the physical state of an element under normal conditions of temperature and atmospheric pressure using the periodic table.

3.6   Compounds and Chemical Formulas
- To apply the law of constant composition to the chemical formula of a compound.
- To relate the number of atoms of each element in a compound to its chemical formula.

3.7   Physical and Chemical Properties
- To classify a property of a substance as physical or chemical.

3.8   Physical and Chemical Changes
- To classify a change in a substance as physical or chemical.

3.9   Law of Conservation of Mass
- To apply the conservation of mass law to a chemical reaction.

3.10   Law of Conservation of Energy
- To distinguish between potential energy and kinetic energy.
- To identify forms of energy including heat, light, chemical, electrical, mechanical, and nuclear energy.
- To apply the conservation of energy law to a chemical reaction.

3.11   Law of Conservation of Mass and Energy
- To apply the conservation of mass and energy law to a chemical change.

4.1   Evidence for Atoms: The Dalton Model
- To describe an atom based upon Dalton's five proposals.

4.2   Evidence for Subatomic Particles: The Thomson Model
- To state the relative charge and mass of the electron and proton.
- To describe the Thomson model of the atom.

4.3   Evidence for a Nuclear Atom: The Rutherford Model
- To draw a diagram of the nuclear atom.
- To state the measurements of an atom and its nucleus.
- To state the relative charge and approximate mass of the electron, proton, and neutron.

4.4   Atomic Notation
- To draw a diagram of an atom given its atomic notation.
- To define and illustrate an isotope.

4.5   Atomic Mass Scale
- To gain an understanding of the atomic mass scale.
- To become familiar with the mass spectrometer, the instrument for determining the mass of an isotope.

4.6   Atomic Mass
- To calculate the atomic mass for an element given the mass and percent abundance of each naturally occurring isotope.
- To state the atomic mass of an element by referring to the periodic table of the elements.

4.7   Evidence for Electron Energy Levels: The Bohr Model
- To describe the Bohr model of the atom.
- To understand the relationship between electron energy levels in an atom and the lines in an emission spectrum.

4.8   Principal Energy Levels and Sublevels
- To designate the energy sublevels within a given electron energy level.
- To determine the maximum number of electrons that can occupy a given energy level or sublevel.

4.9   Arrangement of Electrons by Energy Sublevel
- To list the order of sublevels according to increasing energy.
- To write the predicted electron configuration for selected elements.

CHAPTER 5 The Periodic Table

5.1   Systematic Arrangement of the Elements
- To identify the contribution of Döbereiner, Newlands, Meyer, and Mendeleev in establishing the periodic table of the elements.

5.2   The Periodic Law
- To state the original periodic law proposed by Mendeleev.
- To state the modern periodic law based on Moseley's discovery.

5.3   The Periodic Table of the Elements
- To use the following terms in reference to the arrangement of elements in the periodic table:
    - (a) groups (families) and periods (series)
    - (b) representative elements and transition elements
    - (c) metals, semimetals, and nonmetals
    - (d) alkali metals, alkaline earth metals, halogens, and noble gases
    - (e) lanthanide series and actinide series
    - (f) rare earth elements and transuranium elements
- To designate a group of elements in the periodic table using either the American convention (IA–VIIIA) or the IUPAC convention (1–18).

5.4   Periodic Trends
- To predict the trend in atomic size for groups and periods of elements in the periodic table.
- To predict the trend in metallic character for groups and periods of elements in the periodic table.

5.5   Predicting Properties of Elements
- To predict a reasonable value for a physical property given the values for other elements in the same group.
- To predict the general chemical properties of an element given the chemical behavior of other elements in the same group.

5.6   The $s\,p\,d\,f$ Blocks of Elements
- To correlate the $s\,p\,d\,f$ sublevels with the positions of the elements in the periodic table.
- To write the predicted electron configuration for selected elements using the periodic table.

5.7   Predicting Valence Electrons
- To predict the number of valence electrons for a representative element in the periodic table.

5.8   Electron Dot Formulas of Atoms
- To write the electron dot formula for a representative element in the periodic table.

5.9   Ionization Energy
- To state which group of elements has the highest and which has the lowest ionization energy in their row in the periodic table.
- To predict which element in a pair has the higher ionization energy based upon the general trends in the periodic table.

5.10   Predicting Ionic Charges
- To predict an ionic charge for a representative element in the periodic table.
- To predict metal and nonmetal ions which are isoelectronic with a given noble gas element.

5.11   Electron Configuration of Ions
- To write the predicted electron configuration for ions of selected elements.

CHAPTER 6 Naming Chemical Compounds

6.1   IUPAC Systematic Nomenclature
- To classify a compound as a binary ionic compound, ternary ionic compound, binary molecular compound, binary acid, or ternary oxyacid.
- To classify an ion as a monoatomic cation, monoatomic anion, polyatomic cation, or polyatomic anion.

6.2   Monoatomic Ions
- To write both the Stock system and Latin system names for common monoatomic cations.
- To write systematic names and formulas for common monoatomic anions.
- To predict charges for ions of representative metals and nonmetals using the periodic table.

6.3   Polyatomic Ions
- To write systematic names and formulas for common polyatomic ions.

6.4   Writing Chemical Formulas
- To write neutral formula units for compounds containing monoatomic ions.
- To write neutral formula units for compounds containing polyatomic ions.

6.5 Binary Ionic Compounds
- To determine the ionic charge on a cation in a binary ionic compound.
- To write systematic names and formulas for binary ionic compounds.

6.6 Ternary Ionic Compounds
- To determine the ionic charge on a cation in a ternary ionic compound.
- To write systematic names and formulas for ternary ionic compounds.

6.7 Binary Molecular Compounds
- To write systematic names and formulas for binary molecular compounds.

6.8 Binary Acids
- To write systematic names and formulas for binary acids.

6.9 Ternary Oxyacids
- To write systematic names and formulas for ternary oxyacids.

6.10 Acid Salts
- To write systematic names and formulas for acid salts.

6.11 Predicting Chemical Formulas
- To predict the chemical formula of a compound given the formula of a similar compound.

CHAPTER 7 Chemical Formula Calculations

7.1 Avogadro's Number
- To state the value of Avogadro's number: 6.02×10^{23}.
- To state the mass of Avogadro's number of atoms of any element.

7.2 The Mole Concept
- To state the number of entities (atoms, molecules, formula units) in 1 mole of any substance.
- To perform calculations that relate moles of a substance to the number of particles of substance.

7.3 Molar Mass
- To calculate the molar mass of a substance given its chemical formula.

7.4 Mole Calculations I
- To perform calculations that relate the mass of a substance to its number of atoms, molecules, or formula units.

7.5   Percentage Composition
- To calculate the percentage composition of a compound given the chemical formula of the compound.

7.6   Empirical Formula
- To calculate the empirical formula of a compound given the experimental data from its synthesis.
- To calculate the empirical formula of a compound given its percentage composition.

7.7   Molecular Formula
- To calculate the molecular formula for a molecular compound given its empirical formula and molar mass.

7.8   Molar Volume
- To state the value for the molar volume of any gas at standard temperature and pressure.
- To perform calculations that relate molar mass, molar volume, and the density of a gas at standard temperature and pressure.

7.9   Mole Calculations II
- To perform calculations that relate the STP volume of a gas to its mass and number of molecules.

CHAPTER 8 Writing Chemical Equations

8.1   Evidence for Chemical Reactions
- To state four experimental observations that provide evidence for a chemical reaction.

8.2   Writing Chemical Equations
- To write a chemical equation using formulas and symbols when the description of the chemical reaction is given.

8.3   Balancing Chemical Equations
- To become familiar with the general directions for balancing chemical equations by inspection.
- To gain practice in balancing chemical equations by inspection.

8.4   Classifying Chemical Reactions
- To classify a chemical reaction as one of the following types: combination, decomposition, single replacement, double replacement, or neutralization.

8.5   **Combination Reactions**
- To write balanced chemical equations for combination reactions of a metal and oxygen.
- To write balanced chemical equations for combination reactions of a nonmetal and oxygen gas.
- To write balanced chemical equations for combination reactions of a metal and a nonmetal.

8.6   **Decomposition Reactions**
- To write balanced chemical equations for the decomposition reactions of metal hydrogen carbonate compounds.
- To write balanced chemical equations for the decomposition reactions of metal carbonate compounds.
- To write balanced chemical equations for the decomposition reactions of miscellaneous compounds that evolve oxygen gas.

8.7   **Activity Series**
- To predict whether or not a replacement reaction occurs by referring to the activity series for metals.

8.8   **Single–Replacement Reactions**
- To complete and balance single replacement reactions of a metal in an aqueous solution of an ionic compound.
- To complete and balance single replacement reactions of a metal in an acid.
- To complete and balance single replacement reactions of an active metal in water.

8.9   **Solubility Rules**
- To predict whether or not a compound is soluble in water given the solubility rules for ionic compounds.

8.10   **Double–Replacement Reactions**
- To complete and balance double replacement reactions of two aqueous solutions of ionic compounds.

8.11   **Neutralization Reactions**
- To complete and balance neutralization reactions of an acid and a base.

CHAPTER 9 Chemical Equation Calculations

9.1 Interpreting a Chemical Equation
- To relate the coefficients in a balanced chemical equation to:
    - (a) molecules or formula units of reactants and products
    - (b) moles of reactants and products
    - (c) liters of gaseous reactants and products (at the same conditions)
- To verify the conservation of mass law using the molar masses of reactants and products in a balanced chemical equation.

9.2 Mole–Mole Problems
- To relate moles of any two substances participating in a balanced chemical equation.

9.3 Types of Stoichiometry Problems
- To classify the three basic types of stoichiometry problems: mass–mass, mass–volume, and volume–volume.
- To state the three step procedure for solving a stoichiometry problem given the balanced chemical equation.

9.4 Mass–Mass Stoichiometry Problems
- To perform mass–mass stoichiometry calculations.

9.5 Mass–Volume Stoichiometry Problems
- To perform mass–volume stoichiometry calculations.

9.6 Volume–Volume Stoichiometry Problems
- To perform volume–volume stoichiometry calculations.

9.7 Percent Yield
- To calculate the percent yield for a reaction given the actual yield and theoretical yield.

9.8 Experimental Accuracy and Precision
- To express accuracy and precision for an analysis given the experimental results and the theoretical value.

CHAPTER 10 Modern Atomic Theory

10.1 Bohr Model of the Atom
- To describe the Bohr model of the atom.

10.2 Quantum Theory
- To apply the quantum theory to the description of electrons in atoms.

10.3 Quantum Mechanical Model of the Atom
- To describe the quantum mechanical model of the atom in terms of the probability of finding an electron with a given energy.
- To describe the relative sizes and shapes of *s* and *p* orbitals.

10.4 Distribution of Electrons by Orbital
- To designate the maximum number of electrons in a given orbital, subshell, or shell.

10.5 The Four Quantum Numbers
- To state the allowed values for the four quantum numbers that indicate the energy and location of an electron in an atom.

10.6 Orbital Energy Diagrams
- To write out the electron configuration and orbital diagram for the distribution of electrons in atoms of selected elements.
- To draw an orbital energy diagram for the electrons in hydrogen atoms and non-hydrogen atoms.

10.7 Quantum Notation: (*n, l, m, s*)
- To write a set of four quantum numbers to describe the highest energy electron in an atom of an element.

CHAPTER 11 Chemical Bonding

11.1 Valence Electrons and Chemical Bonds
- To describe valence electron changes for the formation of ionic and covalent bonds.
- To predict whether a compound is held together by ionic or covalent bonds.

11.2 The Ionic Bond
- To describe the formation of an ionic bond between a metal atom and nonmetal atom.

11.3 The Covalent Bond
- To describe the formation of a covalent bond between two nonmetal atoms.

11.4 Electron Dot Formulas of Molecules
- To apply the octet rule to the electron dot formula of a molecule given the arrangement of atoms.
- To write the structural formula for a molecule given the electron dot formula.

11.5   Polar Covalent Bonds
- To state the general electronegativity trends for elements in the periodic table.
- To define and give an example of a polar covalent bond.
- To apply delta notation (δ^+ and δ^-) to a polar bond.

11.6   Nonpolar Covalent Bonds
- To define and give an example of a nonpolar covalent bond.
- To identify the seven nonmetallic elements (H, N, O, F, Cl, Br, and I) that occur naturally as diatomic molecules.

11.7   Coordinate Covalent Bonds
- To define and identify a coordinate covalent bond.

11.8   Polyatomic Ions
- To calculate the total number of valence electrons for a polyatomic ion and write the electron dot formula given the arrangement of atoms.
- To write the structural formula for a polyatomic ion given the electron dot formula.

11.9   Properties of Ionic and Molecular Compounds
- To compare the properties of ionic compounds to those of molecular compounds.
- To relate the properties of compounds to ionic or covalent bonds.

CHAPTER 12 The Gaseous State

12.1   Properties of Gases
- To describe five observed properties of a gas.

12.2   Atmospheric Pressure and the Barometer
- To state standard atmospheric pressure in the following units: atmospheres, millimeters of mercury, torr, centimeters of mercury, inches of mercury, pounds per square inch, and kilopascals.
- To convert a given gas pressure into the following units: atm, mm Hg, torr, cm Hg, in. Hg, psi, and kPa.

12.3   Vapor Pressure
- To understand the concept of vapor pressure and the relationship of boiling point to temperature.

12.4   Dalton's Law of Partial Pressures
- To apply Dalton's Law of Partial Pressures to gases in a mixture.
- To become familiar with the procedure of collecting a gas over water.

12.5   Variables Affecting Gas Pressure
- To identify the three variables that directly affect the pressure exerted by a gas.
- To state whether gas pressure increases or decreases with a given change in volume, temperature, or moles of gas.

12.6   Boyle's Law: Pressure/Volume Changes
- To sketch a graph of the pressure/volume relationship for a gas.
- To calculate the new pressure or volume for a gas after a change in one of these conditions using either (a) modified unit analysis or (b) an algebraic method.

12.7   Charles' Law: Volume/Temperature Changes
- To sketch a graph of the volume/temperature relationship for a gas.
- To calculate the new volume or temperature for a gas after a change in one of these conditions using either (a) modified unit analysis or (b) an algebraic method.

12.8   Gay–Lussac's Law: Pressure/Temperature Changes
- To sketch a graph of the pressure/temperature relationship for a gas.
- To calculate the new pressure or temperature for a gas after a change in one of these conditions using either (a) modified unit analysis or (b) an algebraic method.

12.9   Combined Gas Laws
- To calculate a new pressure, volume or temperature for a gas after a change in conditions using either (a) modified unit analysis or (b) an algebraic method.

12.10   Ideal Gas Behavior
- To describe five characteristics of an ideal gas according to the kinetic theory of gases.
- To determine the value of absolute zero from a graph of volume versus temperature or pressure versus temperature.

12.11   Ideal Gas Equation
- To use the ideal gas equation to find the pressure, volume, temperature, or number of moles of gas, given any three of the four variables.
- To calculate the molar mass of a gas using the ideal gas equation.

13.1 The Liquid State
- To describe five observed properties of a liquid.
- To describe the forces of intermolecular attraction in a liquid; that is, dispersion forces, dipole forces, and hydrogen bonding.

13.2 Properties of Liquids
- To relate the properties of compounds in the liquid state to the strength of intermolecular forces.

13.3 Intermolecular Forces
- To state and distinguish the three attractive forces operating between molecules in the liquid state.

13.4 The Solid State
- To describe five observed properties of a solid.

13.5 Crystalline Solids
- To describe three types of crystalline solids; that is, ionic, molecular, and metallic.

13.6 Changes of Physical State
- To calculate heat changes for a substance that involve heat of fusion, specific heat, and heat of vaporization.

13.7 The Water Molecule
- To illustrate the following information for a water molecule.
  - (a) electron dot formula
  - (b) structural formula
  - (c) observed bond angle
  - (d) polar covalent bonds (delta notation)
  - (e) net dipole (arrow notation)

13.8 Physical Properties of Water
- To explain the unusual properties of water.
  - (a) density compared to ice
  - (b) melting point compared to Group VIA/16 hydrogen compounds
  - (c) boiling point compared to Group VIA/16 hydrogen compounds
  - (d) heat of fusion compared to Group VIA/16 hydrogen compounds
  - (e) heat of vaporization compared to Group VIA/16 hydrogen compounds
- To compare the properties of ordinary water and heavy water.

13.9   Chemical Properties of Water
  • To complete and balance equations that illustrate chemical reactions of water.
        (a) electrolysis of water
        (b) reaction of water with active metals
        (c) reaction of water with metal oxides
        (d) reaction of water with nonmetal oxides
  • To complete and balance equations for chemical reactions that produce water.
        (a) combination of hydrogen and oxygen
        (b) oxidation of a hydrocarbon
        (c) neutralization of an acid with a base
        (d) decomposition of a hydrate

13.10 Hydrates
  • To write the chemical formula or IUPAC systematic name for hydrates.
  • To calculate the percentage of water in a hydrate given the chemical formula.
  • To calculate the water of hydration for a hydrate given the anhydrous compound and the percentage water.

13.11 Water Purification
  • To explain the treatment of hard water to produce
        (a) soft water
        (b) deionized water
        (c) distilled water

CHAPTER 14 Solutions

14.1   Gases in a Liquid Solution
  • To indicate how the solubility of a gas in a liquid is affected by temperature and pressure.

14.2   Liquids in a Liquid Solution
  • To be able to predict whether two solvents are miscible or immiscible by applying the *like dissolves like* rule.

14.3   Solids in a Liquid Solution
  • To be able to predict whether a solid compound is soluble or insoluble in water by applying the *like dissolves like* rule.

14.4   The Dissolving Process
  • To describe and diagram the process of dissolving a solid compound composed of (a) molecules and (b) ions.

14.5 Rate of Dissolving
- To state the effect of temperature, stirring, and particle size on the rate of dissolving a solid compound in water.

14.6 Solubility and Temperature
- To see the effects of temperature on solubility for a solid substance in water.

14.7 Unsaturated, Saturated, Supersaturated Solutions
- To state whether a solution is saturated, unsaturated, or supersaturated given its concentration, temperature, and solubility.

14.8 Mass Percent Concentration
- To write three pairs of unit factors given the mass/mass percent concentration of a solution.
- To calculate the unknown quantity for a solution given any two of the following: mass of solute, mass of solvent, mass/mass percent concentration of a solution.

14.9 Molar Concentration
- To write two factors given the molar concentration of a solution.
- To calculate the unknown quantity for a solution given the molar mass of the solute and any two of the following: mass of solute, volume of solution, molar concentration.

14.10 Molal Concentration and Colligative Properties
- To write a pair of unit factors given the molal concentration of a solution.
- To calculate the unknown quantity for a solution given the molar mass of the solute and any two of the following: mass of solute, mass of solution, molal concentration.
- To calculate the unknown quantity for a solution given the molal freezing point constant and any three of the following: mass of solute, molar mass, mass of solution, freezing point lowering.

14.11 Colloids
- To distinguish between a solution and colloid.

CHAPTER 15 Acids and Bases

15.1 Properties of Acids and Bases
- To list properties of acids and bases.
- To classify a solution with a given pH as strongly acidic, weakly acidic, neutral, weakly basic, or strongly basic.

15.2   Acid–Base Indicators
  • To state the color of the following indicators in a solution of given pH: phenolphthalein, methyl red, and bromthymol blue.

15.3   Standard Solutions of Acids and Bases
  • To calculate the unknown quantity for a standard solution of acid or base given any three of the following:
      (a) mass of the solid acid or solid base
      (b) molar mass of the solid acid or solid base
      (c) molarity of the acid or base
      (d) volume of the acid or base

15.4   Acid–Base Titrations
  • To calculate the unknown quantity for the titration of an acid or base solution given any three of the following:
      (a) molarity of the acid
      (b) volume of the acid
      (c) molarity of the base
      (d) volume of the base
  • To express the molarity of an acid or base in terms of mass/mass percent concentration.

15.5   Arrhenius Acid–Base Theory
  • To state whether Arrhenius acids and bases are strong or weak given the degree of ionization in aqueous solution.
  • To identify the Arrhenius acid and base that produce a given salt from a neutralization reaction.

15.6   Brønsted–Lowry Acid–Base Theory
  • To classify the substance acting as a Brønsted–Lowry acid or base in a given neutralization reaction.
  • To designate the stronger Brønsted–Lowry acid and base participating in a reversible reaction.

15.7   Ionization of Water
  • To state each of the following for the ionization of pure water: the equilibrium constant expression, the value for K_w at 25°C, the molar hydrogen ion and hydroxide ion concentrations.
  • To calculate the molar hydroxide ion concentration, $[OH^-]$, given a molar hydrogen ion concentration, $[H^+]$.

15.8   The pH Concept
  • To perform calculations that relate integer pH values to the molar hydrogen ion concentration of a solution.

15.9 Advanced pH and pOH Calculations
- To perform calculations that relate fractional pH values to hydrogen ion concentrations that are not exact powers of 10.
- To perform calculations that relate pOH values to the hydroxide ion concentration of a solution.

15.10 Strong and Weak Electrolytes
- To classify a substance in aqueous solution as a strong or weak acid, a strong or weak base, a soluble or slightly soluble ionic compound.
- To write substances in aqueous solution as ionized or unionized, given the electrolyte strength.

15.11 Net Ionic Equations
- To write a net ionic equation for a chemical reaction given the names or formulas of the reactants and products.

CHAPTER 16 Chemical Equilibrium

16.1 Collision Theory of Reaction Rates
- To state the effect of collision frequency, collision energy, and geometry of molecules on the rate of a chemical reaction.
- To state the effect of concentration, temperature, and catalyst on the rate of a chemical reaction.

16.2 Energy Profiles of Chemical Reactions
- To draw the general energy profile for each of the following:
    - (a) an endothermic reaction
    - (b) an exothermic reaction
    - (c) a catalyzed reaction
- To label each of the following on an energy diagram:
    - (a) vertical and horizontal axes
    - (b) reactants and products
    - (c) transition state
    - (d) energy of activation, E_{act}
    - (e) heat of reaction, ΔH

16.3 Rates of Reaction
- To explain the meaning of the rate equation for a given chemical reaction.
- To calculate the change in the rate of reaction given the rate equation and the change in reactant concentration.

16.4 Law of Chemical Equilibrium
- To describe the concept of dynamic equilibrium for a reversible reaction.
- To write an equilibrium constant expression for any general reversible reaction.

16.5 Concentration Equilibrium Constant, K_c
- To write the equilibrium constant expression for a reversible reaction in the gaseous state.
- To use experimental data to calculate the concentration equilibrium constant, K_c, for a reversible reaction.

16.6 Gaseous State Equilibria Shifts
- To apply LeChatelier's Principle to reversible reactions in the gaseous state.

16.7 Aqueous Solution Equilibria
- To state three forces that drive a partially reversible reaction in aqueous solution to completion.

16.8 Ionization Equilibrium Constant, K_i
- To write the equilibrium constant expression for a weak acid or weak base.
- To use experimental data to calculate the ionization equilibrium constant, K_i, for a weak acid or weak base.

16.9 Weak Acid–Base Equilibria Shifts
- To apply LeChatelier's Principle to aqueous solutions of weak acids or weak bases.

16.10 Solubility Product Equilibrium Constant, K_{sp}
- To write the equilibrium constant expression for a slightly soluble ionic compound.
- To use experimental data to calculate the solubility product constant, K_{sp}, for a slightly soluble ionic compound.

16.11 Dissociation Equilibria Shifts
- To apply LeChatelier's Principle to a saturated solution containing a slightly soluble ionic compound.

CHAPTER 17 Oxidation and Reduction

17.1 Oxidation Numbers
- To assign an oxidation number for an element in each of the following:
    - (a) metals and nonmetals
    - (b) monoatomic and polyatomic ions
    - (c) ionic and molecular compounds

17.2 Oxidation–Reduction Reactions
- To identify the substance oxidized and the substance reduced in a given redox reaction.
- To identify the oxidizing agent and reducing agent in a given redox reaction.

17.3 Balancing Redox Equations: Oxidation Number Method
- To write a balanced chemical equation for a redox reaction using the oxidation number method.

17.4 Balancing Redox Equations: Ion–Electron Method
- To write a balanced ionic equation for a redox reaction using the ion electron (half reaction) method:
    - (a) in acidic solution
    - (b) in basic solution

17.5 Predicting Spontaneous Redox Reactions
- To predict the stronger oxidizing agent and reducing agent given examples from the activity series.
- To predict whether a reaction is spontaneous or nonspontaneous given the activity series.

17.6 Voltaic Cells
- To indicate the anode, cathode, oxidation half–reaction, reduction half–reaction in a spontaneous voltaic cell.

17.7 Electrolytic Cells
- To indicate the anode, cathode, oxidation half–reaction, reduction half–reaction in a nonspontaneous electrochemical cell.

CHAPTER 18 Advanced Chemical Calculations

18.1   Advanced Problem Solving
- To state general techniques for solving chemical calculations including: problem analysis, strategy maps, concept maps, algorithms, visualization, unit analysis, algebraic analysis.

18.2   Chemical Formula Calculations
- To perform chemical formula calculations that relate moles of substance to the following quantities.
    - (a) number of particles (atoms, molecules, or formula units)
    - (b) mass of substance
    - (c) volume of gas
    - (d) volume of aqueous solution

18.3   Chemical Equation Calculations
- To perform chemical equation calculations for the following types of problems.
    - (a) mass–mass stoichiometry
    - (b) mass–volume stoichiometry
    - (c) volume–volume stoichiometry
    - (d) solution stoichiometry

18.4   Limiting Reactant Concept
- To perform chemical equation calculations that involve a limiting reactant given
    - (a) the masses of two reactants
    - (b) the volumes of two gaseous reactants

18.5   Thermochemical Stoichiometry
- To write thermochemical equations for endothermic and exothermic reactions.
- To perform chemical equation calculations that involve the heat of reaction, ΔH.

18.6   Multiple–Reaction Stoichiometry
- To perform chemical equation calculations that involve two or more reactions.

18.7   Advanced Problem–Solving Examples
- To perform calculations that involve two or more chemical principles.

19.1 Natural Radioactivity
- To state the properties of alpha, beta, and gamma radiation.

19.2 Nuclear Equations
- To represent alpha, beta, gamma, positron, neutron, and proton radiation using atomic notation.
- To write balanced nuclear equations for substances involved in nuclear reactions.

19.3 Radioactive Decay Series
- To become familiar with the natural radioactive decay series for: uranium–238, uranium–235, and thorium–232.

19.4 Radioactive Half–life
- To explain the relationship between the activity of a radioactive sample and a click from a Geiger counter.
- To perform calculations relating to the activity and half–life for a given amount of radioactive sample.

19.5 Applications of Radioisotopes
- To study radioisotopes used for age dating, medical treatment and diagnoses, agriculture uses, and research applications.

19.6 Artificial Radioactivity
- To write balanced equations for nuclear reactions caused by a particle bombarding a target nucleus.

19.7 Nuclear Fission
- To describe the process of nuclear fission, including the concepts of chain reaction and critical mass.

19.8 Mass Defect and Binding Energy
- To calculate the mass defect for an isotope, given the isotopic mass and the masses of a proton and a neutron.
- To calculate the binding energy for an isotope, given the mass defect.

19.9 Nuclear Fusion
- To describe the process of nuclear fusion.
- To write a nuclear equation for a given fusion reaction.

19.10 Nuclear Reactors and Power Plants
- To explain the operation of a nuclear reactor, including the following components: core, fuel rods, control rods, moderator, and coolant.
- To explain the basic design of a nuclear power plant, including the reactor core, steam generator, steam turbine, electrical generator.
- To state the purpose of a breeder reactor and write equations for the production of fissionable isotopes.

20.1 Hydrocarbons
- To classify an organic compound as a hydrocarbon or hydrocarbon derivative.
- To classify a hydrocarbon as saturated or unsaturated.
- To classify a hydrocarbon as an alkane, alkene, alkyne, or aromatic.

20.2 Alkanes
- To study the alkane class of compounds including:
  - (a) names and formulas of the first ten members of the alkane class
  - (b) structural isomers
  - (c) alkyl and aryl substituent groups
  - (d) general nomenclature rules of alkanes
  - (e) oxidation and halogenation reactions

20.3 Alkenes and Alkynes
- To study the alkene and alkyne classes of compounds including:
  - (a) names and formulas of simplest members
  - (b) geometric isomers
  - (c) general nomenclature rules
  - (d) oxidation, hydrogenation, and halogenation reactions

20.4 Aromatic Hydrocarbons
- To study the aromatic class of compounds including:
  - (a) structural formulas of benzene
  - (b) ortho, meta, and para isomers

20.5 Hydrocarbon Derivatives
- To recognize the functional group and identify the class of compound for examples of the following hydrocarbon derivatives.
  - (a) organic halide, alcohol, phenol, ether, amine
  - (b) aldehyde, ketone, carboxylic acid, ester, amide

20.6 Organic Halides
- To study the organic halide class of compounds including:
  - (a) names and formulas of simplest members
  - (b) application and uses

20.7 Alcohols, Phenols, and Ethers
- To study the alcohol, phenol, and ether classes of compounds including:
  - (a) names and formulas of simplest members
  - (b) applications and properties

20.8 Amines
- To study the amine class of compounds including:
    - (a) names and formulas of simplest members
    - (b) applications and properties

20.9 Aldehydes and Ketones
- To study the aldehyde and ketone classes of compounds including:
    - (a) names and formulas of simplest members
    - (b) applications and properties

20.10 Carboxylic Acids, Esters, and Amides
- To study the carboxylic acid, ester, and amide classes of compounds including:
    - (a) names and formulas of simplest members
    - (b) applications and properties

CHAPTER 1

A Mathematical Foundation

Section 1.1 Uncertainty in Measurement

2. No physical quantities can be measured with no uncertainty.

4.

	Unit	Quantity		Unit	Quantity
(a)	grams (g)	mass	(b)	milliliters (mL)	volume
(c)	centimeters (cm)	length	(d)	seconds (s)	time

6.

	Maximum	Minimum		Maximum	Minimum
(a)	6.40 cm	6.30 cm	(b)	1.557 g	1.555 g
(c)	30.10 mL	30.00 mL	(d)	60.02 s	60.00 s

Section 1.2 Significant Digits

8.

	Measurement	Significant Digits
(a)	2.50 cm	3
(b)	5.05 cm	3
(c)	2.00 g	3
(d)	1000 g	1
(e)	250 mL	2
(f)	10.0 mL	3
(g)	2.0×10^4 s	2
(h)	1×10^{-3} s	1

Section 1.3 Rounding Off Nonsignificant Digits

10.

	Not Rounded	Rounded to Three Significant Digits
(a)	61.15	61.2
(b)	362.01	362
(c)	2155	2160
(d)	0.3665	0.367
(e)	12.59	12.6
(f)	35.55	35.6
(g)	1.598×10^9	1.60×10^9
(h)	2.6514×10^{-4}	2.65×10^{-4}

Section 1.4 Adding and Subtracting Measurements

12.

		Answer
(a)	45.35 cm – 41.1 cm = 4.25 cm	4.3 cm
(b)	24.9 cm – 2.55 cm = 22.35 cm	22.4 cm
(c)	242.167 g – 175 g = 67.167 g	67 g
(d)	27.55 g – 14.545 g = 13.005 g	13.01 g
(e)	22.10 mL – 10.5 mL = 11.60 mL	11.6 mL
(f)	10.0 mL – 0.15 mL = 9.85 mL	9.9 mL

Section 1.5 Multiplying and Dividing Measurements

14.   Answer

(a) $\dfrac{66.3 \text{ g}}{7.5 \text{ mL}} = 8.84 \text{ g/mL}$ 8.8 g/mL

(b) $\dfrac{12.5 \text{ g}}{4.1 \text{ mL}} = 3.04878 \text{ g/mL}$ 3.0 g/mL

(c) $\dfrac{42.620 \text{ g}}{10.0 \text{ mL}} = 4.262 \text{ g/mL}$ 4.26 g/mL

(d) $\dfrac{91.235 \text{ g}}{10.00 \text{ mL}} = 9.1235 \text{ g/mL}$ 9.124 g/mL

(e) $\dfrac{26.0 \text{ cm}^2}{10.1 \text{ cm}} = 2.5746 \text{ cm}$ 2.57 cm

(f) $\dfrac{9.95 \text{ cm}^2}{0.15 \text{ cm}} = 66.333 \text{ cm}$ 66 cm

(g) $\dfrac{131.78 \text{ cm}^3}{19.25 \text{ cm}} = 6.8457 \text{ cm}^2$ 6.846 cm^2

(h) $\dfrac{131.78 \text{ cm}^3}{19.26 \text{ cm}} = 6.8422 \text{ cm}^2$ 6.842 cm^2

Section 1.6 Exponential Numbers

16.

	Exponential #	Inverse		Exponential #	Inverse
(a)	10^3	$\dfrac{1}{10^{-3}}$	(b)	10^{23}	$\dfrac{1}{10^{-23}}$
(c)	10^{-8}	$\dfrac{1}{10^8}$	(d)	10^{-15}	$\dfrac{1}{10^{15}}$
(e)	$\dfrac{1}{10^3}$	10^{-3}	(f)	$\dfrac{1}{10^{12}}$	10^{-12}
(g)	$\dfrac{1}{10^{-7}}$	10^7	(h)	$\dfrac{1}{10^{-22}}$	10^{22}

18.

	Power of Ten	Number
(a)	1×10^1	10
(b)	1×10^{-1}	0.1
(c)	1×10^5	100,000
(d)	1×10^{-4}	0.0001
(e)	1×10^8	100,000,000
(f)	1×10^{-9}	0.000 000 001
(g)	1×10^0	1
(h)	1×10^{-22}	0.000 000 000 000 000 000 000 1

Section 1.7 Scientific Notation

20.

	Number	Scientific Notation
(a)	1,010,000,000,000,000	1.01×10^{15}
(b)	0.000 000 000 000 456	4.56×10^{-13}
(c)	94,500,000,000,000,000	9.45×10^{16}
(d)	0.000 000 000 000 000 019 50	1.950×10^{-17}

22.

Number	Scientific Notation
0.000 000 000 000 000 000 000 0335 g	3.35×10^{-23} g

Section 1.8 Calculators and Significant Digits

24.

		Calculator Notation		Scientific Notation
(a)	$\dfrac{(4.97 \times 10^8)\,(3.24 \times 10^4)}{(56.71 \times 10^{-2})\,(1.31 \times 10^3)} \ =$	2.17 E10	=	2.17×10^{10}
(b)	$\dfrac{(96.77 \times 10^{-7})\,(0.00181 \times 10^{-8})}{(3.49 \times 10^{10})\,(7.62 \times 10^{-12})} \ =$	6.59 E–16	=	6.59×10^{-16}
(c)	$\dfrac{(1.78 \times 10^2)}{(3.69 \times 10^{-3})} \times \dfrac{(6.02 \times 10^{23})}{(1.6 \times 10^{20})} \ =$	1.8 E08	=	1.8×10^8
(d)	$\dfrac{(16.4 \times 10^{-3})}{(1.186 \times 10^{-7})} \times \dfrac{(4.00 \times 10^6)}{(3.78 \times 10^{-4})} \ =$	1.46 E15	=	1.46×10^{15}
(e)	$\dfrac{(3.111 \times 10^{-6})}{(2.08 \times 10^{-2})} \times \dfrac{(4.55 \times 10^5)}{(8.88 \times 10^9)} \ =$	7.66 E–09	=	7.66×10^{-9}

Section 1.9 Unit Conversion Factors

26.

	Unit Equation	Unit Factors		
(a)	1 day = 24 hours	$\dfrac{1 \text{ day}}{24 \text{ hours}}$	and	$\dfrac{24 \text{ hours}}{1 \text{ day}}$
(b)	12 inches = 1 foot	$\dfrac{12 \text{ inches}}{1 \text{ foot}}$	and	$\dfrac{1 \text{ foot}}{12 \text{ inches}}$
(c)	1 year = 365 days	$\dfrac{1 \text{ year}}{365 \text{ days}}$	and	$\dfrac{365 \text{ days}}{1 \text{ year}}$
(d)	1 yard = 36 inches	$\dfrac{1 \text{ yard}}{36 \text{ inches}}$	and	$\dfrac{36 \text{ inches}}{1 \text{ yard}}$
(e)	100 years = 1 century	$\dfrac{100 \text{ years}}{1 \text{ century}}$	and	$\dfrac{1 \text{ century}}{100 \text{ years}}$
(f)	3 feet = 1 yard	$\dfrac{3 \text{ feet}}{1 \text{ yard}}$	and	$\dfrac{1 \text{ yard}}{3 \text{ feet}}$
(g)	7 days = 1 week	$\dfrac{7 \text{ days}}{1 \text{ week}}$	and	$\dfrac{1 \text{ week}}{7 \text{ days}}$
(h)	1760 yards = 1 mile	$\dfrac{1760 \text{ yards}}{1 \text{ mile}}$	and	$\dfrac{1 \text{ mile}}{1760 \text{ yards}}$
(i)	12 months = 1 year	$\dfrac{12 \text{ months}}{1 \text{ year}}$	and	$\dfrac{1 \text{ year}}{12 \text{ months}}$
(j)	1 mile = 5280 feet	$\dfrac{1 \text{ mile}}{5280 \text{ feet}}$	and	$\dfrac{5280 \text{ feet}}{1 \text{ mile}}$

Section 1.10 Problem Solving by Unit Analysis

28. related given value $\times \dfrac{\text{unit}}{\text{factor(s)}}$ = units in answer

(a) $225 \text{ hours} \times \dfrac{1 \text{ work week}}{40 \text{ hours}} = 5.62$ work weeks

(b) $\left(26 \text{ miles} \times \dfrac{1760 \text{ yards}}{1 \text{ mile}}\right) + 385 \text{ yards} = 46{,}145$ yards

(c) $0.305 \text{ grams} \times \dfrac{1 \text{ karat}}{0.200 \text{ grams}} = 1.53$ karat

(d) $20.0 \text{ gallons} \times \dfrac{3.78 \text{ liters}}{1 \text{ gallon}} = 75.6$ liters

(e) $1 \text{ hour} \times \dfrac{60 \text{ minutes}}{1 \text{ hour}} \times \dfrac{60 \text{ seconds}}{1 \text{ minute}} \times \dfrac{186{,}000 \text{ miles}}{1 \text{ second}}$
$= 6.70 \times 10^8$ miles

(f) $\dfrac{3.00 \times 10^{10} \text{ cm}}{1 \text{ second}} \times \dfrac{60 \text{ seconds}}{1 \text{ minute}} \times \dfrac{60 \text{ minutes}}{1 \text{ hour}} \times \dfrac{24 \text{ hours}}{1 \text{ day}} \times \dfrac{365 \text{ days}}{1 \text{ year}}$
$= 9.46 \times 10^{17}$ cm/year

Section 1.11 Percentage

30. (a) $135 \text{ } \cancel{\text{students}} \times \dfrac{11.1 \text{ A's}}{100 \text{ } \cancel{\text{students}}} = 15.0 \text{ A's}$

    (b) $15.0 \text{ } \cancel{\text{g oxygen}} \times \dfrac{100 \text{ g water}}{88.8 \text{ } \cancel{\text{g oxygen}}} = 16.9 \text{ g water}$

    (c) $0.375 \text{ } \cancel{\text{g table salt}} \times \dfrac{39.3 \text{ g sodium}}{100 \text{ } \cancel{\text{g table salt}}} = 0.147 \text{ g sodium}$

    (d) $0.100 \text{ } \cancel{\text{g potassium iodide}} \times \dfrac{100 \text{ g salt}}{0.02 \text{ } \cancel{\text{g potassium iodide}}} = 500 \text{ g salt}$

    (e) oxygen: $2.37 \times 10^{25} \text{ } \cancel{\text{g crust}} \times \dfrac{49.2 \text{ g oxygen}}{100 \text{ } \cancel{\text{g crust}}} = 1.17 \times 10^{25} \text{ g oxygen}$

    silicon: $2.37 \times 10^{25} \text{ } \cancel{\text{g crust}} \times \dfrac{25.7 \text{ g silicon}}{100 \text{ } \cancel{\text{g crust}}} = 6.09 \times 10^{24} \text{ g silicon}$

    aluminum: $2.37 \times 10^{25} \text{ } \cancel{\text{g crust}} \times \dfrac{7.50 \text{ g aluminum}}{100 \text{ } \cancel{\text{g crust}}}$
    $$= 1.78 \times 10^{24} \text{ g aluminum}$$

    (f) $3.87 \times 10^{21} \text{ } \cancel{\text{kg five moons}} \times \dfrac{54.3 \text{ kg Titania}}{100 \text{ } \cancel{\text{kg five moons}}}$
    $$= 2.10 \times 10^{21} \text{ kg Titania}$$

32. Total quantity = 2.554 g copper and zinc
    Quantity of zinc = 2.490 g
    Quantity of copper = total quantity – quantity of zinc
    Quantity of copper = 2.554 g – 2.490 g = 0.064 g
    Percent of zinc: $\dfrac{2.490 \text{ g}}{2.554 \text{ g}} \times 100 = 97.49\% \text{ zinc}$
    Percent of copper: $\dfrac{0.064 \text{ g}}{2.554 \text{ g}} \times 100 = 2.5\% \text{ copper}$

General Exercises

34. Ruler A: 2.9 cm (± 0.1 cm)
    Ruler B: 2.95 cm (± 0.05 cm)

36. 1.000×10^3 mL (± 1 mL)

38.

Not Rounded	Rounded to Three Significant Digits
2.997925×10^{10} cm/s	3.00×10^{10} cm/s

40. Remaining length: 255 cm – 2(25.0 cm) = 205 cm

42.

	Exponential Number	Scientific Notation
(a)	732×10^{-3}	7.32×10^{-1}
(b)	0.00350×10^{-1}	3.50×10^{-4}
(c)	16.6×10^{-6}	1.66×10^{-5}
(d)	0.191×10^{-5}	1.91×10^{-6}

44. $1 \times 10^{100} = 10 \times 10^{99}$

Calculator Notation: 10 E99

46.   Mass of neutron $= 1.67495 \times 10^{-24}$ g

Mass of proton $= 1.67265 \times 10^{-24}$ g

Mass difference: 1.67495×10^{-24} g $- 1.67265 \times 10^{-24}$ g $= 2.30000 \times 10^{-27}$ g

48.   Total distance $= \left(\begin{array}{c}\text{distance from the} \\ \text{earth to the moon}\end{array}\right) + \left(\begin{array}{c}\text{distance from the} \\ \text{moon to Mars}\end{array}\right)$

Total distance: 2.39×10^5 miles $+ 4.84 \times 10^7$ miles $= 4.86 \times 10^7$ miles

50.   Volume $= \dfrac{4}{3} \pi r^3$

$r = 4.32 \times 10^5$ miles

$\pi = 3.14$

Volume $= \dfrac{4}{3} \times 3.14 \times \left(4.32 \times 10^5 \text{ miles}\right)^3 = 3.38 \times 10^{17}$ miles^3

52.   4.1 billion years $= 4.1 \times 10^9$ years

$4.1 \times 10^9 \; \cancel{\text{years}} \times \dfrac{365 \; \cancel{\text{days}}}{1 \; \cancel{\text{year}}} \times \dfrac{24 \; \cancel{\text{hours}}}{1 \; \cancel{\text{day}}} \times \dfrac{60 \text{ minutes}}{1 \; \cancel{\text{hour}}}$

$= 2.2 \times 10^{15}$ minutes

54. $1 \; \cancel{\text{avoirdupois pound}} \times \dfrac{16 \; \cancel{\text{avoirdupois ounces}}}{1 \; \cancel{\text{avoirdupois pound}}} \times \dfrac{28.4 \text{ grams}}{1 \; \cancel{\text{avoirdupois ounce}}}$

$= 454$ grams

CHAPTER 2 Measurement

Section 2.1 The Metric System

2. The only true statement is (d).
   Corrected Statements
   (a) The English system *does not use* a basic unit for length, mass, and volume.
   (b) The English system is *not* a decimal system that uses prefixes related by a power of 10.
   (c) The English system is *not* used exclusively throughout the scientific community.

4.
	Quantity	Metric Prefix	Symbol
(a)	10^{-2}	centi-	c
(b)	0.001	milli-	m
(c)	10^{-3}	milli-	m
(d)	1000	kilo-	k
(e)	10^3	kilo-	k
(f)	0.01	centi-	c
(g)	10^{-1}	deci-	d
(h)	0.1	deci-	d
(i)	10^{-9}	nano-	n
(j)	0.000 001	micro-	μ

6.
	Symbol	Metric Unit		Symbol	Metric Unit
(a)	m	meter	(b)	μs	microsecond
(c)	kg	kilogram	(d)	mL	milliliter
(e)	dm	decimeter	(f)	cal	calorie
(g)	cL	centiliter	(h)	m^2	square meter
(i)	ng	nanogram	(j)	mm^3	cubic millimeter

Section 2.2 Metric Unit Conversion Factors

8.

Unit Factors

(a) $\dfrac{1000 \text{ mm}}{1 \text{ m}}$ and $\dfrac{1 \text{ m}}{1000 \text{ mm}}$

Unit Factors

(b) $\dfrac{10 \text{ dL}}{1 \text{ L}}$ and $\dfrac{1 \text{ L}}{10 \text{ dL}}$

8.

 Unit Factors   Unit Factors

(c) $\dfrac{1\ g}{10^6\ \mu g}$ and $\dfrac{10^6\ \mu g}{1\ g}$ (d) $\dfrac{10\ dm}{1\ m}$ and $\dfrac{1\ m}{10\ dm}$

(e) $\dfrac{1\ kL}{1000\ L}$ and $\dfrac{1000\ L}{1\ kL}$ (f) $\dfrac{10^9\ ns}{1\ s}$ and $\dfrac{1\ s}{10^9\ ns}$

10.

 Unit Factors   Unit Factors

(a) $\dfrac{1\ m}{10^9\ nm}$ and $\dfrac{10^9\ nm}{1\ m}$ (b) $\dfrac{10^6\ \mu m}{1\ m}$ and $\dfrac{1\ m}{10^6\ \mu m}$

(c) $\dfrac{100\ cg}{1\ g}$ and $\dfrac{1\ g}{100\ cg}$ (d) $\dfrac{1\ mL}{1\ cm^3}$ and $\dfrac{1\ cm^3}{1\ mL}$

(e) $\dfrac{1\ L}{10\ dL}$ and $\dfrac{10\ dL}{1\ L}$ (f) $\dfrac{1000\ cal}{1\ kcal}$ and $\dfrac{1\ kcal}{1000\ cal}$

Section 2.3 Metric Problems by Unit Analysis

12. Choose one or more unit factors that will allow conversion of the given units to the units of the unknown quantity.

Section 2.4 Metric-Metric Unit Conversions

14. (a) $120\ \cancel{mm} \times \dfrac{1\ \cancel{m}}{1000\ \cancel{mm}} \times \dfrac{100\ cm}{1\ \cancel{m}} = 12\ cm$

(b) $14.5\ \cancel{dL} \times \dfrac{1\ \cancel{L}}{10\ \cancel{dL}} \times \dfrac{100\ cL}{1\ \cancel{L}} = 145\ cL$

(c) $255\ \cancel{mg} \times \dfrac{1\ \cancel{g}}{1000\ \cancel{mg}} \times \dfrac{10\ dg}{1\ \cancel{g}} = 2.55\ dg$

(d) $1.56 \times 10^{-3}\ \cancel{km} \times \dfrac{1000\ \cancel{m}}{1\ \cancel{km}} \times \dfrac{10\ dm}{1\ \cancel{m}} = 15.6\ dm$

(e) $1.81\ \cancel{mL} \times \dfrac{1\ \cancel{L}}{1000\ \cancel{mL}} \times \dfrac{10^6\ \mu L}{1\ \cancel{L}} = 1810\ \mu L\ (1.81 \times 10^3\ \mu L)$

(f) $8.15 \times 10^4\ \cancel{ms} \times \dfrac{1\ \cancel{s}}{1000\ \cancel{ms}} \times \dfrac{10^9\ ns}{1\ \cancel{s}} = 8.15 \times 10^{10}\ ns$

(g) $0.55\ \cancel{dm} \times \dfrac{1\ \cancel{m}}{10\ \cancel{dm}} \times \dfrac{1000\ mm}{1\ \cancel{m}} = 55\ mm$

(h) $3.5\ \cancel{kL} \times \dfrac{1000\ \cancel{L}}{1\ \cancel{kL}} \times \dfrac{1000\ mL}{1\ \cancel{L}} = 3{,}500{,}000\ mL\ (3.5 \times 10^6\ mL)$

(i) $0.326\ \cancel{kg} \times \dfrac{1000\ \cancel{g}}{1\ \cancel{kg}} \times \dfrac{100\ cg}{1\ \cancel{g}} = 32{,}600\ cg\ (3.26 \times 10^4\ cg)$

(j) $0.000222\ \cancel{cm} \times \dfrac{1\ \cancel{m}}{100\ \cancel{cm}} \times \dfrac{10^9\ nm}{1\ \cancel{m}} = 2220\ nm\ (2.22 \times 10^3\ nm)$

Section 2.5 Metric-English Unit Conversions

16.   (a) $12.0\;\cancel{in.} \times \dfrac{2.54\text{ cm}}{1\;\cancel{in.}} = 30.5\text{ cm}$

       (b) $2.20\;\cancel{lb} \times \dfrac{454\text{ g}}{1\;\cancel{lb}} = 999\text{ g}$

       (c) $0.500\;\cancel{qt} \times \dfrac{946\text{ mL}}{1\;\cancel{qt}} = 473\text{ mL}$

       (d) $4.00\;\cancel{qt} \times \dfrac{946\text{ cm}^3}{1\;\cancel{qt}} = 3780\text{ cm}^3$

18.   (a) $175\;\cancel{lb} \times \dfrac{454\;\cancel{g}}{1\;\cancel{lb}} \times \dfrac{1\text{ kg}}{1000\;\cancel{g}} = 79.5\text{ kg}$

       (b) $1250\;\cancel{mL} \times \dfrac{1\;\cancel{qt}}{946\;\cancel{mL}} \times \dfrac{1\text{ gallon}}{4\;\cancel{qt}} = 0.330\text{ gallon}$

       (c) $0.500\;\cancel{qt} \times \dfrac{946\;\cancel{mL}}{1\;\cancel{qt}} \times \dfrac{1\text{ L}}{1000\;\cancel{mL}} = 0.473\text{ L}$

       (d) $0.375\;\cancel{kg} \times \dfrac{1000\;\cancel{g}}{1\;\cancel{kg}} \times \dfrac{1\text{ lb}}{454\;\cancel{g}} = 0.826\text{ lb}$

       (e) $72\;\cancel{in.} \times \dfrac{2.54\;\cancel{cm}}{1\;\cancel{in.}} \times \dfrac{1\text{ m}}{100\;\cancel{cm}} = 1.8\text{ m}$

       (f) $800.0\;\cancel{m} \times \dfrac{100\;\cancel{cm}}{1\;\cancel{m}} \times \dfrac{1\;\cancel{in.}}{2.54\;\cancel{cm}} \times \dfrac{1\;\cancel{ft}}{12\;\cancel{in.}} \times \dfrac{1\text{ yd}}{3\;\cancel{ft}} = 875\text{ yd}$

       (g) $152\;\cancel{cm} \times \dfrac{1\;\cancel{in.}}{2.54\;\cancel{cm}} \times \dfrac{1\text{ ft}}{12\;\cancel{in.}} = 4.99\text{ ft}$

       (h) $1.5 \times 10^4\;\cancel{dg} \times \dfrac{1\;\cancel{g}}{10\;\cancel{dg}} \times \dfrac{1\text{ lb}}{454\;\cancel{g}} = 3.3\text{ lb}$

       (i) $2.20\;\cancel{lb} \times \dfrac{454\;\cancel{g}}{1\;\cancel{lb}} \times \dfrac{1\text{ kg}}{1000\;\cancel{g}} = 0.999\text{ kg}$

       (j) $\dfrac{1\;\cancel{mi}}{4} \times \dfrac{5280\;\cancel{ft}}{1\;\cancel{mi}} \times \dfrac{12\;\cancel{in.}}{1\;\cancel{ft}} \times \dfrac{2.54\;\cancel{cm}}{1\;\cancel{in.}} \times \dfrac{1\;\cancel{m}}{100\;\cancel{cm}} \times \dfrac{1\text{ km}}{1000\;\cancel{m}}$

                                                            $= 0.402\text{ km}$

20. $\dfrac{0.959\;\cancel{dollar}}{\cancel{gallon}} \times \dfrac{100\text{ cents}}{1\;\cancel{dollar}} \times \dfrac{1\;\cancel{gallon}}{4\;\cancel{qt}} \times \dfrac{1\;\cancel{qt}}{946\;\cancel{mL}} \times \dfrac{1000\;\cancel{mL}}{1\text{ L}} = \dfrac{25.3\text{ cents}}{\text{L}}$

22. $1\;\cancel{mi} \times \dfrac{5280\;\cancel{ft}}{1\;\cancel{mi}} \times \dfrac{12\;\cancel{in.}}{1\;\cancel{ft}} \times \dfrac{2.54\;\cancel{cm}}{1\;\cancel{in.}} \times \dfrac{1\text{ m}}{100\;\cancel{cm}} = 1610\text{ m}$

    Thus, one mile is longer than 1500 meters.

Section 2.6 Volume by Calculation

24. $5.00 \text{ cm} \times \dfrac{1 \text{ m}}{100 \text{ cm}} \times \dfrac{1000 \text{ mm}}{1 \text{ m}} = 50.0 \text{ mm}$

$50.0 \text{ mm} \times 50.0 \text{ mm} \times 25.0 \text{ mm} = 62{,}500 \text{ mm}^3 \ (6.25 \times 10^4 \text{ mm}^3)$

26. $\dfrac{(3.68 \text{ cm}^3)}{(30.5 \text{ cm})(75.0 \text{ cm})} = 1.61 \times 10^{-3} \text{ cm}$

28. $500.0 \text{ cm}^3 \times \dfrac{1 \text{ mL}}{1 \text{ cm}^3} = 500.0 \text{ mL}$

$500.0 \text{ cm}^3 \times \dfrac{1 \text{ mL}}{1 \text{ cm}^3} \times \dfrac{1 \text{ L}}{1000 \text{ mL}} = 0.5000 \text{ L}$

30. $1.20 \text{ L} \times \dfrac{1000 \text{ mL}}{1 \text{ L}} \times \dfrac{1 \text{ cm}^3}{1 \text{ mL}} \times \dfrac{1 \text{ in.}}{2.54 \text{ cm}} \times \dfrac{1 \text{ in.}}{2.54 \text{ cm}} \times \dfrac{1 \text{ in.}}{2.54 \text{ cm}} = 73.2 \text{ in.}^3$

Section 2.7 Volume by Displacement

32. volume of hydrogen gas:
212 mL water = 212 mL hydrogen gas produced (212 cm^3 = 0.212 L)

Section 2.8 Density

34.

Gas	Rise or Fall	Gas	Rise or Fall
(a) helium	rise	(b) carbon monoxide	rise
(c) nitrous oxide	fall	(d) ammonia	rise

36. (a) $10.0 \text{ g} \times \dfrac{1 \text{ cm}^3}{8.90 \text{ g}} \times \dfrac{1 \text{ mL}}{1 \text{ cm}^3} = 1.12 \text{ mL}$

(b) $0.500 \text{ g} \times \dfrac{1 \text{ mL}}{3.12 \text{ g}} = 0.160 \text{ mL}$

(c) $33.5 \text{ g} \times \dfrac{1 \text{ mL}}{1.59 \text{ g}} = 21.1 \text{ mL}$

(d) $0.899 \text{ kg} \times \dfrac{1000 \text{ g}}{1 \text{ kg}} \times \dfrac{1 \text{ mL}}{0.792 \text{ g}} = 1140 \text{ mL}$

(e) $1.00 \text{ kg} \times \dfrac{1000 \text{ g}}{1 \text{ kg}} \times \dfrac{1 \text{ cm}^3}{0.25 \text{ g}} \times \dfrac{1 \text{ mL}}{\text{cm}^3} = 4000 \text{ mL} \ (4.00 \times 10^3 \text{ mL})$

38.   Density

    (a) jet fuel: $0.775 \times \dfrac{1.00\text{g}}{\text{mL}} = 0.775 \text{ g/mL}$

    (b) gasohol: $0.801 \times \dfrac{1.00\text{g}}{\text{mL}} = 0.801 \text{ g/mL}$

    (c) mercury: $13.6 \times \dfrac{1.00\text{g}}{\text{mL}} = 13.6 \text{ g/mL}$

    (d) salt water: $1.05 \times \dfrac{1.00\text{g}}{\text{mL}} = 1.05 \text{ g/mL}$

    (e) water: $1.00 \times \dfrac{1.00\text{g}}{\text{mL}} = 1.00 \text{ g/mL}$

Section 2.9 Temperature

40.

	Scale	Boiling Point of Water
(a)	Fahrenheit	212°F
(b)	Kelvin	373 K
(c)	Celsius	100°C

42.   (a) $\left(19°C \times \dfrac{180°F}{100°C}\right) + 32°F = 66°F$

       (b) $\left(-175°C \times \dfrac{180°F}{100°C}\right) + 32°F = -283°F$

       (c) $\left(1115°C \times \dfrac{180°F}{100°C}\right) + 32°F = 2039°F$

       (d) $\left(-273°C \times \dfrac{180°F}{100°C}\right) + 32°F = -459°F$

44.   (a) 275 K – 273 = 0°C

       (b) 100 K – 273 = –173°C

       (c) 298 K – 273 = 25°C

       (d) 3 K – 273 = –270°C

Section 2.10 Heat and Specific Heat

46. The specific heat of water is: $\dfrac{1.00 \text{ cal}}{1 \text{ g} \cdot °C}$

48. $2.45 \times 10^7 \cancel{\text{g}} \times \dfrac{1.00 \cancel{\text{cal}}}{1 \cancel{\text{g}} \cdot \cancel{°C}} \times (28 - 17)°C \times \dfrac{1 \text{ kcal}}{1000 \cancel{\text{cal}}} = 2.7 \times 10^5 \text{ kcal } (lost)$

    (Note: The answer has two significant digits because of the subtraction.)

50. $35.5 \cancel{\text{g}} \times \dfrac{0.0902 \text{ cal}}{1 \cancel{\text{g}} \cdot \cancel{°C}} \times (50.0 - 45.0)°C = 16 \text{ cal}$

    (Note: The answer has two significant digits because of the subtraction.)

52.
$$\frac{35.7 \text{ cal}}{75.0 \text{ g } (43.9 - 28.9)^\circ\text{C}} = 0.0317 \text{ cal/g} \cdot {}^\circ\text{C}$$

54.
$$\frac{\text{g} \cdot {}^\circ\text{C}}{0.0308 \text{ cal}} \times \frac{52.5 \text{ cal}}{(35.7 - 25.1)^\circ\text{C}} = 161 \text{ g}$$

56.
$$\frac{\text{g} \cdot {}^\circ\text{C}}{0.293 \text{ cal}} \times \frac{750 \text{ cal}}{8.92 \text{ g}} = 290^\circ\text{C}$$

Section 2.11 The International System of Measurement (SI)

58. (a) $143,000 \text{ Mg} \times \dfrac{10^6 \text{ g}}{1 \text{ Mg}} \times \dfrac{1 \text{ Gg}}{10^9 \text{ g}} = 143 \text{ Gg}$

(b) $10.0 \text{ nL} \times \dfrac{1 \text{ L}}{10^9 \text{ nL}} \times \dfrac{10^6 \text{ } \mu\text{L}}{1 \text{ L}} = 0.0100 \text{ } \mu\text{L}$

(c) $0.000\,000\,035 \text{ Pm} \times \dfrac{10^{15} \text{ m}}{1 \text{ Pm}} \times \dfrac{1 \text{ km}}{1000 \text{ m}} = 3.5 \times 10^4 \text{ km}$

(d) $75 \text{ ms} \times \dfrac{1 \text{ s}}{1000 \text{ ms}} \times \dfrac{10^{12} \text{ ps}}{1 \text{ s}} = 7.5 \times 10^{10} \text{ ps}$

60.
$$\frac{0.0332 \text{ cal}}{\text{g} \cdot {}^\circ\text{C}} \times \frac{4.184 \text{ J}}{1 \text{ cal}} \times \frac{1000 \text{ g}}{1 \text{ kg}} \times \frac{1 {}^\circ\text{C}}{1 \text{ K}} = 139 \text{ J/kg} \cdot \text{K}$$

General Exercises

62. $300 \text{ ft} \times \dfrac{12 \text{ in.}}{1 \text{ ft}} \times \dfrac{2.54 \text{ cm}}{1 \text{ in.}} \times \dfrac{1 \text{ m}}{100 \text{ cm}} = 91.4 \text{ m}$

$160 \text{ ft} \times \dfrac{12 \text{ in.}}{1 \text{ ft}} \times \dfrac{2.54 \text{ cm}}{1 \text{ in.}} \times \dfrac{1 \text{ m}}{100 \text{ cm}} = 48.8 \text{ m}$

Playing Area: $91.4 \text{ m} \times 48.8 \text{ m} = 4460 \text{ m}^2$

64. $1.31 \times 10^{25} \text{ lb} \times \dfrac{454 \text{ g}}{1 \text{ lb}} \times \dfrac{1 \text{ kg}}{1000 \text{ g}} = 5.95 \times 10^{24} \text{ kg}$

66. $2.50 \text{ kg} \times \dfrac{1000 \text{ g}}{1 \text{ kg}} \times \dfrac{1000 \text{ mg}}{1 \text{ g}} \times \dfrac{1 \text{ grain}}{64.8 \text{ mg}} \times \dfrac{\text{aspirin tablet}}{5 \text{ grain}}$

$= 7720 \text{ aspirin tablets}$

68. $\dfrac{1 \text{ cycle}}{305 \text{ cm}} \times \dfrac{100 \text{ cm}}{1 \text{ m}} \times \dfrac{3.00 \times 10^8 \text{ m}}{\text{s}} \times \dfrac{1 \text{ megacycle}}{10^6 \text{ cycles}} = 98.4 \text{ megacycles/s}$

70. $589 \text{ nm} \times \dfrac{1 \text{ m}}{10^9 \text{ nm}} \times \dfrac{100 \text{ cm}}{1 \text{ m}} \times \dfrac{10^8 \text{ Å}}{1 \text{ cm}} = 5890 \text{ Å}$

72. Volume of opal: $57.5 \text{ mL} - 50.0 \text{ mL} = 7.5 \text{ mL}$

Density of opal: $\dfrac{15.357 \text{ g}}{7.5 \text{ mL}} = \dfrac{2.0 \text{ g}}{\text{mL}}$

74. $1 \; \cancel{\text{drop water}} \times \dfrac{1 \; \cancel{\text{mL water}}}{20 \; \cancel{\text{drops water}}} \times \dfrac{1.00 \; \cancel{\text{g water}}}{1 \; \cancel{\text{mL water}}} \times$

$\dfrac{3.34 \times 10^{22} \text{ molecules water}}{1 \; \cancel{\text{g water}}} = 1.67 \times 10^{21} \text{ molecules water}$

76. $11.95 \; \cancel{\text{kcal}} \times \dfrac{1000 \; \cancel{\text{cal}}}{1 \; \cancel{\text{kcal}}} \times \dfrac{4.184 \text{ J}}{1 \; \cancel{\text{cal}}} = 50{,}000 \text{ J} \; (5.000 \times 10^{4} \text{ J})$

78. $10.0 \text{ g} \times \dfrac{0.0920 \text{ cal}}{1 \text{ g} \cdot {}^{\circ}\text{C}} \times (T_{final} - 22.7){}^{\circ}\text{C} = 27.8 \text{ cal}$

$T_{final} = \left(\dfrac{27.8 \; \cancel{\text{cal}}}{10.0 \; \cancel{\text{g}}} \times \dfrac{1 \; \cancel{\text{g}} \cdot {}^{\circ}\text{C}}{0.0920 \; \cancel{\text{cal}}} \right) + 22.7{}^{\circ}\text{C} = 52.9{}^{\circ}\text{C}$

80. Heat lost by water = Heat gained by metal

Heat lost by water: $75.0 \; \cancel{\text{g}} \times \dfrac{1.00 \text{ cal}}{1 \; \cancel{\text{g}} \cdot \cancel{{}^{\circ}\text{C}}} \times (80.0 - 78.3)\cancel{{}^{\circ}\text{C}} = 130 \text{ cal}$

Specific heat of metal: $\dfrac{130 \text{ cal}}{10.0 \text{ g} \, (78.3 - 20.5){}^{\circ}\text{C}} = \dfrac{0.22 \text{ cal}}{\text{g} \cdot {}^{\circ}\text{C}}$

Since the specific heat is ~ 0.215 cal/g · °C, the unknown metal is aluminum.

82. Volume = $\pi \, r^2 h$

$r = 1.95 \text{ cm}$

Volume = $1 \; \cancel{\text{kg}} \times \dfrac{1000 \; \cancel{\text{g}}}{1 \; \cancel{\text{kg}}} \times \dfrac{\text{cm}^3}{21.50 \; \cancel{\text{g}}} = 46.51 \text{ cm}^3$

$\pi \, r^2 h = 46.51 \text{ cm}^3$

$h = \dfrac{46.51 \text{ cm}^3}{\pi \cdot r^2} = \dfrac{46.51 \text{ cm}^3}{3.14 \times (1.95 \text{ cm})^2} = 3.90 \text{ cm}$

Note: diameter = 2 × radius = 2 × 1.95 cm = 3.90 cm
    diameter = height

CHAPTER 3 Matter and Energy

Section 3.1 Physical States of Matter

2.

	State	Compressibility
(a)	solid	negligible
(b)	liquid	negligible
(c)	gas	high

4.   Normal conditions are the conditions at which the pressure exerted on a substance is equal to the atmospheric pressure at sea level and the temperature of a substance is equivalent to room temperature (~25°C).

6.

	Change	Heat Energy		Change	Heat Energy
(a)	solid to liquid	absorbed	(b)	liquid to solid	released
(c)	gas to liquid	released	(d)	liquid to gas	absorbed
(e)	solid to gas	absorbed	(f)	gas to solid	released

Section 3.2 Physical State and Energy

8.   If the molecular motion of a molecule increases twofold, the kinetic energy of the molecule increases fourfold. If the molecular motion of a molecule decreases by one-half, the kinetic energy decreases by one-fourth. Thus, as the molecular motion increases or decreases, kinetic energy increases or decreases by the square of the velocity.

10. (a)   The kinetic energy of carbon dioxide decreases because the temperature decreases. (Kinetic energy and temperature are directly related).
     (b)   The velocity of carbon dioxide molecules decreases because the kinetic energy is lower.

12. At the same temperature, the average velocity of lighter gas molecules is *greater* than the average velocity of heavier gas molecules.

14. If two gases have the same kinetic energy, the average velocity of lighter gas molecules is *greater* than the average velocity of heavier gas molecules.

Section 3.3 Classification of Matter

16.

	Substance	Classification		Substance	Classification
(a)	iodine	element	(b)	silver ore	mixture
(c)	nitrogen dioxide	compound	(d)	ocean water	mixture
(e)	auto emissions	mixture	(f)	alloy wheels	mixture
(g)	iron	element	(h)	steel (Mn in Fe)	mixture

18.

	Substance	Classification		Substance	Classification
(a)	earth's crust	mixture	(b)	atmosphere	mixture
(c)	oxygen	element	(d)	ozone (O_3)	compound
(e)	seawater	mixture	(f)	sulfur oxide	compound
(g)	soft drink	mixture	(h)	titanium	element

Section 3.4 Names and Symbols of the Elements

20.   Uranium is not one of the earth's most ten abundant elements.

22.

	Symbol	Element		Symbol	Element
(a)	As	arsenic	(b)	Ba	barium
(c)	Be	beryllium	(d)	Cd	cadmium
(e)	Cl	chlorine	(f)	Ge	germanium
(g)	Co	cobalt	(h)	Cu	copper
(i)	Al	aluminum	(j)	B	boron
(k)	Au	gold	(l)	Cr	chromium
(m)	Mn	manganese	(n)	Hg	mercury
(o)	Ne	neon	(p)	P	phosphorus
(q)	Ra	radium	(r)	Sr	strontium
(s)	Si	silicon	(t)	Ag	silver
(u)	Pb	lead	(v)	N	nitrogen
(w)	S	sulfur	(x)	Se	selenium

24.

	Atomic Number	Element	Symbol
(a)	at. no. 1	hydrogen	H
(b)	at. no. 15	phosphorus	P
(c)	at. no. 79	gold	Au
(d)	at. no. 53	iodine	I
(e)	at. no. 6	carbon	C
(f)	at. no. 38	strontium	Sr
(g)	at. no. 82	lead	Pb
(h)	at. no. 20	calcium	Ca

Section 3.5 Metals, Nonmetals, and Semimetals

26.   Arsenic is another element that is used in the semiconductor industry because it is a semimetal.

28.

	Property	Classification
(a)	heat conductor	metal
(b)	gaseous state	nonmetal
(c)	malleable	metal
(d)	dull appearance	nonmetal
(e)	low density	nonmetal
(f)	electrical insulator	nonmetal
(g)	high melting point	metal
(h)	ductile	metal
(i)	reacts with metals	nonmetal
(j)	reacts with nonmetals	metal

30.

	Element	Physical State		Element	Physical State
(a)	cobalt	solid	(b)	germanium	solid
(c)	argon	gas	(d)	titanium	solid
(e)	nitrogen	gas	(f)	bromine	liquid
(g)	hydrogen	gas	(h)	mercury	liquid
(i)	barium	solid	(j)	antimony	solid

Section 3.6 Compounds and Chemical Formulas

32. The composition of C: H: O in vitamin C must be in the ratio 9: 1: 12 by mass as predicted from the law of constant composition.

34.

	Atomic Composition	Formula
(a)	2 carbon, 6 hydrogen, 1 oxygen	C_2H_6O
(b)	2 carbon, 2 chlorine, 4 fluorine	$C_2Cl_2F_4$
(c)	20 carbon, 30 hydrogen, 1 oxygen	$C_{20}H_{30}O$
(d)	5 carbon, 11 hydrogen, 2 oxygen, 1 nitrogen, 1 sulfur	$C_5H_{11}O_2NS$
(e)	14 carbon, 18 hydrogen, 5 oxygen, 2 nitrogen	$C_{14}H_{18}O_5N_2$

36.

	Chemical Formula	Total Number of Atoms
(a)	$C_{27}H_{45}OH$	74
(b)	$CH_3(CH_2)_{16}CO_2H$	56
(c)	$C_3H_5(C_{17}H_{35}O_2)_3$	170
(d)	$NH_2(CH_2)_4CH(CO_2H)NH_2$	24
(e)	$HO_2C(CH_2)_2CH(NH_2)COOH$	19

Section 3.7 Physical and Chemical Properties

38.

	Property		Property
(a)	physical	(b)	chemical
(c)	physical	(d)	physical
(e)	chemical		

40.

	Property		Property
(a)	physical	(b)	chemical
(c)	physical	(d)	physical
(e)	physical	(f)	chemical
(g)	physical	(h)	chemical
(i)	chemical	(j)	chemical

Section 3.8 Physical and Chemical Changes

42.

	Observation	Classification
(a)	burning, combustion (rapid oxidation)	chemical
(b)	rusting, tarnishing (slow oxidation)	chemical
(c)	changing color, odor, or taste	chemical
(d)	evolving gas bubbles from a mixture	chemical
(e)	forming an insoluble substance upon mixing two solutions	chemical
(f)	changing by melting or boiling	physical
(g)	releasing energy as heat or light	chemical

44.

	Change		Change
(a)	physical	(b)	chemical
(c)	physical	(d)	physical
(e)	chemical	(f)	physical
(g)	physical	(h)	chemical
(i)	physical	(j)	chemical

Section 3.9 Law of Conservation of Mass

46.   85 g potassium nitrite + 16 g oxygen = 101 g potassium nitrate

48.   53.453 g ammonium chloride – 36.451 g hydrogen chloride

$$= 17.002 \text{ g ammonia}$$

Section 3.10 Law of Conservation of Energy

50.   On a playground swing the potential energy is greatest when the swing is at its highest point. As the swing descends, it loses potential energy and gains kinetic energy, having its greatest kinetic energy at its lowest point. As the swing ascends, it loses kinetic energy and gains potential energy.

52.   From the law of conservation of energy, 210,000 kilocalories of heat energy were required to convert the water to steam.

54.   (a) $1.000 \text{ g ammonia} \times \dfrac{649 \text{ cal}}{1 \text{ g ammonia}} = 649 \text{ cal}$

       (b)   1.000 g ammonia – 0.824 g nitrogen = 0.176 g hydrogen

56.   Forms of Energy
        (a)   chemical energy is changed into electrical energy
        (b)   electrical energy is changed into mechanical energy
        (c)   mechanical energy is changed into mechanical energy
        (d)   electrical energy and chemical energy are changed into heat energy
        (e)   heat energy is changed into mechanical energy
        (f)   mechanical energy is changed into mechanical energy
        (g)   mechanical energy is changed into mechanical energy
        (h)   mechanical energy is changed into mechanical energy
        (i)   mechanical energy and electrical energy are changed into chemical energy
        (j)   chemical energy and electrical energy are changed into light energy

Section 3.11 Law of Conservation of Mass and Energy

58.   No, the total amount of matter and energy before the process equals the total amount of matter and energy after.

60.   According to the law of conservation of mass and energy, the mass and energy of the gasoline and oxygen must equal the mass and energy of the carbon dioxide, water, and heat. Since the amount of mass converted to energy during the reaction is insignificant, the mass of the gasoline and oxygen essentially equals the mass of the carbon dioxide and water.

General Exercises

62.   The pressure should be *decreased* in order to convert the liquid to a gas.

64.   No, some oxygen molecules have a higher velocity than others, but the *average* velocity of each molecule is identical.

66.   Statement   Change
        (a)   a change in physical state but not chemical formula   physical
        (b)   a change in chemical formula but not physical state   chemical

68.   Forms of Energy
        (1)   nuclear
        (2)   heat
        (3)   mechanical
        (4)   electrical

70.

	Element	Name	Symbol
(a)	at. no. 104	unnilquadium	Unq
(b)	at. no. 105	unnilpentium	Unp
(c)	at. no. 106	unnilhexium	Unh
(d)	at. no. 107	unnilseptium	Uns
(e)	at. no. 108	unniloctium	Uno
(f)	at. no. 109	unnilennium	Une
(g)	at. no. 117	ununseptium	Uus
(h)	at. no. 130	untrinilium	Utn
(i)	at. no. 146	unquadhexium	Uqh
(j)	at. no. 168	unhexoctium	Uho

CHAPTER 4

Atomic Theory and Structure

Section 4.1 Evidence for Atoms: The Dalton Model

2. (1) Law of Conservation of Mass
    (2) Law of Constant Composition

4. No, atoms are composed of smaller particles (protons, neutrons, and electrons) and can be separated into those smaller particles.

Section 4.2 Evidence for Subatomic Particles: The Thomson Model

6. The proton (p^+) is the simplest particle that was observed in canal rays.

8. | Relative Charge of Proton | Relative Mass of Proton |
    |---|---|
    | 1+ | 1836 times the mass of an electron |

10. The homogeneous consistency in the plum pudding model was analogous to the protons in an atom.

Section 4.3 Evidence for a Nuclear Atom: The Rutherford Model

12. According to the Rutherford Model, an atom contains negatively charged electrons that travel in circular orbits about a dense, positively charged nucleus, like the planets in orbit around the sun.

14. | Diameter of an Atom | Diameter of an Atomic Nucleus |
    |---|---|
    | ~ 10^{-8} cm | ~ 10^{-13} cm |

16. | Particle | Approximate Mass (in amu) |
    |---|---|
    | electron (e^-) | ~ 0 |
    | proton (p^+) | ~ 1 |
    | neutron (n°) | ~ 1 |

Section 4.4 Atomic Notation

18.

	Isotope	Neutrons		Isotope	Neutrons
(a)	hydrogen-3	$3 - 1 = 2\, n°$	(b)	Sr-90	$90 - 38 = 52\, n°$
(c)	carbon-14	$14 - 6 = 8\, n°$	(d)	U-235	$235 - 92 = 143\, n°$
(e)	cobalt-60	$60 - 27 = 33\, n°$	(f)	Pt-145	$145 - 78 = 67\, n°$
(g)	aluminum-27	$27 - 13 = 14\, n°$	(h)	Pu-239	$239 - 94 = 145\, n°$

20.

(a) $\begin{pmatrix} 12\,n° \\ 12\,p^+ \end{pmatrix}$ $12e-$ (b) $\begin{pmatrix} 16\,n° \\ 15\,p^+ \end{pmatrix}$ $15e-$

(c) $\begin{pmatrix} 18\,n° \\ 17\,p^+ \end{pmatrix}$ $17e-$ (d) $\begin{pmatrix} 22\,n° \\ 18\,p^+ \end{pmatrix}$ $18e-$

(e) $\begin{pmatrix} 30\,n° \\ 26\,p^+ \end{pmatrix}$ $26e-$ (f) $\begin{pmatrix} 78\,n° \\ 53\,p^+ \end{pmatrix}$ $53e-$

22.   Yes, the mass number is dependent upon the number of protons and neutrons found within an atom's nucleus. Since the number of neutrons in an atom of a particular element can vary, two different elements can have the same mass number.

24.

Atomic Notation	Atomic Number	Mass Number	Number of Protons	Number of Neutrons	Number of Electrons
$^{56}_{26}$Fe	26	56	26	30	26
$^{67}_{30}$Zn	30	67	30	37	30
$^{78}_{34}$Se	34	78	34	44	34
$^{88}_{38}$Sr	38	88	38	50	38
$^{120}_{50}$Sn	50	120	50	70	50
$^{131}_{54}$Xe	54	131	54	77	54

Section 4.5 Atomic Mass Scale

26.   Atomic masses must be expressed on a relative atomic mass scale because atoms are too small to weigh directly and weight values given in grams would be too awkward to work with.

28.

	Isotope	Magnetic Field		Isotope	Magnetic Field
(a)	$^{27}_{13}$Al	decreased	(b)	$^{45}_{21}$Sc	increased
(c)	$^{68}_{30}$Zn	increased	(d)	$^{90}_{40}$Zr	increased

Section 4.6 Atomic Mass

30.

	Isotope	Isotopic Mass		Isotope	Isotopic Mass
(a)	$^{9}_{4}$Be	9.012182 amu	(b)	$^{27}_{13}$Al	26.981539 amu
(c)	$^{31}_{15}$P	30.973762 amu	(d)	$^{75}_{33}$As	74.92159 amu

32.
quizzes: $73 \times 0.10 = 7.3$
homework: $95 \times 0.10 = 9.5$
tests: $75 \times 0.40 = 30$
lab experiment: $92 \times 0.20 = 18$
final exam: $58 \times 0.20 = \underline{12}$
        Weighted average score $= 77$

34.	Fe-54:	53.940 amu × 0.0582	=	3.14 amu
	Fe-56:	55.935 amu × 0.9166	=	51.27 amu
	Fe-57:	56.935 amu × 0.0219	=	1.25 amu
	Fe-58:	57.933 amu × 0.0033	=	0.19 amu
		Atomic Mass	=	55.85 amu

36.	Pt-190:	189.960 amu × 0.000127	=	0.0241 amu
	Pt-192:	191.9612 amu × 0.0078	=	1.5 amu
	Pt-194:	193.963 amu × 0.329	=	63.8 amu
	Pt-195:	194.965 amu × 0.338	=	65.9 amu
	Pt-196:	195.965 amu × 0.253	=	49.6 amu
	Pt-198:	197.968 amu × 0.0721	=	14.3 amu
		Atomic Mass	=	195.1 amu

38.	Ne-20:	19.992 amu × 0.9092	=	18.18 amu
	Ne-21:	20.994 amu × 0.0026	=	0.055 amu
	Ne-22:	21.991 amu × 0.0882	=	1.94 amu
		Atomic Mass	=	20.18 amu

40. The other naturally occurring isotope of bromine is Br-81. This is found by determining what isotopic mass must be averaged with Br-79 to give an atomic mass for bromine of ~ 80 amu.

42. No, the periodic table lists the mass number, not the atomic mass, of the most stable isotope of promethium.

Section 4.7 Evidence for Electron Energy Levels: The Bohr Model

44. Red

46. 1150 nm

48. The emission line spectrum of hydrogen was the experimental evidence that supported the concept of electron energy levels in an atom.

50. The amount of electrical energy required to excite an electron to a higher level is equal to the same amount of light energy released when the electron falls to the ground state.

52.

	Radiant (Light) Energy	Energy Level Transition
(a)	infrared line	5 to 3 or 5 to 4
(b)	ultraviolet line	5 to 1

54.   2 to 1 is the least energetic energy-level change because the electron drops the shortest distance.

56.   4 to 2
        $\lambda = 490$ nm
        A wavelength of 490 nm corresponds to the blue-green line found in the emission spectrum of hydrogen.

58.   5 to 2
        $\lambda = 430$ nm
        A wavelength of 430 nm corresponds to the violet line found in the emission spectrum of hydrogen.

Section 4.8 Principal Energy Levels and Sublevels

60.   Fine lines in the emission spectra of the elements suggested the existence of sublevels within principal energy levels.

62.

	Principal Level	Number of Sublevels
(a)	first	1 (1s)
(b)	third	3 (3s 3p 3d)
(c)	fifth	5 (5s 5p 5d 5f 5g)
(d)	sixth	6 (6s 6p 6d 6f 6g 6h)

64.

	Sublevel	Max. # of Electrons
(a)	an s sublevel	2 e⁻
(b)	a p sublevel	6 e⁻
(c)	a d sublevel	10 e⁻
(d)	an f sublevel	14 e⁻

66.

	Principal Level	Max. # of Electrons
(a)	fifth	$2\,e^- + 6\,e^- + 10\,e^- + 14\,e^- + 18\,e^- = 50\,e^-$
(b)	sixth	$2\,e^- + 6\,e^- + 10\,e^- + 14\,e^- + 18\,e^- + 22\,e^- = 72\,e^-$

Section 4.9 Arrangement of Electrons by Energy Sublevel

68. <u>Filling Diagram</u>   The 6s sublevel follows the 5p sublevel.

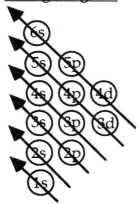

70.

	Element	Electron Configuration
(a)	B	$1s^2\,2s^2\,2p^1$
(b)	F	$1s^2\,2s^2\,2p^5$
(c)	Mn	$1s^2\,2s^2\,2p^6\,3s^2\,3p^6\,4s^2\,3d^5$
(d)	Ni	$1s^2\,2s^2\,2p^6\,3s^2\,3p^6\,4s^2\,3d^8$
(e)	Al	$1s^2\,2s^2\,2p^6\,3s^2\,3p^1$
(f)	Ar	$1s^2\,2s^2\,2p^6\,3s^2\,3p^6$
(g)	As	$1s^2\,2s^2\,2p^6\,3s^2\,3p^6\,4s^2\,3d^{10}\,4p^3$
(h)	Sn	$1s^2\,2s^2\,2p^6\,3s^2\,3p^6\,4s^2\,3d^{10}\,4p^6\,5s^2\,4d^{10}\,5p2$

72.

	Electron Configuration	Element
(a)	$1s^2\,2s^2\,2p^5$	F
(b)	$1s^2\,2s^2\,2p^6\,3s^2\,3p^6$	Ar
(c)	$1s^2\,2s^2\,2p^6\,3s^2\,3p^6\,4s^2\,3d^{10}\,4p^6\,5s^2\,4d^5$	Tc
(d)	$1s^2\,2s^2\,2p^6\,3s^2\,3p^6\,4s^2\,3d^{10}\,4p^6\,5s^2\,4d^{10}\,5p^5$	I

General Exercises

74. If the Houston Astrodome represents the size of a typical atom, then a lead BB in the middle of the Astrodome represents an atomic nucleus.

76. Mass of a proton:

$$1.60 \times 10^{-19} \; \text{coulomb} \times \frac{1 \text{ g}}{9.57 \times 10^4 \; \text{coulomb}} = 1.67 \times 10^{-24} \text{ g}$$

78. | Three Isotopes of Hydrogen | Atomic Notation |
|---|---|
| (a) protium | $_1^1\mathrm{H}$ |
| (b) deuterium | $_1^2\mathrm{H}$ |
| (c) tritium | $_1^3\mathrm{H}$ |

80. An algebraic method must be used to solve this problem.

Let X = the unknown abundance of B-10
Let $1.000 - X$ = the unknown abundance of B-11
The percent abundance of B-10 + the percent abundance of B-11 = 100%
$X\% + (1.000 - X)\% = 100\%$
$X + (1.000 - X) = 1.000$ (Divide percents by 100)

B-10: $10.013\ \text{amu} \times X \quad = \quad 10.013\,X$
B-11: $11.009\ \text{amu} \times (1 - X) = \underline{11.009\,(1 - X)}$
     Atomic Mass $\quad = \quad 10.811\ \text{amu}$

$10.013\,X + 11.009(1 - X) = 10.811$ (Solve for X)
$10.013\,X + 11.009 - 11.009\,X = 10.811$
$0.996\,X = 0.198$

Abundance of B-10: $X = \dfrac{0.198}{0.996} = 0.199$

Abundance of B-11: $1.000 - X = 1.000 - 0.199 = 0.801$

Percent abundance of B-10 = $0.199 \times 100 = 19.9\%$
Percent abundance of B-11 = $0.801 \times 100 = 80.1\%$

82. Since the dominant lines in the emission spectrum of neon occur between 600 and 650 nm, the observed color is reddish-orange.

84. The greater of the two frequencies is the most energetic because energy and frequency are directly related.
The frequency with the higher energy is 5×10^{11} cycles/s.

86. $\lambda = 120\ \text{nm}$
A wavelength of 120 nm corresponds to the ultraviolet region of the spectrum.

88. $\lambda = 1900\ \text{nm}$
A wavelength of 1900 nm corresponds to the infrared region of the spectrum.

90.   The fourth main energy level can hold a maximum of 32 electrons because of the 4*s*, 4*p*, 4*d*, and 4*f* sublevels. Yet, the fourteen 4*f* electrons are not found in the fourth row of the periodic table, they are found in the sixth row. In addition, the ten 4*d* electrons are not found in the fourth row of the periodic table, they are found in the fifth row.

CHAPTER 5

The Periodic Table

Section 5.1 Systematic Arrangement of the Elements

2.   Beginning with hydrogen, oxygen (O) would complete the octave.
        Beginning with fluorine, sulfur (S) would complete the octave.

4.   Mendeleev had not included the noble gases in his periodic table of 1871
        because the noble gases had not yet been discovered.

Section 5.2 The Periodic Law

6.   Ar and K   Although argon has a greater atomic mass than potassium, it
                      precedes potassium on the periodic table because of
                      its lower atomic number.

        Co and Ni   Although cobalt has a greater atomic mass than nickel, it
                      precedes nickel on the periodic table because of
                      its lower atomic number.

8.   By studying x-ray emission from excited nuclei, Moseley discovered that
        the elements have a stepwise increase in nuclear charge.

Section 5.3 The Periodic Table of the Elements

10.   Periods and series

12.   Transition elements

14.   Metals

16.   Semimetals

18.	Family	Group Number
(a)	boron group	IIIA/13
(b)	oxygen group	VIA/16
(c)	nickel group	VIII/10
(d)	copper group	IB/11

20. Actinide series

22. Transuranium elements

24.

	IUPAC	American		IUPAC	American
(a)	Group 2	IIA	(b)	Group 4	IVB
(c)	Group 6	VIB	(d)	Group 8	VIII
(e)	Group 9	VIII	(f)	Group 10	VIII
(g)	Group 12	IIB	(h)	Group 14	IVA
(i)	Group 16	VIA	(j)	Group 18	VIIIA

26.

	Element		Element
(a)	Sb	(b)	Mg
(c)	Br	(d)	Th
(e)	Sc	(f)	Se
(g)	Pt	(h)	Rn

Section 5.4 Periodic Trends

28. Decreases

30. Decreases

32.

	Metallic Character		Metallic Character
(a)	B < **Al**	(b)	Na < **K**
(c)	Mg < **Ba**	(d)	H < **Fe**
(e)	**K** > Ca	(f)	**Mg** > Al
(g)	**Fe** > Cu	(h)	**S** > Ar

(Note: The element with the greater metallic character is in bold)

Section 5.5 Predicting Properties of Elements

34. Predicted atomic radius of Cl: $0.115 - (0.133 - 0.115) = \sim 0.097$ nm

Predicted density of Br: $\dfrac{1.56 + 4.97}{2} = \sim 3.27$ g/mL

Predicted boiling point of I: $58.8 + [58.8 - (-34.6)] = \sim 152.2°C$

36. Predicted boiling point of Ar: $-152 + [-152 - (-107)] = \sim -197°C$

Predicted atomic radius of Kr: $\dfrac{0.180 + 0.210}{2} = \sim 0.195$ nm

Predicted density of Xe: $3.48 + (3.48 - 1.66) = \sim 5.30$ g/mL

38.

	Compound	Formula		Compound	Formula
(a)	potassium fluoride	KF	(b)	calcium fluoride	CaF_2
(c)	boron bromide	BBr_3	(d)	germanium iodide	GeI_4

40.

	Compound	Formula		Compound	Formula
(a)	strontium chloride	$SrCl_2$	(b)	strontium bromide	$SrBr_2$
(c)	magnesium iodide	MgI_2	(d)	beryllium fluoride	BeF_2

42.

	Compound	Formulas		Compound	Formulas
(a)	nitrogen oxide	N_2O_3 N_2O_5	(b)	arsenic oxide	As_2O_3 As_2O_5
(c)	phosphorus sulfide	P_2S_3 P_2S_5	(d)	antimony sulfide	Sb_2S_3 Sb_2S_5

Section 5.6 The *s, p, d, f* Blocks of Elements

44. The *p* sublevel

46. The *f* sublevel

48. The 5*f* sublevel

50.

	Element	Highest Sublevel		Element	Highest Sublevel
(a)	He	1s	(b)	K	4s
(c)	U	5f	(d)	Pd	4d
(e)	Be	2s	(f)	Co	3d
(g)	Si	3p	(h)	Pt	5d
(i)	Ho	4f	(j)	Unp	6d

52.

	Element	Electron Configuration
(a)	B	$1s^2 2s^2 2p^1$ or [He] $2s^2 2p^1$
(b)	Ti	$1s^2 2s^2 2p^6 3s^2 3p^6 4s^2 3d^2$ or [Ar] $4s^2 3d^2$
(c)	Na	$1s^2 2s^2 2p^6 3s^1$ or [Ne] $3s^1$
(d)	O	$1s^2 2s^2 2p^4$ or [He] $2s^2 2p^4$
(e)	Ge	$1s^2 2s^2 2p^6 3s^2 3p^6 4s^2 3d^{10} 4p^2$ or [Ar] $4s^2 3d^{10} 4p^2$
(f)	Ba	$1s^2 2s^2 2p^6 3s^2 3p^6 4s^2 3d^{10} 4p^6 5s^2 4d^{10} 5p^6 6s^2$ or [Xe] $6s^2$
(g)	Pd	$1s^2 2s^2 2p^6 3s^2 3p^6 4s^2 3d^{10} 4p^6 5s^2 4d^8$ or [Kr] $5s^2 4d^8$
(h)	Kr	$1s^2 2s^2 2p^6 3s^2 3p^6 4s^2 3d^{10} 4p^6$ or [Ar] $4s^2 3d^{10} 4p^6$
(i)	Al	$1s^2 2s^2 2p^6 3s^2 3p^1$ or [Ne] $3s^2 3p^1$
(j)	Si	$1s^2 2s^2 2p^6 3s^2 3p^2$ or [Ne] $3s^2 3p^2$

Section 5.7 Predicting Valence Electrons

54.

	Group	Valence Electrons		Group	Valence Electrons
(a)	IIA/2	2	(b)	IVA/14	4
(c)	VIA/16	6	(d)	VIIIA/18	8

56.

	Element	Valence Electrons		Element	Valence Electrons
(a)	He	2	(b)	Pb	4
(c)	Se	6	(d)	Ne	8
(e)	Cs	1	(f)	Ga	3
(g)	Sb	5	(h)	Br	7

Section 5.8 Electron Dot Formulas of Atoms

58.

	Element	Dot Formula		Element	Dot Formula
(a)	He	 H̤e·	(b)	Pb	 ·Ṗb:
(c)	Se	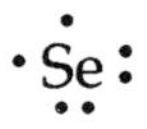 ·S̤e:	(d)	Ne	 :N̤e:
(e)	Cs	 Cs·	(f)	Ga	 ·G̤a·
(g)	Sb	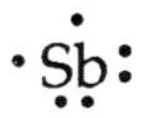 ·Ṣb:	(h)	Br	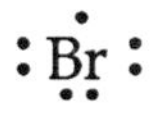 :Ḅr:

Section 5.9 Ionization Energy

60.   Increases

62.   Group IA/1

64.

	Ionization Energy		Ionization Energy
(a)	Rb > **Cs**	(b)	He > **Ar**
(c)	B > **Al**	(d)	F > **I**
(e)	**Mg** < Si	(f)	**Pb** < Bi
(g)	**Ca** < Ga	(h)	**P** < Cl
(i)	**Sc** < Zn	(j)	H > **Li**

(Note: The element with the lower ionization energy is in bold)

Section 5.10 Predicting Ionic Charges

66.

	Group	Ionic Charge		Group	Ionic Charge
(a)	IVA/14	4–	(b)	VA/15	3–
(c)	VIA/16	2–	(d)	VIIA/17	1–

68.

	Ion	Charge		Ion	Charge
(a)	Ga ion	3+	(b)	Cs ion	1+
(c)	Ra ion	2+	(d)	Pb ion	4+
(e)	Br ion	1–	(f)	S ion	2–
(g)	P ion	3–	(h)	I ion	1–

70.

	Ion	Isoelectronic with Krypton
(a)	Rb^+	yes
(b)	Ca^{2+}	no
(c)	Y^{3+}	yes
(d)	Br^-	yes
(e)	Se^{2-}	yes
(f)	As^{3+}	no

Section 5.11 Electron Configuration of Ions

72.

	Ion	Electron Configuration
(a)	Sr^{2+}	$1s^2\,2s^2\,2p^6\,3s^2\,3p^6\,4s^2\,3d^{10}\,4p^6$ or [Kr]
(b)	Y^{3+}	$1s^2\,2s^2\,2p^6\,3s^2\,3p^6\,4s^2\,3d^{10}\,4p^6$ or [Kr]
(c)	Fe^{3+}	$1s^2\,2s^2\,2p^6\,3s^2\,3p^6\,3d^5$ or [Ar] $3d^5$
(d)	Ti^{4+}	$1s^2\,2s^2\,2p^6\,3s^2\,3p^6$ or [Ar]

74.

	Ion	Electron Configuration
(a)	Br^-	$1s^2\,2s^2\,2p^6\,3s^2\,3p^6\,4s^2\,3d^{10}\,4p^6$ or [Kr]
(b)	Te^{2-}	$1s^2\,2s^2\,2p^6\,3s^2\,3p^6\,4s^2\,3d^{10}\,4p^6\,5s^2\,4d^{10}\,5p^6$ or [Xe]
(c)	As^{3-}	$1s^2\,2s^2\,2p^6\,3s^2\,3p^6\,4s^2\,3d^{10}\,4p^6$ or [Kr]
(d)	O^{2-}	$1s^2\,2s^2\,2p^6$ or [Ne]

General Exercises

76.

Triad	
yellow gas	Cl
reddish-brown liquid	Br
violet solid	I

78.

	European	IUPAC		European	IUPAC
(a)	Group IIA	Group 2	(b)	Group IIB	Group 12
(c)	Group IVA	Group 4	(d)	Group IVB	Group 14
(e)	Group VIA	Group 6	(f)	Group VIIIB	Group 18

80.

	Element	Electron Configuration
(a)	Sr	[Kr] $5s^2$
(b)	Ru	[Kr] $5s^2\,4d^6$
(c)	Sb	[Kr] $5s^2\,4d^{10}\,5p^3$
(d)	Cs	[Xe] $6s^1$
(e)	W	[Xe] $6s^2\,4f^{14}\,5d^4$
(f)	Bi	[Xe] $6s^2\,4f^{14}\,5d^{10}\,6p^3$
(g)	Ra	[Rn] $7s^2$
(h)	Ac	[Rn] $7s^2\,6d^1$

80. | Element | | Electron Configuration |
       |---|---|---|
       | (i) | Pu | $[Rn] \, 7s^2 \, 5f^6$ |
       | (j) | Unh | $[Rn] \, 7s^2 \, 5f^{14} \, 6d^4$ |

82.   Magnesium has two *s* electrons. Aluminum has two *s* electrons and one *p* electron. Therefore, the ionization energy for aluminum is less than that for magnesium because *s* electrons are more difficult to remove than *p* electrons.

84.   Ion
       H^+ Hydrogen loses an electron like the Group IA/1 elements.
       H^- Hydrogen gains an electron like the Group VIIA/17 elements.

CHAPTER 6

Naming Chemical Compounds

Section 6.1 IUPAC Systematic Nomenclature

2.

	Compound	Classification		Compound	Classification
(a)	CO_2	binary molecular	(b)	$HF_{(aq)}$	binary acid
(c)	$H_3PO_{4(aq)}$	ternary oxyacid	(d)	Co_2O_3	binary ionic
(e)	$Zn_3(PO_4)_2$	ternary ionic			

4.

	Ion	Classification		Ion	Classification
(a)	Bi^{3+}	monoatomic cation	(b)	ClO_3^-	polyatomic anion
(c)	H_3O^+	polyatomic cation	(d)	N^{3-}	monoatomic anion

Section 6.2 Monoatomic Ions

6.

	Monoatomic Cation	Formula
(a)	lithium ion	Li^+
(b)	aluminum ion	Al^{3+}
(c)	zinc ion	Zn^{2+}
(d)	strontium ion	Sr^{2+}

8.

	Monoatomic Cation	Formula
(a)	lead(II) ion	Pb^{2+}
(b)	nickel(II) ion	Ni^{2+}
(c)	tin(IV) ion	Sn^{4+}
(d)	manganese(II) ion	Mn^{2+}

10.

	Monoatomic Cation	Formula
(a)	cupric ion	Cu^{2+}
(b)	mercuric ion	Hg^{2+}
(c)	ferrous ion	Fe^{2+}
(d)	plumbic ion	Pb^{4+}

12. | Monoatomic Anion | Formula
(a) chloride ion | Cl^-
(b) bromide ion | Br^-
(c) sulfide ion | S^{2-}
(d) nitride ion | N^{3-}

Section 6.3 Polyatomic Ions

14. | Polyatomic Anion | Systematic Name
(a) CN^- | cyanide ion
(b) NO_3^- | nitrate ion
(c) CrO_4^{2-} | chromate ion
(d) HSO_4^- | hydrogen sulfate ion

16. | Polyatomic Ion | Formula
(a) hydrogen sulfite ion | HSO_3^-
(b) chlorite ion | ClO_2^-
(c) sulfate ion | SO_4^{2-}
(d) perchlorate ion | ClO_4^-

Section 6.4 Writing Chemical Formulas

18. | Ions | | Binary Compound
(a) $Ba^{2+} + 2\,Cl^-$ | = | $BaCl_2$
(b) $3\,Li^+ + N^{3-}$ | = | Li_3N
(c) $Cd^{2+} + S^{2-}$ | = | CdS
(d) $3\,Mg^{2+} + 2\,P^{3-}$ | = | Mg_3P_2
(e) $Pb^{4+} + 2\,S^{2-}$ | = | PbS_2

20. | Ions | | Ternary Compound
(a) $Fe^{3+} + 3\,HCO_3^-$ | = | $Fe(HCO_3)_3$
(b) $2\,Cu^+ + CO_3^{2-}$ | = | Cu_2CO_3
(c) $Hg^{2+} + 2\,CN^-$ | = | $Hg(CN)_2$
(d) $Sn^{4+} + 4\,C_2H_3O_2^-$ | = | $Sn(C_2H_3O_2)_4$

22. | Ions | | Ternary Compound
(a) $Pb^{4+} + 2\,SO_4^{2-}$ | = | $Pb(SO_4)_2$
(b) $Sn^{2+} + 2\,ClO_2^-$ | = | $Sn(ClO_2)_2$
(c) $Co^{2+} + 2\,OH^-$ | = | $Co(OH)_2$
(d) $3\,Hg_2^{2+} + 2\,PO_4^{3-}$ | = | $(Hg_2)_3(PO_4)_2$

Section 6.5 Binary Ionic Compounds

24.
	Binary Ionic Compound	Formula
(a)	lithium oxide	Li_2O
(b)	strontium oxide	SrO
(c)	zinc chloride	$ZnCl_2$
(d)	nickel(II) fluoride	NiF_2

26.
	Binary Ionic Compound	Formula
(a)	manganese(II) nitride	Mn_3N_2
(b)	iron(II) bromide	$FeBr_2$
(c)	tin(IV) fluoride	SnF_4
(d)	cobalt(II) sulfide	CoS

28.
	Binary Ionic Compound	Formula
(a)	plumbous oxide	PbO
(b)	ferric phosphide	FeP
(c)	mercuric iodide	HgI_2
(d)	cuprous chloride	$CuCl$

Section 6.6 Ternary Ionic Compounds

30.
	Ternary Ionic Compound	Formula
(a)	potassium nitrate	KNO_3
(b)	magnesium perchlorate	$Mg(ClO_4)_2$
(c)	silver sulfate	Ag_2SO_4
(d)	aluminum dichromate	$Al_2(Cr_2O_7)_3$

32.
	Ternary Ionic Compound	Formula
(a)	manganese(II) acetate	$Mn(C_2H_3O_2)_2$
(b)	copper(II) chlorite	$Cu(ClO_2)_2$
(c)	tin(II) phosphate	$Sn_3(PO_4)_2$
(d)	iron(III) hypochlorite	$Fe(ClO)_3$

34.
	Ternary Ionic Compound	Formula
(a)	cuprous chlorite	$CuClO_2$
(b)	plumbic sulfite	$Pb(SO_3)_2$
(c)	mercuric chlorate	$Hg(ClO_3)_2$
(d)	ferrous chromate	$FeCrO_4$

Section 6.7 Binary Molecular Compounds

36.

	Binary Molecular Compound	Systematic Name
(a)	HCl	hydrogen chloride
(b)	BrF_3	bromine trifluoride
(c)	I_2O_4	diiodine tetraoxide
(d)	Cl_2O_3	dichlorine trioxide

38.

	Binary Molecular Compound	Formula
(a)	chlorine dioxide	ClO_2
(b)	tribromine octaoxide	Br_3O_8
(c)	tetraphosphorus heptasulfide	P_4S_7
(d)	sulfur hexafluoride	SF_6

Section 6.8 Binary Acids

40.

	Binary Acid	Formula
(a)	hydrochloric acid	$HCl_{(aq)}$
(b)	hydroiodic acid	$HI_{(aq)}$
(c)	hydrosulfuric acid	$H_2S_{(aq)}$

Section 6.9 Ternary Oxyacids

42.

	Ternary Oxyacid	Systematic Name
(a)	$HClO_{4(aq)}$	perchloric acid
(b)	$HIO_{(aq)}$	hypoiodous acid
(c)	$HBrO_{2(aq)}$	bromous acid
(d)	$H_2SeO_{4(aq)}$	selenic acid

44.

	Ternary Oxyacid	Formula
(a)	sulfuric acid	$H_2SO_{4(aq)}$
(b)	nitrous acid	$HNO_{2(aq)}$
(c)	iodous acid	$HIO_{2(aq)}$
(d)	bromic acid	$HBrO_{3(aq)}$

Section 6.10 Acid Salts

46.

	Acids Salts	Formula
(a)	barium dihydrogen phosphate	$Ba(H_2PO_4)_2$
(b)	silver monohydrogen phosphate	Ag_2HPO_4
(c)	cuprous hydrogen carbonate	$CuHCO_3$
(d)	iron(III) hydrogen sulfate	$Fe(HSO_4)_3$

Section 6.11 Predicting Chemical Formulas

48. (a) Given: aluminum nitride   =   AlN
                 gallium nitride   =   GaN
     (b) Given: titanium oxide   = TiO_2
                 zirconium oxide   = ZrO_2

50. (a) Given: iron(III) sulfate   = $Fe_2(SO_4)_3$
                 iron(III) selenate = $Fe_2(SeO_4)_3$
     (b) Given: scandium nitrate   = $Sc(NO_3)_3$
                 lanthanum nitrate   = $La(NO_3)_3$

52. (a) Given: phosphorous acid   = $H_3PO_{3(aq)}$
                 arsenous acid   = $H_3AsO_{3(aq)}$
     (b) Given: sulfuric acid   = $H_2SO_{4(aq)}$
                 selenic acid   = $H_2SeO_{4(aq)}$

General Exercises

54.
	Substance	Ionic Charge
(a)	chlorine gas molecules	0
(b)	chloride ions	1–
(c)	hypochlorite ions	1–
(d)	chlorine compounds	0

56.
	Polyatomic Anion	Valence Electrons
(a)	$BrO^{?-}$	$7 + 6 + (1\ e^- \text{ from charge}) = 14$
(b)	$S_2O_8^{?-}$	$2(6) + 8(6) + (1\ e^- \text{ from charge}) = 61$
(c)	$HCO_2^{?-}$	$1 + 4 + 2(6) + (1\ e^- \text{ from charge}) = 18$
(d)	$CNO^{?-}$	$4 + 5 + 6 + (1\ e^- \text{ from charge}) = 16$

The polyatomic anions with an even number of valence electrons are (a), (c), and (d). Thus, BrO^-, HCO_2^-, and CNO^- are the polyatomic anions that have a 1– charge.

58.

Ions	lithium ion	copper(II) ion	iron(III) ion	lead(IV) ion
chloride ion	Li^+ Cl^- LiCl	Cu^{2+} $2\,Cl^-$ $CuCl_2$	Fe^{3+} $3\,Cl^-$ $FeCl_3$	Pb^{4+} $4\,Cl^-$ $PbCl_4$
iodide ion	Li^+ I^- LiI	Cu^{2+} $2\,I^-$ CuI_2	Fe^{3+} $3\,I^-$ FeI_3	Pb^{4+} $4\,I^-$ PbI_4
phosphide ion	$3\,Li^+$ P^{3-} Li_3P	$3\,Cu^{2+}$ $2\,P^{3-}$ Cu_3P_2	Fe^{3+} P^{3-} FeP	$3\,Pb^{4+}$ $4\,P^{3-}$ Pb_3P_4
sulfide ion	$2\,Li^+$ S^{2-} Li_2S	Cu^{2+} S^{2-} CuS	$2\,Fe^{3+}$ $3\,S^{2-}$ Fe_2S_3	Pb^{4+} $2\,S^{2-}$ PbS_2

60.

Ions	sodium ion	iron(II) ion	calcium ion	cobalt(III) ion
hydroxide ion	Na^+ OH^- NaOH	Fe^{2+} $2\,OH^-$ $Fe(OH)_2$	Ca^{2+} $2\,OH^-$ $Ca(OH)_2$	Co^{3+} $3\,OH^-$ $Co(OH)_3$
sulfate ion	$2\,Na^+$ SO_4^{2-} Na_2SO_4	Fe^{2+} SO_4^{2-} $FeSO_4$	Ca^{2+} SO_4^{2-} $CaSO_4$	$2\,Co^{3+}$ $3\,SO_4^{2-}$ $Co_2(SO_4)_3$
acetate ion	Na^+ $C_2H_3O_2^-$ $NaC_2H_3O_2$	Fe^{2+} $2\,C_2H_3O_2^-$ $Fe(C_2H_3O_2)_2$	Ca^{2+} $2\,C_2H_3O_2^-$ $Ca(C_2H_3O_2)_2$	Co^{3+} $3\,C_2H_3O_2^-$ $Co(C_2H_3O_2)_3$
phosphate ion	$3\,Na^+$ PO_4^{3-} Na_3PO_4	$3\,Fe^{2+}$ $2\,PO_4^{3-}$ $Fe_3(PO_4)_2$	$3\,Ca^{2+}$ $2\,PO_4^{3-}$ $Ca_3(PO_4)_2$	Co^{3+} PO_4^{3-} $CoPO_4$

62.

	Compound	Suffix Ending		Compound	Suffix Ending
(a)	KI	-ide	(b)	$HI_{(aq)}$	-ic acid
(c)	KIO	-ite	(d)	$HIO_{(aq)}$	-ous acid
(e)	KIO_2	-ite	(f)	$HIO_{2(aq)}$	-ous acid
(g)	KIO_3	-ate	(h)	$HIO_{3(aq)}$	-ic acid
(i)	KIO_4	-ate	(j)	$HIO_{4(aq)}$	-ic acid

64.

	Chemical Name	Common Name	Formula
(a)	acetic acid	vinegar solution	$HC_2H_3O_{2(aq)}$
(b)	aqueous nitrogen trihydride	ammonia solution	$NH_{3(aq)}$
(c)	aqueous magnesium hydroxide	milk of magnesia	$Mg(OH)_{2(aq)}$
(d)	aqueous sodium bisulfate	"bowl cleaner"	$NaHSO_{4(aq)}$

66.   Binary Compound   Formula
    (a) boron tribromide BBr_3
    (b) trisilicon tetranitride Si_3N_4
    (c) diarsenic trioxide As_2O_3
    (d) diantimony pentaoxide Sb_2O_5

68.   Name   Formula
    manganese(IV) oxide MnO_2

70. Given: lutetium chloride   = $LuCl_3$
                   lawrencium chloride = $LrCl_3$

Chemical Formula Calculations

Section 7.1 Avogadro's Number

2.

	Element	Average Mass		Element	Average Mass
(a)	H	1.0 g	(b)	Li	6.9 g
(c)	C	12.0 g	(d)	P	31.0 g
(e)	Ca	40.1 g	(f)	Zn	65.4 g
(g)	As	74.9 g	(h)	U	238.0 g

Section 7.2 The Mole Concept

4. (a) 6.02×10^{23} atoms Cu = 1 mol Cu atoms
    (b) 6.02×10^{23} molecules SO_2 = 1 mol SO_2 molecules
    (c) 6.02×10^{23} formula units $CuSO_4$ = 1 mol $CuSO_4$ formula units
    (d) 6.02×10^{23} ions HSO_4^- = 1 mol HSO_4^- ions

6. (a) $2.12 \; \cancel{\text{mol Ar}} \times \dfrac{6.02 \times 10^{23} \text{ atoms Ar}}{1 \; \cancel{\text{mol Ar}}} = 1.28 \times 10^{24}$ atoms Ar

    (b) $7.10 \; \cancel{\text{mol NF}_3} \times \dfrac{6.02 \times 10^{23} \text{ molecules NF}_3}{1 \; \cancel{\text{mol NF}_3}}$
    $= 4.27 \times 10^{24}$ molecules NF_3

    (c) $0.552 \; \cancel{\text{mol Ag}_2\text{SO}_4} \times \dfrac{6.02 \times 10^{23} \text{ formula units Ag}_2\text{SO}_4}{1 \; \cancel{\text{mol Ag}_2\text{SO}_4}}$
    $= 3.32 \times 10^{23}$ formula units Ag_2SO_4

    (d) $0.112 \; \cancel{\text{mol CO}_3^{2-}} \times \dfrac{6.02 \times 10^{23} \text{ ions CO}_3^{2-}}{1 \; \cancel{\text{mol CO}_3^{2-}}} = 6.74 \times 10^{22}$ ions CO_3^{2-}

8. (a) $7.88 \times 10^{24} \; \cancel{\text{atoms Se}} \times \dfrac{1 \text{ mol Se}}{6.02 \times 10^{23} \; \cancel{\text{atoms Se}}} = 13.1$ mol Se

    (b) $5.55 \times 10^{25} \; \cancel{\text{molecules H}_2\text{S}} \times \dfrac{1 \text{ mol H}_2\text{S}}{6.02 \times 10^{23} \; \cancel{\text{molecules H}_2\text{S}}}$
    $= 92.2$ mol H_2S

    (c) $2.25 \times 10^{22} \; \cancel{\text{formula units SrCO}_3} \times \dfrac{1 \text{ mol SrCO}_3}{6.02 \times 10^{23} \; \cancel{\text{formula units SrCO}_3}}$
    $= 0.0374$ mol $SrCO_3$

8.   (d) 6.55×10^{24} ~~ions CrO$_4^{2-}$~~ $\times \dfrac{1 \text{ mol CrO}_4{}^{2-}}{6.02 \times 10^{23} \text{ ~~ions CrO$_4^{2-}$~~}} = 10.9 \text{ mol CrO}_4{}^{2-}$

Section 7.3 Molar Mass

10.

Element	Molar Mass
(a) F_2	$2(19.0) = 38.0$ g/mol
(b) I_2	$2(126.9) = 253.8$ g/mol
(c) P_4	$4(31.0) = 124.0$ g/mol
(d) S_8	$8(32.1) = 256.8$ g/mol

12.

Molecular Compound	Molar Mass
(a) CH_4	12.0 g $+ 4(1.0)$ g $= 16.0$ g/mol
(b) PI_3	31.0 g $+ 3(126.9)$ g $= 411.7$ g/mol
(c) As_2O_5	$2(74.9)$ g $+ 5(16.0)$ g $= 229.8$ g/mol
(d) $C_3H_5(OH)_3$	$3(12.0)$ g $+ 8(1.0)$ g $+ 3(16.0)$ g $= 92.0$ g/mol

Section 7.4 Mole Calculations I

14.   (a)   MM of Kr = 83.8 g/mol

1.21×10^{24} ~~atoms Kr~~ $\times \dfrac{1 \text{ ~~mol Kr~~}}{6.02 \times 10^{23} \text{ ~~atoms Kr~~}} \times \dfrac{83.8 \text{ g Kr}}{1 \text{ ~~mol Kr~~}} = 168 \text{ g Kr}$

(b)   MM of $N_2O = 2(14.0)$ g $+ 16.0 = 44.0$ g/mol

6.33×10^{22} ~~molecules N$_2$O~~ $\times \dfrac{1 \text{ ~~mol N$_2$O~~}}{6.02 \times 10^{23} \text{ ~~molecules N$_2$O~~}} \times$

$\dfrac{44.0 \text{ g N}_2\text{O}}{1 \text{ ~~mol N$_2$O~~}} = 4.63 \text{ g N}_2\text{O}$

(c)   MM of $Mg(ClO_4)_2 = 24.3$ g $+ 2(35.5)$ g $+ 8(16.0)$ g $= 223.3$ g/mol

4.17×10^{21} ~~formula units Mg(ClO$_4$)$_2$~~ $\times$

$\dfrac{1 \text{ ~~mol Mg(ClO$_4$)$_2$~~}}{6.02 \times 10^{23} \text{ ~~formula units Mg(ClO$_4$)$_2$~~}} \times \dfrac{223.3 \text{ g Mg(ClO}_4)_2}{1 \text{ ~~mol Mg(ClO$_4$)$_2$~~}}$

$= 1.55 \text{ g Mg(ClO}_4)_2$

16.   (a)   MM of Pt = 195.1 g/mol

7.57 ~~g Pt~~ $\times \dfrac{1 \text{ ~~mol Pt~~}}{195.1 \text{ ~~g Pt~~}} \times \dfrac{6.02 \times 10^{23} \text{ atoms Pt}}{1 \text{ ~~mol Pt~~}} = 2.34 \times 10^{22} \text{ atoms Pt}$

(b)   MM of $C_2H_6 = 2(12.0)$ g $+ 6(1.0)$ g $= 30.0$ g/mol

3.88 ~~g C$_2$H$_6$~~ $\times \dfrac{1 \text{ ~~mol C$_2$H$_6$~~}}{30.0 \text{ ~~g C$_2$H$_6$~~}} \times \dfrac{6.02 \times 10^{23} \text{ molecules C}_2\text{H}_6}{1 \text{ ~~mol C$_2$H$_6$~~}}$

$= 7.79 \times 10^{22} \text{ molecules C}_2\text{H}_6$

16. (c) MM of $AlCl_3$ = 27.0 g + 3(35.5) g = 133.5 g/mol

$$0.152 \text{ g AlCl}_3 \times \frac{1 \text{ mol AlCl}_3}{133.5 \text{ g AlCl}_3} \times \frac{6.02 \times 10^{23} \text{ formula units AlCl}_3}{1 \text{ mol AlCl}_3}$$
$$= 6.85 \times 10^{20} \text{ formula units AlCl}_3$$

18. (a) MM of CH_4 = 12.0 g + 4(1.0) g = 16.0 g/mol

$$\frac{16.0 \text{ g CH}_4}{1 \text{ mol CH}_4} \times \frac{1 \text{ mol CH}_4}{6.02 \times 10^{23} \text{ molecules CH}_4}$$
$$= 2.66 \times 10^{-23} \text{ g/molecule CH}_4$$

(b) MM of NH_3 = 14.0 g + 3(1.0) g = 17.0 g/mol

$$\frac{17.0 \text{ g NH}_3}{1 \text{ mol NH}_3} \times \frac{1 \text{ mol NH}_3}{6.02 \times 10^{23} \text{ molecules NH}_3}$$
$$= 2.82 \times 10^{-23} \text{ g/molecule NH}_3$$

(c) MM of SO_3 = 32.1 g + 3(16.0) g = 80.1 g/mol

$$\frac{80.1 \text{ g SO}_3}{1 \text{ mol SO}_3} \times \frac{1 \text{ mol SO}_3}{6.02 \times 10^{23} \text{ molecules SO}_3}$$
$$= 1.33 \times 10^{-22} \text{ g/molecule SO}_3$$

(d) MM of N_2O_5 = 2(14.0) g + 5(16.0) g = 108.0 g/mol

$$\frac{108.0 \text{ g N}_2\text{O}_5}{1 \text{ mol N}_2\text{O}_5} \times \frac{1 \text{ mol N}_2\text{O}_5}{6.02 \times 10^{23} \text{ molecules N}_2\text{O}_5}$$
$$= 1.79 \times 10^{-22} \text{ g/molecule N}_2\text{O}_5$$

Section 7.5 Percentage Composition

20. MM of $C_3H_5O_3(NO_2)_3$ = 3(12.0) g C + 5(1.0) g H + 9(16.0) g O +
$$3(14.0) \text{ g N}$$
$$= 36.0 \text{ g C} + 5.0 \text{ g H} + 144.0 \text{ g O} + 42.0 \text{ g N}$$
$$= 227.0 \text{ g C}_3\text{H}_5\text{O}_3(\text{NO}_2)_3$$

$$\frac{36.0 \text{ g C}}{227.0 \text{ g C}_3\text{H}_5\text{O}_3(\text{NO}_2)_3} \times 100 = 15.9\% \text{ C}$$

$$\frac{5.0 \text{ g H}}{227.0 \text{ g C}_3\text{H}_5\text{O}_3(\text{NO}_2)_3} \times 100 = 2.2\% \text{ H}$$

$$\frac{144.0 \text{ g O}}{227.0 \text{ g C}_3\text{H}_5\text{O}_3(\text{NO}_2)_3} \times 100 = 63.4\% \text{ O}$$

$$\frac{42.0 \text{ g N}}{227.0 \text{ g C}_3\text{H}_5\text{O}_3(\text{NO}_2)_3} \times 100 = 18.5\% \text{ N}$$

22. MM of $C_5H_{11}NSO_2$ = 5(12.0) g C + 11(1.0) g H + 14.0 g N + 32.1 g S +
$$2(16.0) \text{ g O}$$
$$= 60.0 \text{ g C} + 11.0 \text{ g H} + 14.0 \text{ g N} + 32.1 \text{g S} + 32.0 \text{ g O}$$
$$= 149.1 \text{ g C}_5\text{H}_{11}\text{NSO}_2$$

22.

$$\frac{60.0 \text{ g C}}{149.1 \text{ g C}_5\text{H}_{11}\text{NSO}_2} \times 100 = 40.2\% \text{ C}$$

$$\frac{11.0 \text{ g H}}{149.1 \text{ g C}_5\text{H}_{11}\text{NSO}_2} \times 100 = 7.4\% \text{ H}$$

$$\frac{14.0 \text{ g N}}{149.1 \text{ g C}_5\text{H}_{11}\text{NSO}_2} \times 100 = 9.4\% \text{ N}$$

$$\frac{32.1 \text{ g S}}{149.1 \text{ g C}_5\text{H}_{11}\text{NSO}_2} \times 100 = 21.5\% \text{ S}$$

$$\frac{32.0 \text{ g O}}{149.1 \text{ g C}_5\text{H}_{11}\text{NSO}_2} \times 100 = 21.5\% \text{ O}$$

24.

$$\begin{aligned}
\text{MM of C}_{55}\text{H}_{70}\text{MgN}_4\text{O}_6 &= 55(12.0) \text{ g C} + 70(1.0) \text{ g H} + 24.3 \text{ g Mg} + \\
&\qquad 4(14.0) \text{ g N} + 6(16.0) \text{ g O} \\
&= 660.0 \text{ g C} + 70.0 \text{ g H} + 24.3 \text{ g Mg} + 56.0 \text{ g N} + \\
&\qquad 96.0 \text{ g O} \\
&= 906.3 \text{ g C}_{55}\text{H}_{70}\text{MgN}_4\text{O}_6
\end{aligned}$$

$$\frac{660.0 \text{ g C}}{906.3 \text{ g C}_{55}\text{H}_{70}\text{MgN}_4\text{O}_6} \times 100 = 72.8\% \text{ C}$$

$$\frac{70.0 \text{ g H}}{906.3 \text{ g C}_{55}\text{H}_{70}\text{MgN}_4\text{O}_6} \times 100 = 7.7\% \text{ H}$$

$$\frac{24.3 \text{ g Mg}}{906.3 \text{ g C}_{55}\text{H}_{70}\text{MgN}_4\text{O}_6} \times 100 = 2.7\% \text{ Mg}$$

$$\frac{56.0 \text{ g N}}{906.3 \text{ g C}_{55}\text{H}_{70}\text{MgN}_4\text{O}_6} \times 100 = 6.2\% \text{ N}$$

$$\frac{96.0 \text{ g O}}{906.3 \text{ g C}_{55}\text{H}_{70}\text{MgN}_4\text{O}_6} \times 100 = 10.6\% \text{ O}$$

26.

$$\begin{aligned}
\text{MM of HgNa}_2\text{C}_{20}\text{H}_8\text{Br}_2\text{O}_6 &= 200.6 \text{ g Hg} + 2(23.0) \text{ g Na} + 20(12.0) \text{ g C} + \\
&\qquad 8(1.0) \text{ g H} + 2(79.9) \text{ g Br} + 6(16.0) \text{ g O} \\
&= 200.6 \text{ g Hg} + 46.0 \text{ g Na} + 240.0 \text{ g C} + 8.0 \text{ g H} \\
&\qquad + 159.8 \text{ g Br} + 96.0 \text{ g O} \\
&= 750.4 \text{ g HgNa}_2\text{C}_{20}\text{H}_8\text{Br}_2\text{O}_6
\end{aligned}$$

$$\frac{200.6 \text{ g Hg}}{750.4 \text{ g HgNa}_2\text{C}_{20}\text{H}_8\text{Br}_2\text{O}_6} \times 100 = 26.7\% \text{ Hg}$$

$$\frac{46.0 \text{ g Na}}{750.4 \text{ g HgNa}_2\text{C}_{20}\text{H}_8\text{Br}_2\text{O}_6} \times 100 = 6.1\% \text{ Na}$$

$$\frac{240.0 \text{ g C}}{750.4 \text{ g HgNa}_2\text{C}_{20}\text{H}_8\text{Br}_2\text{O}_6} \times 100 = 32.0\% \text{ C}$$

$$\frac{8.0 \text{ g H}}{750.4 \text{ g HgNa}_2\text{C}_{20}\text{H}_8\text{Br}_2\text{O}_6} \times 100 = 1.1\% \text{ H}$$

$$\frac{159.8 \text{ g Br}}{750.4 \text{ g HgNa}_2\text{C}_{20}\text{H}_8\text{Br}_2\text{O}_6} \times 100 = 21.3\% \text{ Br}$$

$$\frac{96.0 \text{ g O}}{750.4 \text{ g HgNa}_2\text{C}_{20}\text{H}_8\text{Br}_2\text{O}_6} \times 100 = 12.8\% \text{ O}$$

Section 7.6 Empirical Formula

28. $0.500 \ \cancel{g \ Ni} \times \dfrac{1 \ mol \ Ni}{58.7 \ \cancel{g \ Ni}} = 0.00852 \ mol \ Ni$

    $0.704 \ g \ Ni_xO_y - 0.500 \ g \ Ni = 0.204 \ g \ O$

    $0.204 \ \cancel{g \ O} \times \dfrac{1 \ mol \ O}{16.0 \ \cancel{g \ O}} = 0.0128 \ mol \ O$

    $\dfrac{Ni \ 0.00852}{0.00852} \dfrac{O \ 0.0128}{0.00852} = Ni_{1.00}O_{1.50}$

    The empirical formula is Ni_2O_3.

30. $1.925 \ \cancel{g \ Cu} \times \dfrac{1 \ mol \ Cu}{63.5 \ \cancel{g \ Cu}} = 0.03031 \ mol \ Cu$

    $2.410 \ g \ Cu_xO_y - 1.925 \ g \ Cu = 0.485 \ g \ O$

    $0.485 \ \cancel{g \ O} \times \dfrac{1 \ mol \ O}{16.0 \ \cancel{g \ O}} = 0.0303 \ mol \ O$

    $\dfrac{Cu \ 0.03031}{0.0303} \dfrac{O \ 0.0303}{0.0303} = Cu_{1.00}O_{1.00}$

    The empirical formula is CuO.

32. $0.715 \ \cancel{g \ Ti} \times \dfrac{1 \ mol \ Ti}{47.9 \ \cancel{g \ Ti}} = 0.0149 \ mol \ Ti$

    $2.836 \ g \ Ti_xCl_y - 0.715 \ g \ Ti = 2.121 \ g \ Cl$

    $2.121 \ \cancel{g \ Cl} \times \dfrac{1 \ mol \ Cl}{35.5 \ \cancel{g \ Cl}} = 0.0597 \ mol \ Cl$

    $\dfrac{Ti \ 0.0149}{0.0149} \dfrac{Cl \ 0.0597}{0.0149} = Ti_{1.00}Cl_{4.01}$

    The empirical formula is $TiCl_4$.

34. (a) $55.0 \ \cancel{g \ K} \times \dfrac{1 \ mol \ K}{39.1 \ \cancel{g \ K}} = 1.41 \ mol \ K$

    $45.0 \ \cancel{g \ O} \times \dfrac{1 \ mol \ O}{16.0 \ \cancel{g \ O}} = 2.81 \ mol \ O$

    $\dfrac{K \ 1.41}{1.41} \dfrac{P \ 2.81}{1.41} = K_{1.00}O_{1.99}$

    The empirical formula is KO_2.

    (b) $68.0 \ \cancel{g \ V} \times \dfrac{1 \ mol \ V}{50.9 \ \cancel{g \ V}} = 1.34 \ mol \ V$

    $32.0 \ \cancel{g \ O} \times \dfrac{1 \ mol \ O}{16.0 \ \cancel{g \ O}} = 2.00 \ mol \ O$

    $\dfrac{V \ 1.34}{1.34} \dfrac{O \ 2.00}{1.34} = V_{1.00}O_{1.49}$

    The empirical formula is V_2O_3.

34. (c) $74.0 \cancel{\text{g Zr}} \times \dfrac{1 \text{ mol Zr}}{91.2 \cancel{\text{g Zr}}} = 0.811 \text{ mol Zr}$

$26.0 \cancel{\text{g O}} \times \dfrac{1 \text{ mol O}}{16.0 \cancel{\text{g O}}} = 1.63 \text{ mol O}$

$\dfrac{\text{Zr}_{0.811}}{0.811} \dfrac{\text{O}_{1.63}}{0.811} = \text{Zr}_{1.00}\text{O}_{2.01}$

The empirical formula is ZrO_2.

(d) $89.7 \cancel{\text{g Bi}} \times \dfrac{1 \text{ mol Bi}}{209.0 \cancel{\text{g Bi}}} = 0.429 \text{ mol Bi}$

$10.3 \cancel{\text{g O}} \times \dfrac{1 \text{ mol O}}{16.0 \cancel{\text{g O}}} = 0.644 \text{ mol O}$

$\dfrac{\text{Bi}_{0.429}}{0.429} \dfrac{\text{O}_{0.644}}{0.429} = \text{Bi}_{1.00}\text{O}_{1.50}$

The empirical formula is Bi_2O_3.

36. $30.7 \cancel{\text{g C}} \times \dfrac{1 \text{ mol C}}{12.0 \cancel{\text{g C}}} = 2.56 \text{ mol C}$

$7.74 \cancel{\text{g H}} \times \dfrac{1 \text{ mol H}}{1.0 \cancel{\text{g H}}} = 7.74 \text{ mol H}$

$20.5 \cancel{\text{g O}} \times \dfrac{1 \text{ mol O}}{16.0 \cancel{\text{g O}}} = 1.28 \text{ mol O}$

$41.0 \cancel{\text{g S}} \times \dfrac{1 \text{ mol S}}{32.1 \cancel{\text{g S}}} = 1.28 \text{ mol S}$

$\dfrac{\text{C}_{2.56}}{1.28} \dfrac{\text{H}_{7.74}}{1.28} \dfrac{\text{O}_{1.28}}{1.28} \dfrac{\text{S}_{1.28}}{1.28} = \text{C}_{2.00}\text{H}_{6.05}\text{O}_{1.00}\text{S}_{1.00}$

The empirical formula is $\text{C}_2\text{H}_6\text{OS}$.

Section 7.7 Molecular Formula

38. MM of $\text{C}_{10}\text{H}_{12}\text{NO}$ = 10(12.0) g C + 12(1.0) g H + 14.0 g N + 16.0 g O
= 162.0 g/mol $\text{C}_{10}\text{H}_{12}\text{NO}$

quinine: $\dfrac{(\text{C}_{10}\text{H}_{12}\text{NO})_n}{\text{C}_{10}\text{H}_{12}\text{NO}} = \dfrac{325 \text{ g/mol}}{162.0 \text{ g/mol}}$ $n \approx 2$

The molecular formula of quinine is $(\text{C}_{10}\text{H}_{12}\text{NO})_2$ or $\text{C}_{20}\text{H}_{24}\text{N}_2\text{O}_2$.

40. MM of $\text{C}_3\text{H}_8\text{N}$ = 3(12.0) g C + 8(1.0) g H + 14.0 g N
= 58.0 g/mol $\text{C}_3\text{H}_8\text{N}$

hexamethylene diamine: $\dfrac{(\text{C}_3\text{H}_8\text{N})_n}{\text{C}_3\text{H}_8\text{N}} = \dfrac{115 \text{ g/mol}}{58.0 \text{ g/mol}}$ $n \approx 2$

The molecular formula of hexamethylene diamine is $(\text{C}_3\text{H}_8\text{N})_2$ or $\text{C}_6\text{H}_{16}\text{N}_2$.

42. Empirical Formula

$$54.5 \; \cancel{g \; C} \times \frac{1 \; mol \; C}{12.0 \; \cancel{g \; C}} = 4.54 \; mol \; C$$

$$9.15 \; \cancel{g \; H} \times \frac{1 \; mol \; H}{1.0 \; \cancel{g \; H}} = 9.15 \; mol \; H$$

$$36.3 \; \cancel{g \; O} \times \frac{1 \; mol \; O}{16.0 \; \cancel{g \; O}} = 2.27 \; mol \; O$$

$$C \frac{4.54}{2.27} H \frac{9.15}{2.27} O \frac{2.27}{2.27} = C_{2.00}H_{4.03}O_{1.00}$$

The empirical formula is C_2H_4O.

Molecular Formula

MM of C_2H_4O = 2(12.0) g C + 4(1.0) g H + 16.0 g O = 44.0 g/mol C_2H_4O

dioxane: $\frac{(C_2H_4O)_n}{C_2H_4O} = \frac{88 \; g/mol}{44.0 \; g/mol}$ $n \approx 2$

The molecular formula of dioxane is $(C_2H_4O)_2$ or $C_4H_8O_2$.

44. Empirical Formula

$$85.0 \; \cancel{g \; Hg} \times \frac{1 \; mol \; Hg}{200.6 \; \cancel{g \; Hg}} = 0.424 \; mol \; Hg$$

$$15.0 \; \cancel{g \; Cl} \times \frac{1 \; mol \; Cl}{35.5 \; \cancel{g \; Cl}} = 0.423 \; mol \; Cl$$

$$Hg \frac{0.424}{0.423} Cl \frac{0.423}{0.423} = Hg_{1.00}Cl_{1.00}$$

The empirical formula is HgCl.

Molecular Formula

MM of HgCl = 200.6 g Hg + 35.5 g Cl = 236.1 g/mol HgCl

mercurous chloride: $\frac{(HgCl)_n}{HgCl} = \frac{470 \; g/mol}{236.1 \; g/mol}$ $n \approx 2$

The molecular formula of mercurous chloride is $(HgCl)_2$ or Hg_2Cl_2.

46. Empirical Formula

$$40.0 \; \cancel{g \; C} \times \frac{1 \; mol \; C}{12.0 \; \cancel{g \; C}} = 3.33 \; mol \; C$$

$$6.72 \; \cancel{g \; H} \times \frac{1 \; mol \; H}{1.0 \; \cancel{g \; H}} = 6.72 \; mol \; H$$

$$53.3 \; \cancel{g \; O} \times \frac{1 \; mol \; O}{16.0 \; \cancel{g \; O}} = 3.33 \; mol \; O$$

$$C \frac{3.33}{3.33} H \frac{6.72}{3.33} O \frac{3.33}{3.33} = C_{1.00}H_{2.02}O_{1.00}$$

The empirical formula is CH_2O.

46.   Molecular Formula
MM of CH_2O = 12.0 g C + 2(1.0) g H + 16.0 g O = 30.0 g/mol CH_2O

galactose: $\dfrac{(CH_2O)_n}{CH_2O} = \dfrac{180\ g/mol}{30.0\ g/mol}$ $n \approx 6$

The molecular formula of galactose is $(CH_2O)_6$ or $C_6H_{12}O_6$.

Section 7.8 Molar Volume

48.   STP conditions: 273 K and 760 mm Hg

50.

Gas	Molecules	Mass	Vol @ STP
radon, Rn	6.02×10^{23}	222.0 g	22.4 L
hydrogen sulfide, H_2S	6.02×10^{23}	34.1 g	22.4 L
phosphine, PH_3	6.02×10^{23}	34.0 g	22.4 L
butane, C_4H_{10}	6.02×10^{23}	58.0 g	22.4 L

52.   (a) MM of Xe = 131.3 g/mol Xe

Density of Xe (at STP): $\dfrac{131.3\ g}{1\ \cancel{mol}} \times \dfrac{1\ \cancel{mol}}{22.4\ L} = 5.86\ g/L$

(b) MM of F_2 = 2(19.0) g F = 38.0 g/mol F_2

Density of F_2 (at STP): $\dfrac{38.0\ g}{\cancel{mol}} \times \dfrac{1\ \cancel{mol}}{22.4\ L} = 1.70\ g/L$

(c) MM of C_3H_8 = 3(12.0) g C + 8(1.0) g H = 44.0 g/mol C_3H_8

Density of C_3H_8 (at STP): $\dfrac{44.0\ g}{\cancel{mol}} \times \dfrac{1\ \cancel{mol}}{22.4\ L} = 1.96\ g/L$

(d) MM of SO_3 = 32.1 g S + 3(16.0) g O = 80.1 g/mol SO_3

Density of SO_3 (at STP): $\dfrac{80.1\ g}{\cancel{mol}} \times \dfrac{1\ \cancel{mol}}{22.4\ L} = 3.58\ g/L$

54.   (a) MM of isobutane: $\dfrac{22.4\ \cancel{L}}{mol} \times \dfrac{2.59\ g}{\cancel{L}} = 58.0\ g/mol$

(b) MM of silane: $\dfrac{22.4\ \cancel{L}}{mol} \times \dfrac{1.43\ g}{\cancel{L}} = 32.0\ g/mol$

(c) MM of Freon-22: $\dfrac{22.4\ \cancel{L}}{mol} \times \dfrac{3.86\ g}{\cancel{L}} = 86.5\ g/mol$

(d) MM of nitric oxide: $\dfrac{22.4\ \cancel{L}}{mol} \times \dfrac{1.34\ g}{\cancel{L}} = 30.0\ g/mol$

Section 7.9 Mole Calculations II

56. (a) MM of He = 4.0 g/mol He

$$0.250 \ \cancel{\text{g He}} \times \frac{1 \ \cancel{\text{mol He}}}{4.0 \ \cancel{\text{g He}}} \times \frac{22.4 \ \text{L He}}{1 \ \cancel{\text{mol He}}} = 1.40 \ \text{L He}$$

(b) MM of N_2 = 2(14.0) g N = 28.0 g/mol N_2

$$5.05 \ \cancel{\text{g N}_2} \times \frac{1 \ \cancel{\text{mol N}_2}}{28.0 \ \cancel{\text{g N}_2}} \times \frac{22.4 \ \text{L N}_2}{1 \ \cancel{\text{mol N}_2}} = 4.04 \ \text{L N}_2$$

(c) MM of CO = 12.0 g C + 16.0 g O = 28.0 g/mol CO

$$0.885 \ \cancel{\text{g CO}} \times \frac{1 \ \cancel{\text{mol CO}}}{28.0 \ \cancel{\text{g CO}}} \times \frac{22.4 \ \text{L CO}}{1 \ \cancel{\text{mol CO}}} = 0.708 \ \text{L CO}$$

58. (a) $2.22 \times 10^{22} \ \cancel{\text{molecules CH}_4} \times \dfrac{1 \ \cancel{\text{mol CH}_4}}{6.02 \times 10^{23} \ \cancel{\text{molecules CH}_4}} \times$

$$\frac{22.4 \ \text{L CH}_4}{1 \ \cancel{\text{mol CH}_4}} = 0.826 \ \text{L CH}_4$$

(b) $4.18 \times 10^{24} \ \cancel{\text{molecules C}_2\text{H}_6} \times \dfrac{1 \ \cancel{\text{mol C}_2\text{H}_6}}{6.02 \times 10^{23} \ \cancel{\text{molecules C}_2\text{H}_6}} \times$

$$\frac{22.4 \ \text{L C}_2\text{H}_6}{1 \ \cancel{\text{mol C}_2\text{H}_6}} = 156 \ \text{L C}_2\text{H}_6$$

(c) $5.09 \times 10^{21} \ \cancel{\text{molecules C}_3\text{H}_8} \times \dfrac{1 \ \cancel{\text{mol C}_3\text{H}_8}}{6.02 \times 10^{23} \ \cancel{\text{molecules C}_3\text{H}_8}} \times$

$$\frac{22.4 \ \text{L C}_3\text{H}_8}{1 \ \cancel{\text{mol C}_3\text{H}_8}} = 0.189 \ \text{L C}_3\text{H}_8$$

60.

Gas	Molecules	Atoms	Mass	Vol @ STP
HCl	1.15×10^{22}	2.30×10^{22}	0.697 g	0.428 L
Cl_2	2.14×10^{24}	4.27×10^{24}	252 g	79.6 L
Cl_2O	6.92×10^{22}	2.08×10^{23}	10.0 g	2.57 L
ClO_2	7.58×10^{21}	2.27×10^{22}	0.850 g	0.282 L

HCl:

$$1.15 \times 10^{22} \ \cancel{\text{molecules HCl}} \times \frac{2 \ \text{atoms HCl}}{1 \ \cancel{\text{molecule HCl}}}$$

$$= 2.30 \times 10^{22} \ \text{atoms HCl}$$

60. HCl:

$$1.15 \times 10^{22} \; \text{molecules HCl} \times \frac{1 \; \text{mol HCl}}{6.02 \times 10^{23} \; \text{molecules HCl}} \times$$

$$\frac{36.5 \; \text{g HCl}}{1 \; \text{mol HCl}} = 0.697 \; \text{g HCl}$$

$$1.15 \times 10^{22} \; \text{molecules HCl} \times \frac{1 \; \text{mol HCl}}{6.02 \times 10^{23} \; \text{molecules HCl}} \times$$

$$\frac{22.4 \; \text{L HCl}}{1 \; \text{mol HCl}} = 0.428 \; \text{L HCl}$$

Cl_2:

$$4.27 \times 10^{24} \; \text{atoms Cl}_2 \times \frac{1 \; \text{molecule Cl}_2}{2 \; \text{atoms Cl}_2} = 2.14 \times 10^{24} \; \text{molecules Cl}_2$$

$$2.14 \times 10^{24} \; \text{molecules Cl}_2 \times \frac{1 \; \text{mol Cl}_2}{6.02 \times 10^{23} \; \text{molecules Cl}_2} \times \frac{71.0 \; \text{g Cl}_2}{1 \; \text{mol Cl}_2}$$
$$= 252 \; \text{g Cl}_2$$

$$2.14 \times 10^{24} \; \text{molecules Cl}_2 \times \frac{1 \; \text{mol Cl}_2}{6.02 \times 10^{23} \; \text{molecules Cl}_2} \times \frac{22.4 \; \text{L Cl}_2}{1 \; \text{mol Cl}_2}$$
$$= 79.6 \; \text{L Cl}_2$$

Cl_2O:

$$10.0 \; \text{g Cl}_2\text{O} \times \frac{1 \; \text{mol Cl}_2\text{O}}{87.0 \; \text{g Cl}_2\text{O}} \times \frac{6.02 \times 10^{23} \; \text{molecules Cl}_2\text{O}}{1 \; \text{mol Cl}_2\text{O}}$$
$$= 6.92 \times 10^{22} \; \text{molecules Cl}_2\text{O}$$

$$6.92 \times 10^{22} \; \text{molecules Cl}_2\text{O} \times \frac{3 \; \text{atoms Cl}_2\text{O}}{1 \; \text{molecules Cl}_2\text{O}}$$
$$= 2.08 \times 10^{23} \; \text{atoms Cl}_2\text{O}$$

$$10.0 \; \text{g Cl}_2\text{O} \times \frac{1 \; \text{mol Cl}_2\text{O}}{87.0 \; \text{g Cl}_2\text{O}} \times \frac{22.4 \; \text{L Cl}_2\text{O}}{1 \; \text{mol Cl}_2\text{O}} = 2.57 \; \text{L Cl}_2\text{O}$$

ClO_2:

$$0.282 \; \text{L ClO}_2 \times \frac{1 \; \text{mol ClO}_2}{22.4 \; \text{L ClO}_2} \times \frac{67.5 \; \text{g ClO}_2}{1 \; \text{mol ClO}_2} = 0.850 \; \text{g ClO}_2$$

$$0.282 \; \text{L ClO}_2 \times \frac{1 \; \text{mol ClO}_2}{22.4 \; \text{L ClO}_2} \times \frac{6.02 \times 10^{23} \; \text{molecules ClO}_2}{1 \; \text{mol ClO}_2}$$
$$= 7.58 \times 10^{21} \; \text{molecules ClO}_2$$

$$7.58 \times 10^{21} \; \text{molecules ClO}_2 \times \frac{3 \; \text{atoms ClO}_2}{1 \; \text{molecule ClO}_2}$$
$$= 2.27 \times 10^{22} \; \text{atoms ClO}_2$$

General Exercises

62. $$0.200 \; \text{g C} \times \frac{1 \; \text{mol C}}{12.0 \; \text{g C}} \times \frac{6.02 \times 10^{23} \; \text{atoms C}}{1 \; \text{mol C}} = 1.00 \times 10^{22} \; \text{atoms C}$$

1.00×10^{22} atoms C > 1×10^{12} atoms C (1 trillion)

Yes, the number of carbon atoms in 0.200 g is greater than one trillion carbon atoms.

64. $0.001 \text{ g Cu} \times \dfrac{1 \text{ mol Cu}}{63.5 \text{ g Cu}} \times \dfrac{6.02 \times 10^{23} \text{ atoms Cu}}{1 \text{ mol Cu}} = 9 \times 10^{18} \text{ atoms Cu}$

66. $1 \text{ mol furry moles} \times \dfrac{6.02 \times 10^{23} \text{ furry moles}}{1 \text{ mol furry moles}} \times \dfrac{17 \text{ cm}}{1 \text{ furry mole}} \times \dfrac{1 \text{ m}}{100 \text{ cm}} \times$

$\dfrac{1 \text{ km}}{1000 \text{ m}} = 1.0 \times 10^{20} \text{ km}$

Ten light years $= 10 \,(9.5 \times 10^{12} \text{ km}) = 9.5 \times 10^{13} \text{ km}$

$1.0 \times 10^{20} \text{ km}$ (1 mol furry moles) $> 9.5 \times 10^{13} \text{ km}$ (10 light-years)

Therefore, one mole of furry moles is longer than the distance light travels in ten years (10 light-years).

68. $0.500 \text{ g Ge} \times \dfrac{1 \text{ mol Ge}}{72.6 \text{ g Ge}} = 0.00689 \text{ mol Ge}$

$0.978 \text{ g Ge}_x\text{Cl}_y - 0.500 \text{ g Ge} = 0.478 \text{ g Cl}$

$0..478 \text{ g Cl} \times \dfrac{1 \text{ mol Cl}}{35.5 \text{ g Cl}} = 0.0135 \text{ mol Cl}$

$\dfrac{\text{Ge } 0.00689}{0.00689} \dfrac{\text{Cl } 0.0135}{0.00689} = \text{Ge}_{1.00}\text{Cl}_{1.96}$

The empirical formula is GeCl_2.

70. MM of $\text{C}_2\text{H}_5\text{OH}$ $= 2(12.0) \text{ g C} + 6(1.0) \text{ g H} + 16.0 \text{ g O}$
$= 46.0 \text{ g/mol C}_2\text{H}_5\text{OH}$

$1 \text{ molecule C}_2\text{H}_5\text{OH} \times \dfrac{1 \text{ mol C}_2\text{H}_5\text{OH}}{6.02 \times 10^{23} \text{ molecules C}_2\text{H}_5\text{OH}} \times \dfrac{46.0 \text{ g C}_2\text{H}_5\text{OH}}{1 \text{ mol C}_2\text{H}_5\text{OH}}$

$\times \dfrac{1 \text{ mL C}_2\text{H}_5\text{OH}}{0.789 \text{ g C}_2\text{H}_5\text{OH}} = 9.68 \times 10^{-23} \text{ mL C}_2\text{H}_5\text{OH}$

72. MM of $\text{C}_6\text{H}_{12}\text{O}_6$ $= 6(12.0) \text{ g C} + 12(1.0) \text{ g H} + 6(16.0) \text{ g O}$
$= 180.0 \text{ g/mol C}_{12}\text{H}_{22}\text{O}_{11}$

$1.00 \text{ g C}_6\text{H}_{12}\text{O}_6 \times \dfrac{1 \text{ mol C}_6\text{H}_{12}\text{O}_6}{180.0 \text{ g C}_6\text{H}_{12}\text{O}_6} \times \dfrac{6 \text{ mol C}}{1 \text{ mol C}_6\text{H}_{12}\text{O}_6} \times$

$\dfrac{6.02 \times 10^{23} \text{ atoms C}}{1 \text{ mol C}} = 2.01 \times 10^{22} \text{ atoms C}$

74. $10.0 \text{ g Fe} \times \dfrac{1 \text{ mol Fe}}{55.8 \text{ g Fe}} \times \dfrac{1 \text{ mol Fe}_2\text{O}_3}{2 \text{ mol Fe}} \times \dfrac{159.6 \text{ g Fe}_2\text{O}_3}{1 \text{ mol Fe}_2\text{O}_3} = 14.3 \text{ g Fe}_2\text{O}_3$

76. Volume of Al atom in nm^3: $(0.255 \text{ nm})^3 = 0.0166 \text{ nm}^3$

Volume of Al atom in cm^3: $\dfrac{\text{atom Al}}{0.0166 \text{ nm}^3} \times \left(\dfrac{10^9 \text{ nm}}{1 \text{ m}}\right)^3 \times \left(\dfrac{1 \text{ m}}{100 \text{ cm}}\right)^3$

$$= \dfrac{6.02 \times 10^{22} \text{ atoms Al}}{cm^3}$$

$$\dfrac{6.02 \times 10^{22} \text{ atoms Al}}{cm^3} \times \dfrac{cm^3}{2.70 \text{ g Al}} \times \dfrac{27.0 \text{ g Al}}{1 \text{ mol Al}} = \dfrac{6.02 \times 10^{23} \text{ atoms Al}}{\text{mol Al}}$$

CHAPTER 8

Writing Chemical Equations

Section 8.1 Evidence for Chemical Reactions

2. (a) The production of an odor (a gas) is evidence of a chemical reaction.
   (b) The combustion of a flaming splint is evidence of a chemical reaction.
   (c) A heat energy change is evidence of a chemical reaction.

Section 8.2 Writing Chemical Equations

4. (a) $Cu_{(s)} + F_{2(g)} \rightarrow CuF_{2(s)}$
   (b) $Fe(HCO_3)_{2(s)} \rightarrow FeCO_{3(s)} + CO_{2(g)} + H_2O_{(g)}$
   (c) $Mn_{(s)} + H_2SO_{4(aq)} \rightarrow MnSO_{4(aq)} + H_{2(g)}$
   (d) $Na_2CrO_{4(aq)} + CaS_{(aq)} \rightarrow CaCrO_{4(s)} + Na_2S_{(aq)}$
   (e) $HNO_{3(aq)} + NH_4OH_{(aq)} \rightarrow NH_4NO_{3(aq)} + H_2O_{(l)}$

Section 8.3 Balancing Chemical Equations

6. If a chemical equation is impossible to balance, it is probably because the original equation had an incorrect subscript in a chemical formula.

8. (a) $Sr_{(s)} + 2\,H_2O_{(l)} \rightarrow Sr(OH)_{2(aq)} + H_{2(g)}$
   (b) $2\,H_3PO_{4(aq)} + 3\,Mn(OH)_{2(aq)} \rightarrow Mn_3(PO_4)_{2(s)} + 6\,H_2O_{(l)}$
   (c) $3\,H_{2(g)} + N_{2(g)} \rightarrow 2\,NH_{3(g)}$
   (d) $2\,Al(HCO_3)_{3(s)} \rightarrow Al_2(CO_3)_{3(s)} + 3\,CO_{2(g)} + 3\,H_2O_{(g)}$
   (e) $K_2SO_{4(aq)} + Ba(OH)_{2(aq)} \rightarrow BaSO_{4(s)} + 2\,KOH_{(aq)}$

10. (a) $2\,Fe_{(s)} + 3\,Cd(NO_3)_{2(aq)} \rightarrow 2\,Fe(NO_3)_{3(aq)} + 3\,Cd_{(s)}$
    (b) $2\,HClO_{4(aq)} + Ba(OH)_{2(aq)} \rightarrow Ba(ClO_4)_{2(s)} + 2\,HOH_{(l)}$
    (c) $3\,Sn_{(s)} + 2\,P_{(s)} \rightarrow Sn_3P_{2(g)}$
    (d) $Fe_2(CO_3)_{3(s)} \rightarrow Fe_2O_{3(s)} + 3\,CO_{2(g)}$
    (e) $Co(NO_3)_{2(aq)} + H_2S_{(g)} \rightarrow CoS_{(s)} + 2\,HNO_{3(aq)}$

Section 8.4 Classifying Chemical Reactions

12. Refer to reactions in exercise 8.

Classification		Classification
(a) single replacement	(b)	neutralization
(c) combination	(d)	decomposition
(e) double replacement		

14. Refer to the reactions in exercise 10.

Classification		Classification
(a) single replacement	(b)	neutralization
(c) combination	(d)	decomposition
(e) double replacement		

Section 8.5 Combination Reactions

General Form: $A + Z \rightarrow AZ$

16. nonmetal + oxygen gas $\rightarrow$ nonmetal oxide

    (a) $2\,C_{(s)} + O_{2(g)} \rightarrow 2\,CO_{(g)}$

    (b) $4\,P_{(s)} + 3\,O_{2(g)} \rightarrow 2\,P_2O_{3(s)}$

    (c) $2\,N_{2(g)} + 5\,O_{2(g)} \rightarrow 2\,N_2O_{5(g)}$

    (d) $2\,Cl_{2(g)} + 3\,O_{2(g)} \rightarrow 2\,Cl_2O_{3(g)}$

18.   (a) $4\,Cr_{(s)} + 3\,O_{2(g)} \rightarrow 2\,Cr_2O_{3(s)}$

    (b) $2\,Cr_{(s)} + N_{2(g)} \rightarrow 2\,CrN_{(s)}$

    (c) $S_{(s)} + O_{2(g)} \rightarrow SO_{2(g)}$

    (d) $2\,S_{(s)} + 3\,O_{2(g)} \xrightarrow{Pt} 2\,SO_{3(g)}$

20.   (a) $2\,Na + I_2 \rightarrow 2\,NaI$

    (b) $2\,Ca + O_2 \rightarrow 2\,CaO$

    (c) $3\,Zn + 2\,P \rightarrow Zn_3P_2$

    (d) $2\,K + F_2 \rightarrow 2\,KF$

22.   (a) $4\,Al + 3\,O_2 \rightarrow 2\,Al_2O_3$

    (b) $Zn + F_2 \rightarrow ZnF_2$

    (c) $2\,K + S \rightarrow K_2S$

    (d) $3\,Ba + N_2 \rightarrow Ba_3N_2$

Section 8.6 Decomposition Reactions

General Form: $AZ \rightarrow A + Z$

24. metal hydrogen carbonate $\rightarrow$ metal carbonate + water + carbon dioxide
  (a) $2\, Au(HCO_3)_{3(s)} \rightarrow Au_2(CO_3)_{3(s)} + 3\, H_2O_{(g)} + 3\, CO_{2(g)}$
  (b) $Sn(HCO_3)_{4(s)} \rightarrow Sn(CO_3)_{2(s)} + 2\, H_2O_{(g)} + 2\, CO_{2(g)}$

26. metal carbonate $\rightarrow$ metal oxide + carbon dioxide
  (a) $Cr_2(CO_3)_{3(s)} \rightarrow Cr_2O_{3(s)} + 3\, CO_{2(g)}$
  (b) $Pb(CO_3)_{2(s)} \rightarrow PbO_{2(s)} + 2\, CO_{2(g)}$

28. oxygen-containing compounds $\rightarrow$ oxygen gas
  (a) $Ca(NO_3)_{2(s)} \rightarrow Ca(NO_2)_{2(s)} + O_{2(g)}$
  (b) $2\, AgClO_{3(s)} \rightarrow 2\, AgCl_{(s)} + 3\, O_{2(g)}$

30. oxygen-containing compounds $\rightarrow$ oxygen gas
  (a) $Sr(ClO_3)_2 \rightarrow SrCl_2 + 3\, O_2$
  (b) $2\, NaClO_3 \rightarrow 2\, NaCl + 3\, O_2$
  (c) $2\, Al(NO_3)_3 \rightarrow 2\, Al(NO_2)_3 + 3\, O_2$
  (d) $2\, CsNO_3 \rightarrow 2\, CsNO_2 + O_2$

Section 8.7 Activity Series

32.

	Element	Placed In:	Observation
(a)	Ag	$Ni(NO_3)_{2(aq)}$	no reaction; Ni > Ag
(b)	Sn	$Ni(NO_3)_{2(aq)}$	no reaction; Ni > Sn
(c)	Co	$Ni(NO_3)_{2(aq)}$	reaction; Co > Ni
(d)	Mn	$Ni(NO_3)_{2(aq)}$	reaction; Mn > Ni

34.

	Element	Placed In:	Observation
(a)	Fe	$H_2SO_{4(aq)}$	reaction; Fe > (H)
(b)	Mn	$H_2SO_{4(aq)}$	reaction; Mn > (H)
(c)	Cd	$H_2SO_{4(aq)}$	reaction; Cd > (H)
(d)	Au	$H_2SO_{4(aq)}$	no reaction; (H) > Au

36.

	Element	Placed In:	Observation
(a)	Ba	$H_2O_{(l)}$	reaction; Ba is an active metal
(b)	Mn	$H_2O_{(l)}$	no reaction; Mn is not an active metal
(c)	Sn	$H_2O_{(l)}$	no reaction; Sn is not an active metal
(d)	K	$H_2O_{(l)}$	reaction; K is an active metal

38.

	Element	Placed In:	Observation
(a)	Pb	$ZnCl_{2(aq)}$	no reaction; Zn > Pb
(b)	Mg	$FeSO_{4(aq)}$	reaction; Mg > Fe
(c)	Cu	$H_2SO_{4(aq)}$	no reaction; (H) > Cu
(d)	Sn	$HCl_{(aq)}$	reaction; Sn > (H)

Section 8.8 Single-Replacement Reactions

General Form: $A + BZ \rightarrow AZ + B$

40. $metal_1 + aqueous\ solution_1 \rightarrow metal_2 + aqueous\ solution_2$ or *NR*

(a) $Ni_{(s)} + Pb(C_2H_3O_2)_{2(aq)} \rightarrow Pb_{(s)} + Ni(C_2H_3O_2)_{2(aq)}$

(b) $Pb_{(s)} + Ni(C_2H_3O_2)_{2(aq)} \rightarrow$ *NR*

(c) $Fe_{(s)} + HgSO_{4(aq)} \rightarrow Hg_{(l)} + FeSO_{4(aq)}$

(d) $Hg_{(l)} + FeSO_{4(aq)} \rightarrow$ *NR*

42. metal + aqueous acid $\rightarrow$ aqueous solution + hydrogen gas or *NR*

(a) $Co_{(s)} + 2\,HCl_{(aq)} \rightarrow CoCl_{2(aq)} + H_{2(g)}$

(b) $Hg_{(l)} + H_2SO_{4(aq)} \rightarrow$ *NR*

(c) $2\,Al_{(s)} + 6\,HC_2H_3O_{2(aq)} \rightarrow 2\,Al(C_2H_3O_2)_{3(aq)} + 3\,H_{2(g)}$

(d) $3\,Zn_{(s)} + 2\,H_3PO_{4(aq)} \rightarrow Zn_3(PO_4)_{2(s)} + 3\,H_{2(g)}$

44. metal + water $\rightarrow$ metal hydroxide + hydrogen gas (if active metal)

metal + water $\rightarrow$ *NR* (if not an active metal)

(a) $Ra_{(s)} + 2\,H_2O_{(l)} \rightarrow Ra(OH)_{2(aq)} + H_{2(g)}$

(b) $Au_{(s)} + H_2O_{(l)} \rightarrow$ *NR*

(c) $Tc_{(s)} + H_2O_{(l)} \rightarrow$ *NR*

(d) $2\,Fr_{(s)} + 2\,H_2O_{(l)} \rightarrow 2\,FrOH_{(aq)} + H_{2(g)}$

46. metal + aqueous acid $\rightarrow$ aqueous solution + hydrogen gas

(a) $Ni_{(s)} + 2\,HNO_{3(aq)} \rightarrow Ni(NO_3)_{2(aq)} + H_{2(g)}$

(b) $Mg_{(s)} + H_2SO_{4(aq)} \rightarrow MgSO_{4(aq)} + H_{2(g)}$

metal + water $\rightarrow$ metal hydroxide + hydrogen gas (if active metal)

metal + water $\rightarrow$ *NR* (if not an active metal)

(c) $2\,Na_{(s)} + 2\,H_2O_{(l)} \rightarrow 2\,NaOH_{(aq)} + H_{2(g)}$

(d) $Mg_{(s)} + H_2O_{(l)} \rightarrow$ *NR*

(e) $Ba_{(s)} + 2\,H_2O_{(l)} \rightarrow Ba(OH)_{2(aq)} + H_{2(g)}$

Section 8.9 Solubility Rules

48.

Compound	Solubility		Compound	Solubility
(a) $AgBr$	insoluble	(b)	$PbSO_4$	insoluble
(c) Na_2S	soluble	(d)	$FePO_4$	insoluble
(e) $SrCO_3$	insoluble	(f)	$Co(OH)_2$	insoluble
(g) NiS	insoluble	(h)	$AgCl$	insoluble

Section 8.10 Double-Replacement Reactions

General Form: $AX + BZ \rightarrow AZ + BX$

50. aqueous solution$_1$ + aqueous solution$_2$ → precipitate + aqueous solution$_3$
   (a) $2\,AgC_2H_3O_{2(aq)} + SrI_{2(aq)} \rightarrow 2\,AgI_{(s)} + Sr(C_2H_3O_2)_{2(aq)}$
   (b) $FeSO_{4(aq)} + Ca(OH)_{2(aq)} \rightarrow Fe(OH)_{2(s)} + CaSO_{4(aq)}$
   (c) $Sn(NO_3)_{2(aq)} + K_2CrO_{4(aq)} \rightarrow SnCrO_{4(s)} + 2\,KNO_{3(aq)}$

52. aqueous solution$_1$ + aqueous solution$_2$ → precipitate + aqueous solution$_3$
   (a) $SnCl_{2(aq)} + Na_2S_{(aq)} \rightarrow SnS_{(s)} + 2\,NaCl_{(aq)}$
   (b) $Co(NO_3)_{2(aq)} + K_2CrO_{4(aq)} \rightarrow CoCrO_{4(s)} + 2\,KNO_{3(aq)}$

Section 8.11 Neutralization Reactions

General Form: $HX + BOH \rightarrow BX + HOH$

54. aqueous acid + aqueous base → aqueous salt + water
   (a) $3\,HBr_{(aq)} + Al(OH)_{3(s)} \rightarrow AlBr_{3(aq)} + 3\,HOH_{(l)}$
   (b) $2\,HClO_{2(aq)} + Mg(OH)_{2(aq)} \rightarrow Mg(ClO_2)_{2(aq)} + 2\,HOH_{(l)}$
   (c) $H_3PO_{4(aq)} + 3\,KOH_{(aq)} \rightarrow K_3PO_{4(aq)} + 3\,HOH_{(l)}$

56. aqueous acid + aqueous base → aqueous salt + water
   (a) $2\,KOH_{(aq)} + H_2CO_{3(aq)} \rightarrow K_2CO_{3(aq)} + 2\,HOH_{(l)}$
   aqueous acid + aqueous base → precipitate + water
   (b) $Sr(OH)_{2(aq)} + 2\,HC_2H_3O_{2(aq)} \rightarrow Sr(C_2H_3O_2)_{2(aq)} + 2\,HOH_{(l)}$

General Exercises

58.   (a) $TiCl_4(s) + 2\,H_2O(g) \rightarrow TiO_2(s) + 4\,HCl(g)$

         (b) $3\,MnO_2(l) + 4\,Al(l) \rightarrow 2\,Al_2O_3(l) + 3\,Mn(l)$

         (c) $3\,Fe(s) + 4\,H_2O(g) \rightarrow Fe_3O_4(s) + 4\,H_2(g)$

         (d) $3\,FeO(l) + 2\,Al(l) \rightarrow Al_2O_3(l) + 3\,Fe(l)$

         (e) $4\,FeS(s) + 7\,O_2(g) \rightarrow 2\,Fe_2O_3(s) + 4\,SO_2(g)$

60.   (a) $2\,C_2H_6(g) + 7\,O_2(g) \rightarrow 4\,CO_2(g) + 6\,H_2O(g)$

         (b) $C_2H_6O(l) + 3\,O_2(g) \rightarrow 2\,CO_2(g) + 3\,H_2O(g)$

         (c) $2\,C_6H_6(g) + 15\,O_2(g) \rightarrow 12\,CO_2(g) + 6\,H_2O(g)$

         (d) $C_6H_6O(l) + 7\,O_2(g) \rightarrow 6\,CO_2(g) + 3\,H_2O(g)$

62.   Blast furnace reaction:

        $Fe_2O_3(l) + 3\,CO(g) \rightarrow 2\,Fe(l) + 3\,CO_2(g)$

CHAPTER 9 — Chemical Equation Calculations

Section 9.1 **Interpreting a Chemical Equation**

2. General Equation: $2A + 3B \rightarrow C + 2D$

    (a) $2 \text{ molecules A} \times \dfrac{3 \text{ molecules B}}{2 \text{ molecules A}} = 3 \text{ molecules B}$

    (b) $2 \text{ moles A} \times \dfrac{1 \text{ mole C}}{2 \text{ moles A}} = 1 \text{ mole C}$

    (c) $2 \text{ volumes gas A} \times \dfrac{2 \text{ volumes gas D}}{2 \text{ volumes gas A}} = 2 \text{ volumes gas D}$

    (d) $1 \text{ molar mass C} \times \dfrac{2 \text{ molar masses A}}{1 \text{ molar mass C}} = 2 \text{ molar masses A}$

4. General Equation: $A + 3B \rightarrow 2C$
    (a) $10.0 \text{ g A} + 15.0 \text{ g B} = 25.0 \text{ g C}$
    (b) $75.0 \text{ g C} - 50.0 \text{ g A} = 25.0 \text{ g B}$

6. (a) $CH_{4(g)} + 2\,O_{2(g)} \xrightarrow{\text{spark}} CO_{2(g)} + 2\,H_2O_{(g)}$
    MM of $CH_4 = 12.0 \text{ g C} + 4(1.0) \text{ g H} = 16.0 \text{ g/mol}$
    MM of $O_2 = 2(16.0) \text{ g O} = 32.0 \text{ g/mol}$
    MM of $CO_2 = 12.0 \text{ g C} + 2(16.0) \text{ g O} = 44.0 \text{ g/mol}$
    MM of $H_2O = 2(1.0) \text{ g H} + 16.0 \text{ g O} = 18.0 \text{ g/mol}$
    $16.0 \text{ g} + 2(32.0) \text{ g} \rightarrow 44.0 \text{ g} + 2(18.0) \text{ g}$
    $80.0 \text{ g} \rightarrow 80.0 \text{ g}$

    (b) $2\,C_2H_{6(g)} + 7\,O_{2(g)} \xrightarrow{\text{spark}} 4\,CO_{2(g)} + 6\,H_2O_{(g)}$
    MM of $C_2H_6 = 2(12.0) \text{ g C} + 6(1.0) \text{ g H} = 30.0 \text{ g/mol}$
    MM of $O_2 = 2(16.0) \text{ g O} = 32.0 \text{ g/mol}$
    MM of $CO_2 = 12.0 \text{ g C} + 2(16.0) \text{ g O} = 44.0 \text{ g/mol}$
    MM of $H_2O = 2(1.0) \text{ g H} + 16.0 \text{ g O} = 18.0 \text{ g/mol}$
    $2(30.0) \text{ g} + 7(32.0) \text{ g} \rightarrow 4(44.0) \text{ g} + 6(18.0) \text{ g}$
    $284.0 \text{ g} \rightarrow 284.0 \text{ g}$

Section 9.2 Mole-Mole Problems

8. $4 P_{(s)} + 5 O_{2(g)} \rightarrow 2 P_2O_{5(s)}$
    Moles of O_2 that react:

    $2.50 \text{ mol P} \times \dfrac{5 \text{ mol } O_2}{4 \text{ mol P}} = 3.13 \text{ mole } O_2 \text{ react}$

    Moles of P_2O_5 produced:

    $2.50 \text{ mol P} \times \dfrac{2 \text{ mol } P_2O_5}{4 \text{ mol P}} = 1.25 \text{ mole } P_2O_5 \text{ produced}$

10. $3 Ba_{(s)} + N_{2(g)} \rightarrow Ba_3N_{2(s)}$
    Moles of Ba that react:

    $0.333 \text{ mol } Ba_3N_2 \times \dfrac{3 \text{ mol Ba}}{1 \text{ mol } Ba_3N_2} = 0.999 \text{ mol Ba react}$

    Moles of N_2 that react:

    $0.333 \text{ mol } Ba_3N_2 \times \dfrac{1 \text{ mol } N_2}{1 \text{ mol } Ba_3N_2} = 0.333 \text{ mol } N_2 \text{ react}$

12. $C_3H_{8(g)} + 5 O_{2(g)} \rightarrow 3 CO_{2(g)} + 4 H_2O_{(g)}$
    Moles of C_3H_8 that react:

    $1.75 \text{ mol } O_2 \times \dfrac{1 \text{ mol } C_3H_8}{5 \text{ mol } O_2} = 0.350 \text{ mol } C_3H_8 \text{ react}$

    Moles of H_2O produced:

    $1.75 \text{ mol } O_2 \times \dfrac{4 \text{ mol } H_2O}{5 \text{ mol } O_2} = 1.40 \text{ mol } H_2O \text{ produced}$

    Moles of CO_2 produced:

    $1.75 \text{ mol } O_2 \times \dfrac{3 \text{ mol } CO_2}{5 \text{ mol } O_2} = 1.05 \text{ mol } CO_2 \text{ produced}$

Section 9.3 Types of Stoichiometry Problems

14.

	Given Quantity	Desired Quantity	Type of Stoichiometry Problem
(a)	volume	volume	volume-volume problem
(b)	mass	mass	mass-mass problem
(c)	volume	mass	mass-volume problem

Section 9.4 Mass-Mass Stoichiometry Problems

16. $2 Zn_{(s)} + O_{2(g)} \rightarrow 2 ZnO_{(s)}$
    MM of O_2 = 32.0 g/mol
    MM of ZnO = 81.4 g/mol

    $1.28 \text{ g ZnO} \times \dfrac{1 \text{ mol ZnO}}{81.4 \text{ g ZnO}} \times \dfrac{1 \text{ mol } O_2}{2 \text{ mol ZnO}} \times \dfrac{32.0 \text{ g } O_2}{1 \text{ mol } O_2} = 0.252 \text{ g } O_2$

18. $2 Bi_{(s)} + 3 Cl_{2(g)} \rightarrow 2 BiCl_{3(s)}$
MM of Cl_2 = 71.0 g/mol
MM of $BiCl_3$ = 315.5 g/mol

$$3.52 \text{ g BiCl}_3 \times \frac{1 \text{ mol BiCl}_3}{315.5 \text{ g BiCl}_3} \times \frac{3 \text{ mol Cl}_2}{2 \text{ mol BiCl}_3} \times \frac{71.0 \text{ g Cl}_2}{1 \text{ mol Cl}_2} = 1.19 \text{ g Cl}_2$$

20. $Cu_{(s)} + 2 AgNO_{3(aq)} \rightarrow Cu(NO_3)_{2(aq)} + 2 Ag_{(s)}$
MM of $AgNO_3$ = 169.9 g/mol
MM of Ag = 107.9 g/mol

$$1.00 \text{ g Ag} \times \frac{1 \text{ mol Ag}}{107.9 \text{ g Ag}} \times \frac{2 \text{ mol AgNO}_3}{2 \text{ mol Ag}} \times \frac{169.9 \text{ g AgNO}_3}{1 \text{ mol AgNO}_3}$$
$$= 1.57 \text{ g AgNO}_3$$

22. Balanced: $2 Co_{(s)} + 3 HgCl_{2(aq)} \rightarrow 2 CoCl_{3(aq)} + 3 Hg_{(l)}$
MM of $HgCl_2$ = 271.6 g/mol
MM of Hg = 200.6 g/mol

$$5.11 \text{ g Hg} \times \frac{1 \text{ mol Hg}}{200.6 \text{ g Hg}} \times \frac{3 \text{ mol HgCl}_2}{3 \text{ mol Hg}} \times \frac{271.6 \text{ g HgCl}_2}{1 \text{ mol HgCl}_2} = 6.92 \text{ g HgCl}_2$$

24. Balanced: $2 Na_3PO_{4(aq)} + 3 Ca(OH)_{2(aq)} \rightarrow Ca_3(PO_4)_{2(s)} + 6 NaOH_{(aq)}$
MM of $Ca(OH)_2$ = 74.1 g/mol
MM of $Ca_3(PO_4)_2$ = 310.3 g/mol

$$2.39 \text{ g Ca}_3(PO_4)_2 \times \frac{1 \text{ mol Ca}_3(PO_4)_2}{310.3 \text{ g Ca}_3(PO_4)_2} \times \frac{3 \text{ mol Ca(OH)}_2}{1 \text{ mol Ca}_3(PO_4)_2} \times$$
$$\frac{74.1 \text{ g Ca(OH)}_2}{1 \text{ mol Ca(OH)}_2} = 1.71 \text{ g Ca(OH)}_2$$

Section 9.5 Mass-Volume Stoichiometry Problems

26. $Ca(ClO_3)_{2(s)} \rightarrow CaCl_{2(s)} + 3 O_{2(g)}$
MM of $Ca(ClO_3)_2$ = 207.1 g/mol

$$2.57 \text{ g Ca(ClO}_3)_2 \times \frac{1 \text{ mol Ca(ClO}_3)_2}{207.1 \text{ g Ca(ClO}_3)_2} \times \frac{3 \text{ mol O}_2}{1 \text{ mol Ca(ClO}_3)_2} \times \frac{22.4 \text{ L O}_2}{1 \text{ mol O}_2} \times$$
$$\frac{1000 \text{ mL O}_2}{1 \text{ L O}_2} = 834 \text{ mL O}_2$$

28. $2 HgO_{(s)} \rightarrow 2 Hg_{(l)} + O_{2(g)}$
MM of HgO = 216.6 g/mol

$$2.50 \text{ g HgO} \times \frac{1 \text{ mol HgO}}{216.6 \text{ g HgO}} \times \frac{1 \text{ mol O}_2}{2 \text{ mol HgO}} \times \frac{22.4 \text{ L O}_2}{1 \text{ mol O}_2} \times \frac{1000 \text{ mL O}_2}{1 \text{ L O}_2}$$
$$= 129 \text{ mL O}_2$$

30. $2\ Na_{(s)} + 2\ H_2O_{(l)} \rightarrow 2\ NaOH_{(aq)} + H_{2(g)}$
MM of Na = 23.0 g/mol

$$75.0\ \cancel{mL\ H_2} \times \frac{1\ \cancel{L\ H_2}}{1000\ \cancel{mL\ H_2}} \times \frac{1\ \cancel{mol\ H_2}}{22.4\ \cancel{L\ H_2}} \times \frac{2\ \cancel{mol\ Na}}{1\ \cancel{mol\ H_2}} \times \frac{23.0\ g\ Na}{1\ \cancel{mol\ Na}}$$
$$= 0.154\ g\ Na$$

32. $MnCl_{2(s)} + H_2SO_{4(aq)} \rightarrow MnSO_{4(aq)} + 2\ HCl_{(g)}$
MM of $MnCl_2$ = 125.9 g/mol

$$49.5\ \cancel{mL\ HCl} \times \frac{1\ \cancel{L\ HCl}}{1000\ \cancel{mL\ HCl}} \times \frac{1\ \cancel{mol\ HCl}}{22.4\ \cancel{L\ HCl}} \times \frac{1\ \cancel{mol\ MnCl_2}}{2\ \cancel{mol\ HCl}} \times$$
$$\frac{125.9\ g\ MnCl_2}{1\ \cancel{mol\ MnCl_2}} = 0.139\ g\ MnCl_2$$

Section 9.6 Volume-Volume Stoichiometry Problems

34. $H_{2(g)} + I_{2(g)} \rightarrow 2\ HI_{(g)}$

$$125\ \cancel{mL\ H_2} \times \frac{2\ mL\ HI}{1\ \cancel{mL\ H_2}} = 250\ mL\ HI$$

36. $2\ Cl_{2(g)} + 3\ O_{2(g)} \rightarrow 2\ Cl_2O_{3(g)}$

(a) $1.75\ \cancel{L\ Cl_2O_3} \times \dfrac{2\ L\ Cl_2}{2\ \cancel{L\ Cl_2O_3}} = 1.75\ L\ Cl_2$

(b) $1.75\ \cancel{L\ Cl_2O_3} \times \dfrac{3\ L\ O_2}{2\ \cancel{L\ Cl_2O_3}} = 2.63\ L\ O_2$

38. $2\ N_{2(g)} + 5\ O_{2(g)} \rightarrow 2\ N_2O_{5(g)}$

(a) $500.0\ \cancel{mL\ N_2O_5} \times \dfrac{2\ mL\ N_2}{2\ \cancel{mL\ N_2O_5}} = 500.0\ mL\ N_2$

(b) $500.0\ \cancel{mL\ N_2O_5} \times \dfrac{5\ mL\ O_2}{2\ \cancel{mL\ N_2O_5}} = 1250\ mL\ O_2$

Section 9.7 Percent Yield

40. Actual yield: 10.4 g acetone
Theoretical yield: 11.6 g acetone

Percent yield: $\dfrac{10.4\ \cancel{g}}{11.6\ \cancel{g}} \times 100 = 89.7\%$

42. Actual yield: 0.725 g KCO_3
Theoretical yield: 0.716 g KCO_3

Percent yield: $\dfrac{0.725\ \cancel{g}}{0.716\ \cancel{g}} \times 100 = 101\%$

Section 9.8 Experimental Accuracy and Precision

44. (a) Error: $\left(\dfrac{15.5\% + 14.2\% + 14.1\%}{3}\right) - 13.2\% = 1.4\%$

     (b) Range: $15.5\% - 14.1\% = 1.4\%$

46. (a) Accuracy: $\left(\dfrac{2.55\% + 2.41\% + 2.35\%}{3}\right) - 2.50\% = -0.06\%$

     (b) Precision: $2.55\% - 2.35\% = 0.20\%$

General Exercises

48. $3\,MnO_{2(s)} + 4\,Al_{(s)} \rightarrow 3\,Mn_{(s)} + 2\,Al_2O_{3(s)}$
     MM of Mn = 54.9 g/mol
     MM of Al = 27.0 g/mol

     $1.00\ \cancel{kg\ Mn} \times \dfrac{1000\ \cancel{g\ Mn}}{1\ \cancel{kg\ Mn}} \times \dfrac{1\ \cancel{mol\ Mn}}{54.9\ \cancel{g\ Mn}} \times \dfrac{4\ \cancel{mol\ Al}}{3\ \cancel{mol\ Mn}} \times \dfrac{27.0\ g\ Al}{1\ \cancel{mol\ Al}}$
     $= 656\ g\ Al$

50. $2\,H_2O_{(l)} \rightarrow 2\,H_{2(g)} + O_{2(g)}$
     MM of H_2O = 18.0 g/mol

     STP milliliter volume of O_2:

     $100.0\ \cancel{mL\ H_2O} \times \dfrac{1.00\ \cancel{g\ H_2O}}{1\ \cancel{mL\ H_2O}} \times \dfrac{1\ \cancel{mol\ H_2O}}{18.0\ \cancel{g\ H_2O}} \times \dfrac{1\ \cancel{mol\ O_2}}{2\ \cancel{mol\ H_2O}} \times \dfrac{22.4\ \cancel{L\ O_2}}{1\ \cancel{mol\ O_2}} \times$
     $\dfrac{1000\ mL\ O_2}{1\ \cancel{L\ O_2}} = 62{,}220\ mL\ O_2$

     STP milliliter volume of H_2:

     $100.0\ \cancel{mL\ H_2O} \times \dfrac{1.00\ \cancel{g\ H_2O}}{1\ \cancel{mL\ H_2O}} \times \dfrac{1\ \cancel{mol\ H_2O}}{18.0\ \cancel{g\ H_2O}} \times \dfrac{2\ \cancel{mol\ H_2}}{2\ \cancel{mol\ H_2O}} \times \dfrac{22.4\ \cancel{L\ H_2}}{1\ \cancel{mol\ H_2}} \times$
     $\dfrac{1000\ mL\ H_2}{1\ \cancel{L\ H_2}} = 124{,}400\ mL\ H_2$

CHAPTER 10 — Modern Atomic Theory

Section 10.1 Bohr Model of the Atom

2. (a) True
    (b) False (Electrons in the Bohr atom lose energy if they drop to an orbit closer to the nucleus.)

4. Of the given series of lines from the emission spectrum of hydrogen, ultraviolet is the most energetic.

6.

	Energy Change	Color of Spectral Line
(a)	2 to 1	not visible
(b)	3 to 2	red
(c)	4 to 2	blue-green
(d)	5 to 1	not visible
(e)	5 to 2	violet
(f)	5 to 3	not visible

8. The greatest limitation for the Bohr model of the atom is that it does not adequately explain the energy states of electrons in atoms other than hydrogen.

Section 10.2 Quantum Theory

10.

	Instrument	Pitch
(a)	piano	quantized
(b)	violin	continuous

12.

	Gauge	Measurement
(a)	digital odometer	quantized
(b)	analog speedometer	continuous

14. 100 photons are responsible for ejecting 100 electrons from a sheet of aluminum foil.

Section 10.3 Quantum Mechanical Model of the Atom

16. (1) The Bohr model of the atom applies only to hydrogen, whereas the quantum mechanical model of the atom applies to all atoms.

(2) In the Bohr model, the energy of an electron is defined in terms of a fixed orbit about the nucleus. In the quantum mechanical model, the energy of an electron is described in terms of its probability of being within a spatial volume surrounding the nucleus (an orbital).

18. Electron probability is the likelihood of finding an electron within a region of space about a nucleus. The region where an electron is most likely to be found (~ 95% probability) is called an orbital.

20.
	Principal Energy Levels	Larger Orbital
(a)	$n = 1$ or $n = 2$	$n = 2$
(b)	$n = 1$ or $n = 3$	$n = 3$
(c)	$n = 2$ or $n = 3$	$n = 3$
(d)	$n = 3$ or $n = 5$	$n = 5$

22.
	Not Allowed
(a)	$n = 0, l = 0$ (n has to be greater than or equal to one)
(c)	$n = 2, l = 2$ (l cannot equal n)

24. (a)   (b)

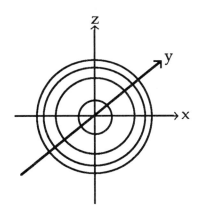 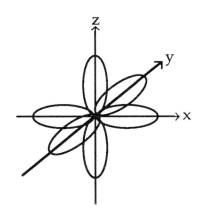

24.   (c)   (d)

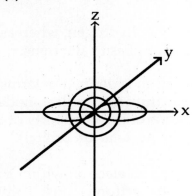   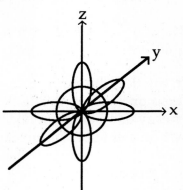

26.	Orbitals	Larger Orbital		Orbitals	Larger Orbital
(a)	$2s$ or $3s$	$3s$	(b)	$2p_x$ or $3p_x$	$3p_x$
(c)	$2p_x$ or $2p_y$	both are equal	(d)	$4p_y$ or $4p_z$	both are equal

28.	Description	Orbital
(a)	spherical orbital in the sixth shell	$6s$
(b)	dumbbell-shaped orbital in the third shell	$3p$

Section 10.4 Distribution of Electrons by Orbital

30.	Orbital	Max. # of Electrons
(a)	$7s$	2 e$^-$
(b)	$6p$	2 e$^-$
(c)	$6d$	2 e$^-$
(d)	$5f$	2 e$^-$

32.	Orbital	Max. # of Electrons
(a)	$n = 1, l = 0$	2 e$^-$
(b)	$n = 2, l = 0$	2 e$^-$
(c)	$n = 3, l = 2$	2 e$^-$
(d)	$n = 4, l = 1$	2 e$^-$

34.	Subshell	Number of Orbitals
(a)	$n = 3, l = 1$	3
(b)	$n = 4, l = 0$	1
(c)	$n = 5, l = 3$	7
(d)	$n = 6, l = 2$	5

36.

	Shell	Number of Subshells
(a)	$n = 5$	5
(b)	$n = 6$	6
(c)	$n = 7$	7
(d)	$n = 8$	8

38.

	Subshell	Max. # of Electrons
(a)	7s	$2\ e^-$
(b)	6p	$2\ e^- + 2\ e^- + 2\ e^- = 6\ e^-$
(c)	5d	$2\ e^- + 2\ e^- + 2\ e^- + 2\ e^- + 2\ e^- = 10\ e^-$
(d)	5f	$2\ e^- + 2\ e^- + 2\ e^- + 2\ e^- + 2\ e^- + 2\ e^- + 2\ e^- = 14\ e^-$

40.

Shell	Max. # of Electrons
$n = 5$	$2\ e^- + 6\ e^- + 10\ e^- + 14\ e^- + 18\ e^- = 50\ e^-$

Section 10.5 The Four Quantum Numbers

42.   Not Allowed
   (a) $n = 0$ (n has to be greater than or equal to one)
   (c) $n = 2.5$ (n has to be a whole number greater than one)

44.   Not Allowed
   (c) $l = 3.5$ (l has to be a whole number)

46.   Not Allowed
   (c) $m = 3.5$ (m has to be a whole number)

48.

	Orbital	3rd Quantum Number
(a)	6s	$m = 0$
(b)	2p	$m = +1, 0, -1$
(c)	3d	$m = +2, +1, 0, -1, -2$
(d)	5f	$m = +3, +2, +1, 0, -1, -2, -3$

50.   Not Allowed
   (a) $s = 0$ (s has to be equal to $+\frac{1}{2}$ or $-\frac{1}{2}$)
   (d) $s = +1$ (s has to be equal to $+\frac{1}{2}$ or $-\frac{1}{2}$)

52.   The second quantum number specifies the shape of the orbital in which an electron is found.

54.   The fourth quantum number specifies the spin of an electron.

Section 10.6 Orbital Energy Diagrams

56.

	Element	Electron Configuration
(a)	Na	$1s^2\,2s^2\,2p^6\,3s^1$
(b)	Ti	$1s^2\,2s^2\,2p^6\,3s^2\,3p^6\,4s^2\,3d^2$
(c)	Ca	$1s^2\,2s^2\,2p^6\,3s^2\,3p^6\,4s^2$
(d)	Se	$1s^2\,2s^2\,2p^6\,3s^2\,3p^6\,4s^2\,3d^{10}\,4p^4$

58. Orbital Diagram

Na: 1s [↑↓] 2s [↑↓] 2p [↑↓][↑↓][↑↓] 3s [↑]

Ti: 1s [↑↓] 2s [↑↓] 2p [↑↓][↑↓][↑↓] 3s [↑↓] 3p [↑↓][↑↓][↑↓] 4s [↑↓] 3d [↑][↑][ ][ ][ ]

Ca: 1s [↑↓] 2s [↑↓] 2p [↑↓][↑↓][↑↓] 3s [↑↓] 3p [↑↓][↑↓][↑↓] 4s [↑↓]

Se: 1s [↑↓] 2s [↑↓] 2p [↑↓][↑↓][↑↓] 3s [↑↓] 3p [↑↓][↑↓][↑↓] 4s [↑↓]

3d [↑↓][↑↓][↑↓][↑↓][↑↓] 4p [↑↓][↑][↑]

60.

Ni: 1s [↑↓] 2s [↑↓] 2p [↑↓][↑↓][↑↓] 3s [↑↓] 3p [↑↓][↑↓][↑↓] 4s [↑↓] 3d [↑↓][↑↓][↑↓][↑][↑]

Nickel has two unpaired electrons.

62. Orbital Energy Diagram

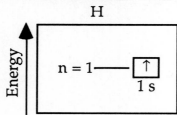

64.   Orbital Energy Diagrams

(a)

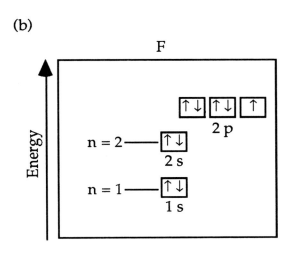

(b)

64.   (c)

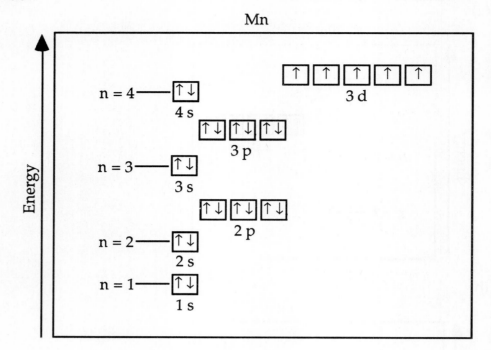

(d)

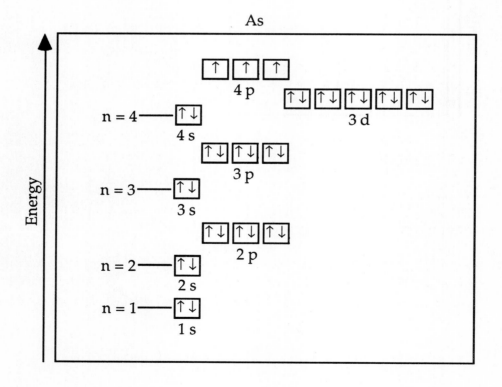

Section 10.7 Quantum Notation: (*n, l, m, s*)

66.

	Element	Quantum Numbers for Highest-Energy Electron
(a)	potassium	$(4, 0, 0, +\frac{1}{2})$
(b)	sulfur	$(3, 1, +1, -\frac{1}{2})$
(c)	nickel	$(3, 2, 0, -\frac{1}{2})$
(d)	bromine	$(4, 1, 0, -\frac{1}{2})$

68.

	Element	Quantum Numbers for Highest-Energy Electron
(a)	Mg	$(3, 0, 0, -\frac{1}{2})$
(b)	P	$(3, 1, -1, +\frac{1}{2})$
(c)	V	$(3, 2, 0, +\frac{1}{2})$
(d)	Ga	$(4, 1, +1, +\frac{1}{2})$

70.

	Quantum Notation	Element
(a)	$(3, 2, 0, +\frac{1}{2})$	V
(b)	$(3, 1, -1, -\frac{1}{2})$	Ar
(c)	$(4, 3, +3, +\frac{1}{2})$	Ce
(d)	$(5, 3, +1, -\frac{1}{2})$	Es

General Exercises

72.   Photon – an individual unit of radiant energy that corresponds to the particle nature of light.
Quantum – a tiny bundle of radiant energy made up of photons.

74.   The 2*s* orbital is higher in energy than the 1*s* orbital. Since higher energy orbitals are farther from the nucleus, the 1*s* orbital is completely contained in the 2*s* orbital.

76.   An atom is more stable with a completely filled *d* subshell than a partially filled one. Thus, one of the 4*s* electrons from copper moves into the 3*d* orbital in order to attain the extra stability.

78.   A lone electron within an orbital spins about its axis creating a weak magnetic field. Paired electrons also spin about their axes, but no overall magnetic field results because the electrons spin in opposite directions and in effect cancel each other out.

CHAPTER 11

Chemical Bonding

Section 11.1 Valence Electrons and Chemical Bonds

2. A nonmetal atom needs valence electrons in order to attain a completely filled octet. A covalent bond forms when nonmetal atoms share their valence electrons in such a fashion so that each atom completes its octet.

4.
Element	Before Reaction	After Reaction
H	1 valence e$^-$	2 valence e$^-$
I	7 valence e$^-$	8 valence e$^-$

6.
	Compound	Bond		Compound	Bond
(a)	N_2O_4	covalent	(b)	$LiClO_3$	ionic
(c)	$FeSO_4$	ionic	(d)	IF_7	covalent

8.
	Substance	Representative Particle
(a)	C_4H_{10}	molecule
(b)	SrI_2	formula unit
(c)	KBr	formula unit
(d)	PbO_2	formula unit
(e)	C_3H_6O	molecule
(f)	UF_4	formula unit

10.
	Substance	Representative Particle
(a)	C_2H_6	molecule
(b)	Cu	atom
(c)	Fe_3O_4	formula unit
(d)	Na_2CO_3	formula unit
(e)	S_8	molecule
(f)	Br_2	molecule

Section 11.2 The Ionic Bond

12.
	Ion	Predicted Charge		Ion	Predicted Charge
(a)	Be ion	2+	(b)	Sr ion	2+
(c)	Ga ion	3+	(d)	Cs ion	1+

14.

	Ion	Predicted Charge		Ion	Predicted Charge
(a)	I ion	1–	(b)	S ion	2–
(c)	Se ion	2–	(d)	P ion	3–

16.

	Ion	Electron Configuration
(a)	Sc^{3+}	$1s^2 \, 2s^2 \, 2p^6 \, 3s^2 \, 3p^6$
(b)	Y^{3+}	$1s^2 \, 2s^2 \, 2p^6 \, 3s^2 \, 3p^6 \, 4s^2 \, 3d^{10} \, 4p^6$
(c)	Ti^{4+}	$1s^2 \, 2s^2 \, 2p^6 \, 3s^2 \, 3p^6$
(d)	Zr^{4+}	$1s^2 \, 2s^2 \, 2p^6 \, 3s^2 \, 3p^6 \, 4s^2 \, 3d^{10} \, 4p^6$

18.

	Ion	Electron Configuration
(a)	Br^-	$1s^2 \, 2s^2 \, 2p^6 \, 3s^2 \, 3p^6 \, 4s^2 \, 3d^{10} \, 4p^6$
(b)	O^{2-}	$1s^2 \, 2s^2 \, 2p^6$
(c)	Se^{2-}	$1s^2 \, 2s^2 \, 2p^6 \, 3s^2 \, 3p^6 \, 4s^2 \, 3d^{10} \, 4p^6$
(d)	N^{3-}	$1s^2 \, 2s^2 \, 2p^6$

20.

	Ion	Isoelectronic With:
(a)	Cl^-	Ar
(b)	I^-	Xe
(c)	O^{2-}	Ne
(d)	P^{3-}	Ar

22.

	Ion	Isoelectronic With:
(a)	F^-	Ne
(b)	Br^-	Kr
(c)	Se^{2-}	Kr
(d)	N^{3-}	Ne

24.
   (a)   Al atom radius > Al ion radius
   (b)   Pb atom radius > Pb ion radius
   (c)   Se atom radius < Se ion radius
   (d)   N atom radius < N ion radius

26.   (d) is not true; cobalt and the cobalt bromide *do not* have similar properties.

Section 11.3 The Covalent Bond

28.
   (a)   The sum of the C and Cl atomic radii is greater than the bond length in C — Cl.
   (b)   The sum of the S and F atomic radii is greater than the bond length in S — F.

30.   (c) is not true; the bond length between nitrogen and oxygen atoms is *less than* the sum of the two atomic radii.

Section 11.4 Electron Dot Formulas of Molecules

32.

	Molecule	Valence Electrons	Electron Dot	Structural
(a)	Cl_2	$7 + 7 = 14\ e^-$	$:\ddot{C}l\!:\!\ddot{C}l\!:$	Cl—Cl
(b)	O_2	$6 + 6 = 12\ e^-$	$\ddot{O}::\ddot{O}$	O=O
(c)	HI	$1 + 7 = 8\ e^-$	$H\!:\!\ddot{I}\!:$	H—I

(d) PH_3 $5 + 3(1) = 8\ e-$

$$H\!:\!\overset{\displaystyle\cdot\cdot}{\underset{\displaystyle\cdot\cdot}{P}}\!:\!H$$

$$\begin{array}{c} H \\ | \\ H\!-\!P\!-\!H \end{array}$$

(e) CH_4 $4 + 4(1) = 8\ e^-$

$$\begin{array}{c} H \\ H\!:\!C\!:\!H \\ H \end{array}$$

$$\begin{array}{c} H \\ | \\ H\!-\!C\!-\!H \\ | \\ H \end{array}$$

(f) NF_3 $5 + 3(7) = 26\ e^-$

$$\begin{array}{c} :\ddot{F}: \\ :\ddot{F}\!:\!N\!:\!\ddot{F}: \end{array}$$

$$\begin{array}{c} F \\ | \\ F\!-\!N\!-\!F \end{array}$$

34.

	Molecule	Valence Electrons	Electron Dot	Structural
(a)	N_2	$2(5) = 10\ e^-$	$:N\!:\!:\!:N:$	N≡N

(b) PI_3 $5 + 3(7) = 26\ e^-$

$$\begin{array}{c} :\ddot{I}: \\ :\ddot{I}\!:\!P\!:\!\ddot{I}: \end{array}$$

$$\begin{array}{c} I \\ | \\ I\!-\!P\!-\!I \end{array}$$

(c) CS_2 $4 + 2(6) = 16\ e^-$ $\ddot{S}::C::\ddot{S}$ S=C=S

(d) CH_3OH $4 + 4(1) + 6 = 14\ e^-$

$$\begin{array}{c} H \\ H\!:\!C\!:\!\ddot{O}\!:\!H \\ H \end{array}$$

$$\begin{array}{c} H \\ | \\ H\!-\!C\!-\!O\!-\!H \\ | \\ H \end{array}$$

(e) H_2O_2 $2(1) + 2(6) = 14\ e^-$ $H\!:\!\ddot{O}\!:\!\ddot{O}\!:\!H$ H—O—O—H

34. | Molecule | Valence Electrons | Electron Dot | Structural |

(f)   HOCN $1 + 6 + 4 + 5 = 16$ e$^-$ H:$\overset{\cdot\cdot}{\underset{\cdot\cdot}{O}}$:C:::N: H—O—C≡N

Section 11.5 Polar Covalent Bonds

36.   Electronegativity across a series in the periodic table generally increases.

38.   Nonmetals are more electronegative than semimetals.

40.

More Electronegative	More Electronegative
(a) Se < **Br**	(b) **O** >H
(c) Te < **S**	(d) **C** > B
(e) **Co** > Ca	(f) Ba < **Be**

(Note: The more electronegative element is in bold.)

42.

Bond	Polarity	Bond	Polarity
(a) H—Cl	$3.0 - 2.1 = 0.9$	(b) H—I	$2.5 - 2.1 = 0.4$
(c) Br—Cl	$3.0 - 2.8 = 0.2$	(d) I—Br	$2.8 - 2.5 = 0.3$
(e) N—O	$3.5 - 3.0 = 0.5$		

44.   Polar Bonds Using Delta Notation

(a) δ^- C—H δ^+

(b) δ^+ Se—O δ^-

(c) δ^+ Ge—Cl δ^-

(d) δ^+ H—Br δ^-

(e) δ^+ P—I δ^-

(Note: δ^- indicates the more electronegative atom and δ^+ indicates the
    more electropositive atom.)

Section 11.6 Nonpolar Covalent Bonds

46.

Bond	Polarity	Classification
(a) I—C	$2.5 - 2.5 = 0$	Nonpolar
(b) C—S	$2.5 - 2.5 = 0$	Nonpolar
(c) S—H	$2.5 - 2.1 = 0.4$	Polar
(d) H—Br	$2.8 - 2.1 = 0.7$	Polar
(e) Te—I	$2.5 - 2.1 = 0.4$	Polar

Thus, (a) and (b) are nonpolar.

48.

Diatomic Molecule	Formula	Diatomic Molecule	Formula
hydrogen	H_2	nitrogen	N_2
oxygen	O_2	fluorine	F_2
chlorine	Cl_2	bromine	Br_2
iodine	I_2		

Section 11.7 Coordinate Covalent Bonds

(Note: Coordinate covalent bonds are indicated by a dash, —)

50.

Formula	Electron Dot Without O	Formula	Electron Dot With O
HOI	H:Ö:Ï:	HOIO	H:Ö:Ï—Ö:

52.

Formula	Electron Dot Without H	Formula	Electron Dot With H
PH_3	H:P:H H	$PH_4{}^+$	$\left[\begin{array}{c} H \\ H:P:H \\ H \end{array}\right]^+$

54.

Formula	Electron Dot Without O	Formula	Electron Dot With O
$PO_3{}^{3-}$	$\left[:\ddot{O}:P:\ddot{O}: \atop :\ddot{O}: \right]^{3-}$	$PO_4{}^{3-}$	$\left[:\ddot{O}: \atop :\ddot{O}:P:\ddot{O}: \atop :\ddot{O}: \right]^{3-}$

56.

Formula	Electron Dot Without H	Formula	Electron Dot With H
$HSO_4{}^-$	$\left[:\ddot{O}: \atop :\ddot{O}:S:\ddot{O}:H \atop :\ddot{O}: \right]^-$	H_2SO_4	$\left[:\ddot{O}: \atop H—\ddot{O}:S:\ddot{O}:H \atop :\ddot{O}: \right]$

Section 11.8 Polyatomic Ions

58.

	Ion	Valence Electrons	Electron Dot	Structural
(a)	BrO^-	$7 + 6 + 1 = 14\ e^-$	$\left[:\ddot{Br}:\ddot{O}: \right]^-$	$\left[Br—O \right]^-$
(b)	$SO_3{}^{2-}$	$4(6) + 2 = 26\ e^-$	$\left[:\ddot{O}:S:\ddot{O}: \atop :\ddot{O}: \right]^{2-}$	$\left[O—S—O \atop \hspace{0.6em}\mid \atop O \right]^{2-}$
(c)	$BO_3{}^{3-}$	$3 + 3(6) + 3 = 24\ e^-$	$\left[:\ddot{O}:B::\ddot{O} \atop :\ddot{O}: \right]^{3-}$	$\left[O—B=O \atop \hspace{0.4em}\mid \atop O \right]^{3-}$
(d)	$HSO_3{}^-$	$1 + 4(6) + 1 = 26\ e^-$	$\left[:\ddot{O}:S:\ddot{O}:H \atop :\ddot{O}: \right]^-$	$\left[O—S—O—H \atop \hspace{0.6em}\mid \atop O \right]^-$

58.

	Ion	Valence Electrons	Electron Dot	Structural
(e)	BrO_3^-	$7 + 3(6) + 1 = 26$ e$^-$	$\left[:\overset{..}{\underset{..}{O}}:\overset{..}{Br}:\overset{..}{\underset{..}{O}}: \atop :\overset{..}{\underset{..}{O}}:\right]^-$	$\left[\begin{array}{c}O-Br-O \\ \mid \\ O\end{array}\right]^-$

60.

	Ion	Valence Electrons	Electron Dot	Structural
(a)	CN^-	$4 + 5 + 1 = 10$ e$^-$	$\left[:C:::N:\right]^-$	$\left[C\equiv N\right]^-$
(b)	HS^-	$1 + 6 + 1 = 8$ e$^-$	$\left[H:\overset{..}{\underset{..}{S}}:\right]^-$	$\left[H-S\right]^-$
(c)	PO_3^{3-}	$5 + 3(6) + 3 = 26$ e$^-$	$\left[:\overset{..}{\underset{..}{O}}:P:\overset{..}{\underset{..}{O}}: \atop :\overset{..}{\underset{..}{O}}:\right]^{3-}$	$\left[\begin{array}{c}O-P-O \\ \mid \\ O\end{array}\right]^{3-}$
(d)	HCO_3^-	$1 + 4 + 3(6) + 1 = 24$ e$^-$	$\left[H:\overset{..}{\underset{..}{O}}:C:\overset{..}{\underset{..}{O}}: \atop :\overset{..}{\underset{..}{O}}:\right]^-$	$\left[\begin{array}{c}H-O-C-O \\ \parallel \\ O\end{array}\right]^-$
(e)	SeO_3^{2-}	$4(6) + 2 = 26$ e$^-$	$\left[:\overset{..}{\underset{..}{O}}:\overset{..}{Se}:\overset{..}{\underset{..}{O}}: \atop :\overset{..}{\underset{..}{O}}:\right]^{2-}$	$\left[\begin{array}{c}O-Se-O \\ \mid \\ O\end{array}\right]^{2-}$

Section 11.9 Properties of Ionic and Molecular Compounds

62.

		Property of Molecular Compound
(a)	physical state	gases, liquids, and solids
(b)	structure	often noncrystalline
(c)	melting point	low (usually below 300°C)
(d)	boiling point	low
(e)	electrical conductivity	nonconductor
(f)	rate of reaction	usually slow

64.

	Property	Ionic or Covalent Bond
(a)	colorless gas	covalent bond
(b)	transparent crystalline solid	ionic bond
(c)	low boiling point	covalent bond
(d)	colorless liquid	covalent bond
(e)	nonconductor in aq. solution	covalent bond
(f)	reacts rapidly in solution	ionic bond

General Exercises

66. A chlorine ion has one more electron than a chlorine atom. As a result, the electrons in the $3p$ subshell repel each other causing the subshell and ion to become larger.

68. The properties of an ionic compound and its constituent elements have no direct or indirect relationship.

70.
	Ions		Formula
(a)	$2\ Bi^{3+} + 3\ S^{2-}$	=	Bi_2S_3
(b)	$3\ Sr^{2+} + 2\ As^{3-}$	=	Sr_3As_2
(c)	$Sc^{3+} + N^{3-}$	=	ScN
(d)	$Ti^{4+} + 2\ O^{2-}$	=	TiO_2

72.
	Ions		Formula
(a)	$Hg^{2+} + 2\ HCO_3^{-}$	=	$Hg(HCO_3)_2$
(b)	$Bi^{3+} + 3\ BrO_3^{-}$	=	$Bi(BrO_3)_3$
(c)	$2\ NH_4^{+} + CO_3^{2-}$	=	$(NH_4)_2CO_3$
(d)	$3\ Hg_2^{2+} + 2\ PO_4^{3-}$	=	$(Hg_2)_3(PO_4)_2$

74. The properties of a covalent compound and its constituent elements have no direct or indirect relationship.

76.
	Ion	Valence Electrons	Electron Dot	Structural
(a)	AsO_3^{3-}	$5 + 3(6) + 3 = 26\ e^-$	$\left[\begin{array}{c} :\ddot{O}:\ddot{A}s:\ddot{O}: \\ :\ddot{O}: \end{array}\right]^{3-}$	$\left[\begin{array}{c} O-As-O \\ | \\ O \end{array}\right]^{3-}$
(b)	SiO_3^{2-}	$4 + 3(6) + 2 = 24\ e^-$	$\left[\begin{array}{c} :\ddot{O}:Si:\ddot{O}: \\ ::\ddot{O}: \end{array}\right]^{2-}$	$\left[\begin{array}{c} O-Si-O \\ || \\ O \end{array}\right]^{2-}$

78. The charge on the outside of the brackets indicates that the overall charge, due to electron loss or gain, is distributed about the entire polyatomic ion.

80.
Molecule	Structural Formulas
NO_2^-	$\left[\text{O=N-O}\right]^-$ and $\left[\text{O-N=O}\right]^-$

82.

Molecule	Valence Electrons	Electron Dot	Structural
XeO_3	$8 + 3(6) = 26$ e$^-$	$:\overset{..}{\underset{..}{O}}:\overset{..}{\underset{..}{Xe}}:\overset{..}{\underset{..}{O}}:$ $:\overset{..}{\underset{..}{O}}:$	O—Xe—O | O

CHAPTER 12

The Gaseous State

Section 12.1 Properties of Gases

2. The density of air is ~ 1 g/L. The density of water is ~ 1 g/mL. Thus, air is approximately 1000 less dense than water.

Section 12.2 Atmospheric Pressure and the Barometer

4.
Units	Standard Atmospheric Pressure
(a) inches of mercury	29.9 in. Hg
(b) pounds per square inch	14.7 psi
(c) kilopascals	101 kPa

6. (a) $7555 \text{ torr} \times \dfrac{76.0 \text{ cm Hg}}{760 \text{ torr}} = 755.5 \text{ cm Hg}$

   (b) $7555 \text{ torr} \times \dfrac{29.9 \text{ in. Hg}}{760 \text{ torr}} = 297 \text{ in. Hg}$

   (c) $7555 \text{ torr} \times \dfrac{14.7 \text{ psi}}{760 \text{ torr}} = 146 \text{ psi}$

   (d) $7555 \text{ torr} \times \dfrac{101 \text{ kPa}}{760 \text{ torr}} = 1000 \text{ kPa}$

8. (a) $99.9 \text{ kPa} \times \dfrac{1.00 \text{ atm}}{101 \text{ kPa}} = 0.989 \text{ atm}$

   (b) $99.9 \text{ kPa} \times \dfrac{760 \text{ mm Hg}}{101 \text{ kPa}} = 752 \text{ mm Hg}$

   (c) $99.9 \text{ kPa} \times \dfrac{14.7 \text{ psi}}{101 \text{ kPa}} = 14.5 \text{ psi}$

   (d) $99.9 \text{ kPa} \times \dfrac{29.9 \text{ in. Hg}}{101 \text{ kPa}} = 29.6 \text{ in. Hg}$

Section 12.3 Vapor Pressure

10.   Water molecules near the surface of the water that have enough kinetic energy can break free from the liquid state and enter the gaseous state. If the liquid water is not in a closed container, eventually all of the molecules will enter the gaseous state. Thus, the vapor pressure of the water drives the liquid to completely evaporate.

12.   When the pressure exerted by a liquid's vapor is equal to the pressure exerted by the atmosphere, the liquid begins to boil.

14.   The temperature at which the vapor pressure of a liquid is equal to the atmospheric pressure is the boiling point. Thus, the boiling point of methanol is 65°C because its vapor pressure at this temperature is 1 atm.

Section 12.4 Dalton's Law of Partial Pressures

16.   The term 'wet gas' refers to a gas collected over water resulting in a mixture of the water vapor with the gaseous sample.

18. $P_{water\ vapor} = 41.2$ mm Hg
$P_{nitrogen} = 731$ mm Hg
$P_{total} = P_{water\ vapor} + P_{nitrogen}$
$P_{total} = 731$ mm Hg $+ 41.2$ mm Hg $= 772$ mm Hg

20. 5.00 atm $\times \dfrac{760 \text{ torr}}{1.00 \text{ atm}} = 3800$ torr

$P_{total} = 3800$ torr
$P_{nitrogen} = 1850$ torr
$P_{hydrogen} = 1150$ torr
$P_{ammonia} = P_{total} - (P_{nitrogen} + P_{hydrogen})$
$P_{ammonia} = 3800$ torr $- (1850$ torr $+ 1150$ torr$) = 800$ torr

Section 12.5 Variables Affecting Gas Pressure

22.   Increasing the temperature of a gas causes the gas molecules to have a greater velocity; thus, they collide with a greater frequency and energy. As a result, the pressure of the gas increases.

24.

	Change	Affect on Pressure	Because
(a)	volume decreases	pressure increases	molecules are closer together and collide more frequently

24.

Change	Affect on Pressure	Because
(b) temperature decreases	pressure decreases	molecules move slower and collide with a lesser frequency and energy
(c) moles of gas decrease	pressure decreases	less molecules cause less collisions

26.

Change	Affect on Pressure
(a) volume decreases	pressure increases
(b) temperature decreases	pressure decreases
(c) moles of gas increase	pressure increases

Section 12.6 Boyle's Law: Pressure / Volume Changes

28. <u>Pressure vs. Reciprocal of Volume</u>

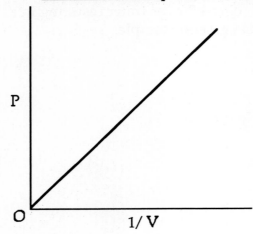

30. $V_1 \times P_{factor} = V_2$

$2.50 \text{ L Ar} \times \dfrac{705 \, \cancel{torr}}{1550 \, \cancel{torr}} = 1.14 \text{ L Ar}$

32. $95.5 \, \cancel{cm \, Hg} \times \dfrac{760 \text{ mm Hg}}{76.0 \, \cancel{cm \, Hg}} = 955 \text{ mm Hg}$

$V_1 \times P_{factor} = V_2$

$1.10 \text{ L Cl}_2 \times \dfrac{955 \, \cancel{mm \, Hg}}{75.0 \, \cancel{mm \, Hg}} = 14.0 \text{ L Cl}_2$

Section 12.7 Charles' Law: Volume / Temperature Changes

34. **Volume vs. Temperature (In Celsius)**

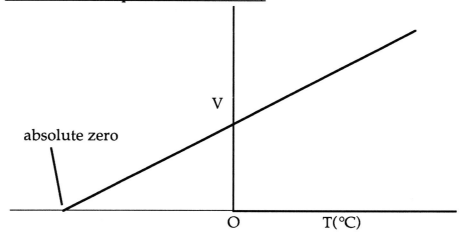

36. $T_1 \times V_{factor} = T_2$ $35°C + 273 = 308 \text{ K}$

$$308 \text{ K} \times \frac{1.00 \text{ L}}{4.50 \text{ L}} = 68.4 \text{ K}$$

$68.4 \text{ K} - 273 = -205°C$

38. $T_1 \times V_{factor} = T_2$ $35°C + 273 = 308 \text{ K}$

$$308 \text{ K} \times \frac{1.26 \text{ L}}{0.500 \text{ L}} = 776 \text{ K}$$

$776 \text{ K} - 273 = 503°C$

Section 12.8 Gay-Lussac's Law: Pressure / Temperature Changes

40. **Pressure vs. Temperature (In Celsius)**

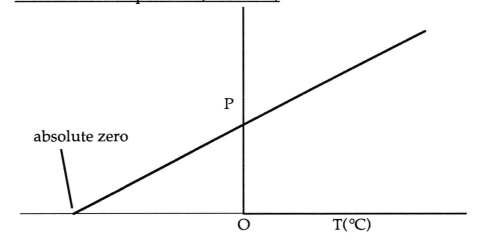

42. $\quad T_1 \times P_{factor} = T_2 \qquad\qquad\qquad 10°C + 273 = 283\ K$

$283\ K \times \dfrac{0.100\ \cancel{atm}}{0.570\ \cancel{atm}} = 49.6\ K$

$49.6\ K - 273 = -223°C$

44. $\quad T_1 \times P_{factor} = T_2 \qquad\qquad\qquad 35°C + 273 = 308\ K$

$308\ K \times \dfrac{745\ \cancel{mm\ Hg}}{650\ \cancel{mm\ Hg}} = 353\ K$

$353\ K - 273 = 80°C$

Section 12.9 Combined Gas Law

46.

	P	V	T
initial	5.00 atm	5.00 L	500°C + 273 = 773 K
final	1.00 atm	V_2	273 K

$V_1 \times P_{factor} \times T_{factor} = V_2$

$5.00\ L \times \dfrac{5.00\ \cancel{atm}}{1.00\ \cancel{atm}} \times \dfrac{273\ \cancel{K}}{773\ \cancel{K}} = 8.83\ L\ NO_2$

48.

	P	V	T
initial	650 mm Hg	25.0 mL	$-25°C + 273 = 248\ K$
final	350 mm Hg	V_2	$25°C + 273 = 298\ K$

$V_1 \times P_{factor} \times T_{factor} = V_2$

$25.0\ mL \times \dfrac{650\ \cancel{mm\ Hg}}{350\ \cancel{mm\ Hg}} \times \dfrac{298\ \cancel{K}}{248\ \cancel{K}} = 55.8\ mL\ gas$

50.

	P	V	T
initial	1.00 atm	0.750 L	273 K
final	P_2	100.0 mL = 0.1000 L	$25°C + 273 = 298\ K$

$P_1 \times V_{factor} \times T_{factor} = P_2$

$1.00\ atm \times \dfrac{0.750\ \cancel{L}}{0.1000\ \cancel{L}} \times \dfrac{298\ \cancel{K}}{273\ \cancel{K}} = 8.19\ atm$

52.

	P	V	T
initial	1.00 atm	1.00 L	273 K
final	2.00 atm	10.0 L	T_2

$$T_1 \times P_{factor} \times V_{factor} = T_2$$

$$273 \text{ K} \times \frac{2.00 \text{ atm}}{1.00 \text{ atm}} \times \frac{10.0 \text{ L}}{1.00 \text{ L}} = 5460 \text{ K}$$

$$5460 \text{ K} - 273 = 5187°C \quad \text{Answer rounded: } 5190°C$$

54.

	P	V	T
initial	75.0 cm Hg	500.0 mL	$-185°C + 273 = 88$ K
final	55.0 cm Hg	225.0 mL	T_2

$$T_1 \times P_{factor} \times V_{factor} = T_2$$

$$88 \text{ K} \times \frac{55.0 \text{ cm Hg}}{75.0 \text{ cm Hg}} \times \frac{225.0 \text{ mL}}{500.0 \text{ mL}} = 29 \text{ K}$$

$$29 \text{ K} - 273 = -244°C$$

Section 12.10 Ideal Gas Behavior

56. An ideal gas is a hypothetical gas that behaves in a consistent and predictable manner (at high temperatures and low pressures).
A real gas is a gas that deviates from the assumptions of the behavior of an ideal gas (especially at high pressures and low temperatures).

58. At a temperature of $-273°C$ (absolute zero), a gas possesses zero kinetic energy.

60. Since the gases are at the same temperature they have the same kinetic energy. Since hydrogen has a lower mass than oxygen, its velocity is faster ($KE = 1/2 \ mv^2$).

62. An ideal gas at 0 K (absolute zero) theoretically occupies zero volume.

Section 12.11 Ideal Gas Equation

64. $V = \dfrac{n \, R \, T}{P}$

$n = 1.25 \text{ mol } O_2$

$T = 25°C + 273 = 298 \text{ K}$

$P = 1200 \text{ torr} \times \dfrac{1.00 \text{ atm}}{760 \text{ torr}} = 1.58 \text{ atm}$

$V = \dfrac{1.25 \text{ mol} \times 298 \text{ K}}{1.58 \text{ atm}} \times \dfrac{0.0821 \text{ atm} \cdot \text{L}}{1 \text{ mol} \cdot \text{K}} = 19.4 \text{ L } O_2$

66. $T = \dfrac{P\,V}{n\,R}$

$P = 725 \; \text{torr} \times \dfrac{1.00 \text{ atm}}{760 \; \text{torr}} = 0.954 \text{ atm}$

$V = 2.15 \text{ L}$

$n = 0.100 \text{ mol Ar}$

$T = \dfrac{0.954 \; \text{atm} \times 2.15 \; \text{L}}{0.100 \; \text{mol}} \times \dfrac{1 \; \text{mol} \cdot \text{K}}{0.0821 \; \text{atm} \cdot \text{L}} = 250 \text{ K}$

$250 \text{ K} - 273 = -23°C$

68. $MM = \dfrac{g\,R\,T}{P\,V}$

$g = 1.95 \text{ g}$

$V = 3.00 \text{ L}$

$P = 760 \; \text{torr} \times \dfrac{1.00 \text{ atm}}{760 \; \text{torr}} = 1.00 \text{ atm}$

$T = 20°C + 273 = 293 \text{ K}$

$MM = \dfrac{1.95 \text{ g} \times 293 \; \text{K}}{1.00 \; \text{atm} \times 3.00 \; \text{L}} \times \dfrac{0.0821 \; \text{atm} \cdot \text{L}}{1 \; \text{mol} \cdot \text{K}} = 15.6 \text{ g/mol}$

70. $MM = \dfrac{g\,R\,T}{P\,V}$

$g = 5.40 \text{ g}$

$V = 1.00 \text{ L}$

$P = 760 \; \text{torr} \times \dfrac{1.00 \text{ atm}}{760 \; \text{torr}} = 1.00 \text{ atm}$

$T = 0°C + 273 = 273 \text{ K}$

$MM = \dfrac{5.40 \text{ g} \times 273 \; \text{K}}{1.00 \; \text{atm} \times 1.00 \; \text{L}} \times \dfrac{0.0821 \; \text{atm} \cdot \text{L}}{1 \; \text{mol} \cdot \text{K}} = 121 \text{ g/mol}$

72. $\dfrac{0.0821 \; \text{atm} \cdot \text{L}}{1 \; \text{mol} \cdot \text{K}} \times \dfrac{101.27 \text{ J}}{1 \; \text{atm} \cdot \text{L}} = 8.31 \text{ J/mol} \cdot \text{K}$

General Exercises

74. $760 \; \text{torr} \times \dfrac{1 \; \text{mm Hg}}{1 \; \text{torr}} \times \dfrac{1 \; \text{cm Hg}}{10 \; \text{mm Hg}} \times \dfrac{1 \; \text{in. Hg}}{2.54 \; \text{cm Hg}} \times \dfrac{1 \; \text{ft. Hg}}{12 \; \text{in. Hg}} \times$ $\dfrac{13.6 \text{ ft } H_2O}{1 \; \text{ft. Hg}} = 33.9 \text{ ft } H_2O$

76. From Figure 12.6: The boiling point of water at 650 torr is ~ 97°C.

78. $P_{hydrogen}$ = 3.15 atm

$P_{chlorine}$ = 50.0 ~~psi~~ $\times \dfrac{1.00 \text{ atm}}{14.7 \text{ ~~psi~~}}$ = 3.40 atm

$P_{hydrogen\ chloride}$ = 2500 ~~torr~~ $\times \dfrac{1.00 \text{ atm}}{760 \text{ ~~torr~~}}$ = 3.29 atm

P_{total} = $P_{hydrogen}$ + $P_{chlorine}$ + $P_{hydrogen\ chloride}$
P_{total} = 3.15 atm + 3.40 atm + 3.29 atm = 9.84 atm

80. P_{total} = 758 mm Hg
$P_{water\ vapor}$ = 13.6 mm Hg
$P_{hydrogen}$ + $P_{water\ vapor}$ = P_{total}
$P_{hydrogen}$ = P_{total} − $P_{water\ vapor}$
$P_{hydrogen}$ = 758 mm Hg − 13.6 mm Hg = 744 mm Hg

	P	V	T
initial	744 mm Hg	79.9 mL	16°C + 273 = 289 K
final	760 mm Hg	V_2	273 K

$V_1 \times P_{factor} \times T_{factor}$ = V_2

79.9 mL $\times \dfrac{744 \text{ ~~mm Hg~~}}{760 \text{ ~~mm Hg~~}} \times \dfrac{273 \text{ ~~K~~}}{289 \text{ ~~K~~}}$ = 73.9 mL H_2

82. $n = \dfrac{P\ V}{R\ T}$

P = 1.00 atm

V = 1.00 ~~cm³~~ $\times \dfrac{1 \text{ ~~mL~~}}{1 \text{ ~~cm³~~}} \times \dfrac{1 \text{ L}}{1000 \text{ ~~mL~~}}$ = 0.00100 L

T = 273 K

$n = \dfrac{1.00 \text{ ~~atm~~} \times 0.00100 \text{ ~~L~~}}{273 \text{ ~~K~~}} \times \dfrac{1 \text{ mol} \cdot \text{ ~~K~~}}{0.0821 \text{ ~~atm~~} \cdot \text{ ~~L~~}}$ = 4.46×10^{-5} mol CO

4.46×10^{-5} ~~mol CO~~ $\times \dfrac{6.02 \times 10^{23} \text{ molecules CO}}{1 \text{ ~~mol CO~~}}$

$= 2.69 \times 10^{19}$ molecules CO

Alternate Method Using Molar Volume:

1.00 ~~cm³ CO~~ $\times \dfrac{1 \text{ ~~mL CO~~}}{1 \text{ ~~cm³ CO~~}} \times \dfrac{1 \text{ ~~L CO~~}}{1000 \text{ ~~mL CO~~}} \times \dfrac{1 \text{ ~~mol CO~~}}{22.4 \text{ ~~L CO~~}} \times$

$\dfrac{6.02 \times 10^{23} \text{ molecules CO}}{1 \text{ ~~mol CO~~}}$ = 2.69×10^{19} molecules CO

(Note: Recall that 1 mol of gas = 22.4 L at STP)

84.   Since the gases are at the same temperature they have the same kinetic energy. Since propane has a lower mass than butane, its velocity is faster.

86.   MM of NH_3 = 14.0 g N + 3(1.0) g H = 17.0 g/mol
        MM of N_2O = 2(14.0) g N + 16.0 g O = 44.0 g/mol
        Since ammonia has a lower mass than nitrous oxide, it has a greater
        molecular velocity. Thus, you would cry before you laugh.

CHAPTER 13 — Liquids, Solids, and Water

Section 13.1 The Liquid State

2.   At the molecular level, liquids have more molecules per unit volume than gases and the forces of molecular attraction are greater in liquids than in gases.

4.

	Substance	Temperature	Physical State
(a)	Ne	$-248°C$	liquid
(b)	Ne	$-225°C$	gas
(c)	Ar	$-187°C$	liquid
(d)	Ar	$-212°C$	solid
(e)	Kr	$-100°C$	gas
(f)	Kr	$-195°C$	solid

Section 13.2 Properties of Liquids

6.   The boiling point of water occurs when the total pressure exerted by the water molecules in the gaseous state above the liquid equals the pressure exerted by the atmosphere.

8.   A water molecule at the surface of the liquid is attracted to adjacent molecules. This attraction, called surface tension, causes a drop of water to have the smallest possible surface area and thus, a spherical shape.

10.

	Property	Value		Property	Value
(a)	vapor pressure	high	(b)	boiling point	low
(c)	viscosity	low	(d)	surface tension	low

Section 13.3 Intermolecular Forces

12. (a) Permanent dipole forces are stronger than temporary dispersion forces for similar molecules.
     (b) A hydrogen bond is a special type of dipole force that is stronger than a normal dipole force.

14.   <u>Molecules</u>   <u>Higher Boiling Point</u>

      (a) CH_3COOH or C_2H_5Cl CH_3COOH

      (b) C_2H_5OH or CH_3OCH_3 C_2H_5OH

16.   <u>Molecules</u>   <u>Higher Surface Tension</u>

      (a) CH_3COOH or C_2H_5Cl CH_3COOH

      (b) C_2H_5OH or CH_3OCH_3 C_2H_5OH

Section 13.4 The Solid State

18.   The molecules in a solid are in a fixed position and cannot move to another position, whereas molecules in a liquid can move and change positions.

20.

	Substance	Temperature	Physical State
(a)	H_2S	$-75.0°C$	liquid
(b)	H_2S	$-50.0°C$	gas
(c)	H_2Se	$-50.0°C$	liquid
(d)	H_2Se	$-25.0°C$	gas
(e)	H_2Te	$-51.5°C$	solid
(f)	H_2Te	$0.0°C$	gas

Section 13.5 Crystalline Solids

22.   <u>Three Types of Crystalline Solids</u>

      (1) ionic solids

      (2) molecular solids

      (3) metallic solids

24.

	Properties	Type of Solid
(a)	wide mp range, malleable, ductile, electrical conductor	metallic solid
(b)	high mp, hard, soluble in H_2O, conducts electricity when melted	ionic solid
(c)	low mp, generally insoluble in H_2O, nonconductor of electricity	molecular solid

26.

	Crystalline Solid	Classification
(a)	S_8	molecular solid
(b)	SO_2	molecular solid
(c)	Ag	metallic solid
(d)	$AgNO_3$	ionic solid

Section 13.6 Changes of Physical State

28. Cooling of Acetone

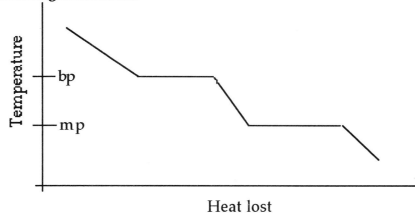

30. Energy released when steam condenses:

$$75.5 \text{ g} \times \frac{540 \text{ cal}}{1 \text{ g}} = 40{,}800 \text{ cal} \quad (40.8 \text{ kcal})$$

32. Energy released when water cools:

$$65.5 \text{ g} \times \frac{1.00 \text{ cal}}{1 \text{ g} \cdot \text{°C}} \times (55.5 - 0.0) \text{°C} = 3{,}640 \text{ cal} \quad (3.64 \text{ kcal})$$

Energy released when water solidifies:

$$65.5 \text{ g} \times \frac{80 \text{ cal}}{1 \text{ g}} = 5{,}240 \text{ cal} \quad (5.24 \text{ kcal})$$

Total heat energy released:
3,640 cal + 5,240 cal = 8,880 cal (8.88 kcal)

34. Energy released when steam condenses:

$$155 \text{ g} \times \frac{540 \text{ cal}}{1 \text{ g}} = 83{,}700 \text{ cal} \quad (83.7 \text{ kcal})$$

Energy released when water cools:

$$155 \text{ g} \times \frac{1.00 \text{ cal}}{1 \text{ g} \cdot \text{°C}} \times (100.0 - 0.0)\text{°C} = 15{,}500 \text{ cal} \quad (15.5 \text{ kcal})$$

Energy released when water solidifies:

$$155 \text{ g} \times \frac{80.0 \text{ cal}}{1 \text{ g}} = 12{,}400 \text{ cal} \quad (12.4 \text{ kcal})$$

Total heat energy released:
83,700 cal + 15,500 cal + 12,400 cal = 111,600 cal (111.6 kcal)

36.   Energy released when steam cools:

$$90.5 \text{ g} \times \frac{0.48 \text{ cal}}{1 \text{ g} \cdot {}^{\circ}\text{C}} \times (110.0 - 100.0){}^{\circ}\text{C} = 434 \text{ cal } (0.434 \text{ kcal})$$

Energy released when steam condenses:

$$90.5 \text{ g} \times \frac{540 \text{ cal}}{1 \text{ g}} = 48{,}900 \text{ cal } (48.9 \text{ kcal})$$

Energy released when water cools:

$$90.5 \text{ g} \times \frac{1.00 \text{ cal}}{1 \text{ g} \cdot {}^{\circ}\text{C}} \times (100.0 - 0.0){}^{\circ}\text{C} = 9{,}050 \text{ cal } (9.05 \text{ kcal})$$

Energy released when water solidifies:

$$90.5 \text{ g} \times \frac{80.0 \text{ cal}}{1 \text{ g}} = 7{,}240 \text{ cal } (7.24 \text{ kcal})$$

Total heat energy released:
434 cal + 48,900 cal + 9,050 cal + 7,240 cal = 65,600 cal (65.5 kcal)

38. $0.500 \text{ kg} = 5.00 \times 10^2 \text{ g}$
Energy released when steam cools:

$$5.00 \times 10^2 \text{ g} \times \frac{0.48 \text{ cal}}{1 \text{ g} \cdot {}^{\circ}\text{C}} \times (150.0 - 100.0){}^{\circ}\text{C} = 12{,}000 \text{ cal } (12.0 \text{ kcal})$$

Energy released when steam condenses:

$$5.00 \times 10^2 \text{ g} \times \frac{540 \text{ cal}}{1 \text{ g}} = 270{,}000 \text{ cal } (270 \text{ kcal})$$

Energy released when water cools:

$$5.00 \times 10^2 \text{ g} \times \frac{1.00 \text{ cal}}{1 \text{ g} \cdot {}^{\circ}\text{C}} \times (100.0 - 0.0){}^{\circ}\text{C} = 50{,}000 \text{ cal } (50.0 \text{ kcal})$$

Energy released when water solidifies:

$$5.00 \times 10^2 \text{ g} \times \frac{80.0 \text{ cal}}{1 \text{ g}} = 40{,}000 \text{ cal } (40.0 \text{ kcal})$$

Energy released when ice cools:

$$5.00 \times 10 \text{ g} \times \frac{0.50 \text{ cal}}{1 \text{ g} \cdot {}^{\circ}\text{C}} \times [0.0 - (-50.0)]{}^{\circ}\text{C} = 12{,}500 \text{ cal } (12.5 \text{ kcal})$$

Total heat energy released:
12,000 cal + 270,000 cal + 50,000 cal + 40,000 cal + 12,500 cal
= 385,000 cal (385 kcal)

Section 13.7 The Water Molecule

40. | Bonding Pairs in Water | Nonbonding Pairs in Water |
      | --- | --- |
      | two | two |

42.   The nonbonding pairs of electrons in water repel the bonding pairs and force them closer together. As a result, the observed bond angle in water is less than 109° (actually 104.5°).

44.   Net Dipole in Water

46.   Hydrogen Bonding in Ammonia

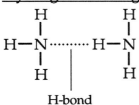

Section 13.8 Physical Properties of Water

48.   As the soft drink freezes, its volume increases because the water it contains undergoes expansion. Thus, if the soft drink freezes, either the cap on the bottle will pop off or the bottle itself will break.

50. | Molecules | Higher Boiling Point |
      | --- | --- |
      | (a) H_2O or H_2Se | H_2O |
      | (b) H_2S or H_2Te | H_2Te |

52. | Molecules | Higher Heat of Vaporization |
      | --- | --- |
      | (a) H_2O or H_2Se | H_2O |
      | (b) H_2S or H_2Te | H_2Te |

54.   MM of H_2Po: 211.0 g/mol

Predicted Values

mp: $-48.9 + [-48.9 - (-60.4)] = \sim -37.4°C$

bp: $-2.2 + [-2.2 - (-41.5)] = \sim 37.1°C$

H_{fusion}: $1670 + (1670 - 599) = \sim 2741$ cal/mol

H_{vapor}: $5570 + (5570 - 4620) = \sim 6520$ cal/mol

(Note: Estimated values based on the interval from H_2Se to H_2Te)

56.

	Property	Higher Value
(a)	molar mass	heavy water
(b)	density	heavy water
(c)	melting point	heavy water
(d)	boiling point	heavy water
(e)	heat of fusion	heavy water
(f)	heat of vaporization	heavy water

Section 13.9 Chemical Properties of Water

58. $2 H_{2(g)} + O_{2(g)} \xrightarrow{\text{spark}} 2 H_2O_{(l)}$

60. (a) $Ba_{(s)} + 2 H_2O_{(l)} \rightarrow Ba(OH)_{2(aq)} + H_{2(g)}$

(b) $Mg_{(s)} + H_2O_{(l)} \rightarrow NR$ (Recall that Mg is not an active metal)

(c) $CaO_{(s)} + H_2O_{(l)} \rightarrow Ca(OH)_{2(aq)}$

(d) $SrO_{(s)} + H_2O_{(l)} \rightarrow Sr(OH)_{2(aq)}$

(e) $N_2O_{3(g)} + H_2O_{(l)} \rightarrow 2 HNO_{2(aq)}$

(f) $N_2O_{5(g)} + H_2O_{(l)} \rightarrow 2 HNO_{3(aq)}$

62. (a) $2 C_4H_{10(g)} + 13 O_{2(g)} \xrightarrow{\text{spark}} 8 CO_{2(g)} + 10 H_2O_{(g)}$

(b) $C_4H_{10}O_{(g)} + 6 O_{2(g)} \xrightarrow{\text{spark}} 4 CO_{2(g)} + 5 H_2O_{(g)}$

(c) $2 HNO_{3(aq)} + Ba(OH)_{2(aq)} \rightarrow Ba(NO_3)_{2(aq)} + 2 HOH_{(l)}$

(d) $H_3PO_{4(aq)} + 3 NaOH_{(aq)} \rightarrow Na_3PO_{4(aq)} + 3 HOH_{(l)}$

(e) $Co(C_2H_3O_2)_2 \cdot 4 H_2O_{(s)} \xrightarrow{\Delta} Co(C_2H_3O_2)_{2(s)} + 4 H_2O_{(g)}$

(f) $KAl(SO_4)_2 \cdot 12 H_2O_{(s)} \xrightarrow{\Delta} KAl(SO_4)_{2(s)} + 12 H_2O_{(g)}$

Section 13.10 Hydrates

64.

	Systematic Name	Chemical Formula
(a)	sodium acetate trihydrate	$NaC_2H_3O_2 \cdot 3 H_2O$
(b)	calcium sulfate dihydrate	$CaSO_4 \cdot 2 H_2O$
(c)	potassium chromate tetrahydrate	$K_2CrO_4 \cdot 4 H_2O$
(d)	zinc sulfate heptahydrate	$ZnSO_4 \cdot 7 H_2O$
(e)	sodium carbonate decahydrate	$Na_2CO_3 \cdot 10 H_2O$
(f)	nickel(II) nitrate hexahydrate	$Ni(NO_3)_2 \cdot 6 H_2O$
(g)	cobalt(III) iodide octahydrate	$CoI_3 \cdot 8 H_2O$
(h)	chromium(III) acetate monohydrate	$Cr(C_2H_3O_2)_3 \cdot H_2O$

66.   (a) Percentage water in $NiCl_2 \cdot 2\,H_2O$
      MM of $NiCl_2$ = 58.7 g + 2(35.5) g = 129.7 g

$$\text{Percentage water: } \frac{2(18.0)\text{ g}}{129.7\text{ g} + 2(18.0)\text{ g}} \times 100 = 21.7\%\ H_2O$$

  (b) Percentage water in $Sr(NO_3)_2 \cdot 6\,H_2O$
      MM of $Sr(NO_3)_2$ = 87.6 g + 2(14.0) g + 6(16.0) g = 211.6 g

$$\text{Percentage water: } \frac{6(18.0)\text{ g}}{211.6\text{ g} + 6(18.0)\text{ g}} \times 100 = 33.8\%\ H_2O$$

  (c) Percentage water in $Co(C_2H_3O_2)_2 \cdot 4\,H_2O$
      MM of $Co(C_2H_3O_2)_2$ = 58.9 g + 4(12.0) g + 6(1.0) g + 4(16.0) g
                              = 176.9 g

$$\text{Percentage water: } \frac{4(18.0)\text{ g}}{176.9\text{ g} + 4(18.0)\text{ g}} \times 100 = 28.9\%\ H_2O$$

  (d) Percentage water in $ZnSO_4 \cdot 7\,H_2O$
      MM of $ZnSO_4$ = 65.4 g + 32.1 g + 4(16.0) g = 161.5 g

$$\text{Percentage water: } \frac{7(18.0)\text{ g}}{161.5\text{ g} + 7(18.0)\text{ g}} \times 100 = 43.8\%\ H_2O$$

  (e) Percentage water in $Cr(NO_3)_3 \cdot 9\,H_2O$
      MM of $Cr(NO_3)_3$ = 52.0 g + 3(14.0) g + 9(16.0) g = 238.0 g

$$\text{Percentage water: } \frac{9(18.0)\text{ g}}{238.0\text{ g} + 9(18.0)\text{ g}} \times 100 = 40.5\%\ H_2O$$

  (f) Percentage water in $KAl(SO_4)_2 \cdot 12H_2O$
      MM of $KAl(SO_4)_2$ = 39.1 g + 27.0 g + 2(32.1) g + 8(16.0) g = 258.3 g

$$\text{Percentage water: } \frac{12(18.0)\text{ g}}{258.3\text{ g} + 12(18.0)\text{ g}} \times 100 = 45.5\%\ H_2O$$

68.   (a) $SrCl_2 \cdot X\,H_2O_{(s)} \xrightarrow{\Delta} SrCl_{2(s)} + X\,H_2O_{(g)}$

$$18.5\ \cancel{g\,H_2O} \times \frac{1\text{ mol }H_2O}{18.0\ \cancel{g\,H_2O}} = 1.03\text{ mol }H_2O$$

$$81.5\ \cancel{g\,SrCl_2} \times \frac{1\text{ mol }SrCl_2}{158.6\ \cancel{g\,SrCl_2}} = 0.514\text{ mol }SrCl_2$$

$$SrCl_2 \cdot \frac{1.03}{0.514}\,H_2O \qquad \frac{1.03}{0.514} \approx 2$$

      Formula: $SrCl_2 \cdot 2\,H_2O$

68. (b) $Ni(NO_3)_2 \cdot X\,H_2O_{(s)} \xrightarrow{\Delta} Ni(NO_3)_{2(s)} + X\,H_2O_{(g)}$

$37.2\;\cancel{g\,H_2O} \times \dfrac{1\;mol\;H_2O}{18.0\;\cancel{g\,H_2O}} = 2.07\;mol\;H_2O$

$62.8\;\cancel{g\,Ni(NO_3)_2} \times \dfrac{1\;mol\;Ni(NO_3)_2}{182.7\;\cancel{g\,Ni(NO_3)_2}} = 0.344\;mol\;Ni(NO_3)_2$

$Ni(NO_3)_2 \cdot \dfrac{2.07}{0.344}\,H_2O \qquad \dfrac{2.07}{0.344} \approx 6$

Formula: $Ni(NO_3)_2 \cdot 6\,H_2O$

(c) $CoSO_4 \cdot X\,H_2O_{(s)} \xrightarrow{\Delta} CoSO_{4(s)} + X\,H_2O_{(g)}$

$10.4\;\cancel{g\,H_2O} \times \dfrac{1\;mol\;H_2O}{18.0\;\cancel{g\,H_2O}} = 0.578\;mol\;H_2O$

$89.6\;g\,\cancel{CoSO_4} \times \dfrac{1\;mol\;CoSO_4}{155.0\;g\,\cancel{CoSO_4}} = 0.578\;mol\;CoSO_4$

$CoSO_4 \cdot \dfrac{0.578}{0.578}\,H_2O \qquad \dfrac{0.578}{0.578} \approx 1$

Formula: $CoSO_4 \cdot H_2O$

(d) $Na_2B_4O_7 \cdot X\,H_2O_{(s)} \xrightarrow{\Delta} Na_2B_4O_{7(s)} + X\,H_2O_{(g)}$

$30.9\;\cancel{g\,H_2O} \times \dfrac{1\;mol\;H_2O}{18.0\;\cancel{g\,H_2O}} = 1.72\;mol\;H_2O$

$69.1\;\cancel{g\,Na_2B_4O_7} \times \dfrac{1\;mol\;Na_2B_4O_7}{201.2\;\cancel{g\,Na_2B_4O_7}} = 0.343\;mol\;Na_2B_4O_7$

$Na_2B_4O_7 \cdot \dfrac{1.72}{0.343}\,H_2O \qquad \dfrac{1.72}{0.343} \approx 5$

Formula: $Na_2B_4O_7 \cdot 5\,H_2O$

Section 13.11 Water Purification

70.

Type of Water	Anions
(a) hard water	Cl^-, CO_3^{2-}, SO_4^{2-}, PO_4^{3-}
(b) soft water	Cl^-, CO_3^{2-}, SO_4^{2-}, PO_4^{3-}
(c) deionized water	negligible
(d) distilled water	negligible

72. $Ca(HCO_3)_{2(aq)} \xrightarrow{\Delta} CaCO_{3(s)} + CO_{2(g)} + H_2O_{(l)}$

General Exercises

74.

Approximate Percent of Water in Humans
(a) total mass: ~ 65%
(b) blood: ~ 80%

76. Network solid: a solid consisting of a three-dimensional network of
    covalent bonds
    Example: SiO_2 (quartz)

78. In the electron sea model, the metallic cations are arranged in a highly
    ordered pattern and are unable to move, while the valence electrons are
    free to move within the crystal.

80. Energy required to heat liquid methanol:
    $$1250 \cancel{g} \times \frac{0.610\ cal}{1\ \cancel{g} \cdot \cancel{°C}} \times (65.2 - 25.0)\cancel{°C} = 30{,}700\ cal\ (30.7\ kcal)$$

    Energy required to vaporize methanol:
    $$1250 \cancel{g} \times \frac{293\ cal}{1\ \cancel{g}} = 366{,}000\ cal\ (366\ kcal)$$

    Total heat energy required:
    30,700 cal + 366,000 cal = 397,000 cal (397 kcal)

82. $2\ H_2O_{2(aq)} \xrightarrow{\Delta} 2\ H_2O_{(l)} + O_{2(g)}$

CHAPTER 14 | Solutions

Section 14.1 Gases in a Liquid Solution

2.
	Change	Solubility of Hydrogen Chloride
(a)	temperature of solution increases	decreases
(b)	partial pressure of HCl decreases	decreases

4. standard solubility × pressure factor = new solubility

$$\frac{1.90 \text{ cm}^3 \text{ N}_2}{100 \text{ cm}^3 \text{ blood}} \times \frac{6.50 \text{ atm}}{1.00 \text{ atm}} = \frac{12.4 \text{ cm}^3 \text{ N}_2}{100 \text{ cm}^3 \text{ blood}}$$

6. $1.00 \text{ atm} \times \dfrac{1.18 \text{ g N}_2\text{O}}{100 \text{ g H}_2\text{O}} \times \dfrac{100 \text{ g H}_2\text{O}}{0.121 \text{ g N}_2\text{O}} = 9.75 \text{ atm}$

Section 14.2 Liquids in a Liquid Solution

8.
(a)	nonpolar solvent + polar solvent =	immiscible
(b)	nonpolar solvent + nonpolar solvent =	miscible

10.
	Solvent	Classification
(a)	C_3H_7OH	polar solvent
(b)	C_5H_{12}	nonpolar solvent
(c)	$C_6H_4(CH_3)_2$	nonpolar solvent
(d)	$C_2H_3Cl_3$	nonpolar solvent

12.
	Solvent	Miscible or Immiscible With Hexane (C_6H_{14})
(a)	C_2H_5OH	immiscible
(b)	$CHCl_3$	miscible
(c)	C_2HCl_3	miscible
(d)	$HC_2H_3O_2$	immiscible

14. Oil, which contains hydrocarbons, is nonpolar. Vinegar, which contains acetic acid, is polar. Since the molecules of oil and vinegar are not alike (they differ in polarity), they are immiscible.

Section 14.3 Solids in a Liquid Solution

16.   (a)   polar solute + nonpolar solvent = insoluble
      (b)   nonpolar solute + nonpolar solvent = soluble
      (c)   ionic solute + nonpolar solvent = insoluble

18.

	Compound	Soluble or Insoluble in Hexane (C_6H_{14})
(a)	C_2HCl_3	soluble
(b)	$Fe(NO_3)_3$	insoluble
(c)	H_2SO_4	insoluble
(d)	$C_{12}H_{26}$	soluble
(e)	$C_6H_4Cl_2$	soluble
(f)	$H_2C_4H_4O_6$	insoluble

20.

	Compound	Formula	Water or Fat Soluble
(a)	cholesterol	$C_{27}H_{46}O$	fat soluble
(b)	citric acid	$C_6H_8O_7$	water soluble
(c)	fructose	$C_6H_{12}O_6$	water soluble
(d)	glycine	$CH_2(NH_2)COOH$	water soluble
(e)	urea	$CO(NH_2)_2$	water soluble
(f)	vitamin K	$CH_3CH(NH_2)COOH$	water soluble

Section 14.4 The Dissolving Process

22.   <u>Sucrose Crystal Dissolving in Aqueous Solution</u>

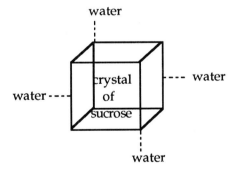

The diagram indicates that the water molecules are attacking the exposed edges of the crystal.

24.   (a)   <u>Cobalt(II) Sulfate Dissolved in Water</u>

24. (b) Nickel(II) Nitrate Dissolved in Water

$$H_2O \cdots Ni^{2+} \cdots OH_2 \qquad H_2O \cdots NO_3^- \cdots OH_2$$

Section 14.5 Rate of Dissolving

26.
	Factor	Rate of Dissolving
(a)	using chilled water rather than tap water	decreases
(b)	shaking the solution	increases
(c)	using powdered rather than crystalline sugar	increases
(d)	using tap water rather than distilled water	no effect

28.
	Dissolves (30°C)		Dissolves (30°C)
(a)	$\dfrac{\sim 85 \text{ g LiCl}}{100 \text{ g H}_2\text{O}}$	(b)	$\dfrac{\sim 108 \text{ g C}_{12}\text{H}_{22}\text{O}_{11}}{100 \text{ g H}_2\text{O}}$

30.
	Max. Solubility (50°C)		Max. Solubility (50°C)
(a)	$\dfrac{\sim 98 \text{ g LiCl}}{100 \text{ g H}_2\text{O}}$	(b)	$\dfrac{\sim 130 \text{ g C}_{12}\text{H}_{22}\text{O}_{11}}{100 \text{ g H}_2\text{O}}$

32.
	Min. Temperature		Min. Temperature
(a)	~ 38°C	(b)	~ 43°C

34.
	Temperature of Saturation		Temperature of Saturation
(a)	~ 65°C	(b)	~ 55°C

Section 14.7 Unsaturated, Saturated, Supersaturated Solutions

36.
	Degree of Saturation
(a)	saturated
(b)	unsaturated
(c)	supersaturated

38.
	Degree of Saturation
(a)	supersaturated
(b)	saturated
(c)	unsaturated

40. $250 \text{ g H}_2\text{O} \times \dfrac{100.0 \text{ g sugar}}{100 \text{ g H}_2\text{O}} = 250 \text{ g sugar}$

Since 250 g of water can dissolve 250 g sugar, 95.0 g sugar will dissolve in 250 g water. Thus, the solution is unsaturated.

42. | Solute Remaining in Solution | | Solute that Crystallizes
     (a) ~ 100 g | (b) ~ 20 g

Section 14.8 Mass Percent Concentration

44. $$\frac{\text{mass of solute}}{\text{mass of solution}} \times 100 = \frac{m}{m}\%$$

  (a) $$\frac{20.0 \text{ g KI}}{20.0 \text{ g KI } + 100.0 \text{ g water}} \times 100 = 16.7\%$$

  (b) $$\frac{2.50 \text{ g AgC}_2\text{H}_3\text{O}_2}{2.50 \text{ g AgC}_2\text{H}_3\text{O}_2 + 95.0 \text{ g water}} \times 100 = 2.56\%$$

  (c) $$\frac{5.57 \text{ g SrCl}_2}{5.57 \text{ g SrCl}_2 + 225.0 \text{ g water}} \times 100 = 2.42\%$$

  (d) $$\frac{50.0 \text{ g sugar}}{50.0 \text{ g sugar } + 250.0 \text{ g water}} \times 100 = 16.7\%$$

46. Solution | Unit Factors

  (a) 3.35% $MgCl_2$

  $$\frac{3.35 \text{ g MgCl}_2}{100.00 \text{ g solution}} \text{ and } \frac{100.00 \text{ g solution}}{3.35 \text{ g MgCl}_2}$$
  $$\frac{96.65 \text{ g H}_2\text{O}}{100.00 \text{ g solution}} \text{ and } \frac{100.00 \text{ g solution}}{96.65 \text{ g H}_2\text{O}}$$
  $$\frac{3.35 \text{ g MgCl}_2}{96.65 \text{ g H}_2\text{O}} \text{ and } \frac{96.65 \text{ g H}_2\text{O}}{3.35 \text{ g MgCl}_2}$$

  (b) 5.25% $Cd(NO_3)_2$

  $$\frac{5.25 \text{ g Cd(NO}_3)_2}{100.00 \text{ g solution}} \text{ and } \frac{100.00 \text{ g solution}}{5.25 \text{ g Cd(NO}_3)_2}$$
  $$\frac{94.75 \text{ g H}_2\text{O}}{100.00 \text{ g solution}} \text{ and } \frac{100.00 \text{ g solution}}{94.75 \text{ g H}_2\text{O}}$$
  $$\frac{5.25 \text{ g Cd(NO}_3)_2}{94.75 \text{ g H}_2\text{O}} \text{ and } \frac{94.75 \text{ g H}_2\text{O}}{5.25 \text{ g Cd(NO}_3)_2}$$

  (c) 6.50% Na_2CrO_4

  $$\frac{6.50 \text{ g Na}_2\text{CrO}_4}{100.00 \text{ g solution}} \text{ and } \frac{100.00 \text{ g solution}}{6.50 \text{ g Na}_2\text{CrO}_4}$$
  $$\frac{93.50 \text{ g H}_2\text{O}}{100.00 \text{ g solution}} \text{ and } \frac{100.00 \text{ g solution}}{93.50 \text{ g H}_2\text{O}}$$
  $$\frac{6.50 \text{ g Na}_2\text{CrO}_4}{93.50 \text{ g H}_2\text{O}} \text{ and } \frac{93.50 \text{ g H}_2\text{O}}{6.50 \text{ g Na}_2\text{CrO}_4}$$

46.   <u>Solution</u>   <u>Unit Factors</u>

(d)   7.25% $ZnSO_4$

$$\frac{7.25 \text{ g } ZnSO_4}{100.00 \text{ g solution}} \text{ and } \frac{100.00 \text{ g solution}}{7.25 \text{ g } ZnSO_4}$$

$$\frac{92.75 \text{ g } H_2O}{100.00 \text{ g solution}} \text{ and } \frac{100.00 \text{ g solution}}{92.75 \text{ g } H_2O}$$

$$\frac{7.25 \text{ g } ZnSO_4}{92.75 \text{ g } H_2O} \text{ and } \frac{92.75 \text{ g } H_2O}{7.25 \text{ g } ZnSO_4}$$

48. (a) $35.0 \text{ g } H_2SO_4 \times \dfrac{100.0 \text{ g solution}}{5.00 \text{ g } H_2SO_4} = 700 \text{ g solution} \quad (7.00 \times 10^2 \text{ g})$

     (b) $10.5 \text{ g } HC_2H_3O_2 \times \dfrac{100.0 \text{ g solution}}{4.50 \text{ g } HC_2H_3O_2} = 233 \text{ g solution}$

50. (a) $10.0 \text{ g solution} \times \dfrac{6.00 \text{ g KOH}}{100.0 \text{ g solution}} = 0.600 \text{ g KOH}$

     (b) $50.0 \text{ g solution} \times \dfrac{5.00 \text{ g } HNO_3}{100.0 \text{ g solution}} = 2.50 \text{ g } HNO_3$

52. (a) $250.0 \text{ g solution} \times \dfrac{90.0 \text{ g } H_2O}{100.0 \text{ g solution}} = 225 \text{ g } H_2O$

     (b) $100.0 \text{ g solution} \times \dfrac{95.0 \text{ g } H_2O}{100.0 \text{ g solution}} = 95.0 \text{ g } H_2O$

Section 14.9   Molar Concentration

54. (a)   MM of KCl $= 39.1 \text{ g} + 35.5 \text{ g} = 74.6 \text{ g/mol}$

         75.0 mL solution = 0.0750 L solution

$$\frac{1.00 \text{ g KCl}}{0.0750 \text{ L solution}} \times \frac{1 \text{ mol KCl}}{74.6 \text{ g KCl}} = 0.179 \text{ } M \text{ KCl}$$

     (b)   MM of $Na_2CrO_4 = 2(23.0) \text{ g} + 52.0 \text{ g} + 4(16.0) \text{ g} = 162.0 \text{ g/mol}$

         75.0 mL solution = 0.0750 L solution

$$\frac{1.00 \text{ g } Na_2CrO_4}{0.0750 \text{ L solution}} \times \frac{1 \text{ mol } Na_2CrO_4}{162.0 \text{ g } Na_2CrO_4} = 0.0823 \text{ } M \text{ } Na_2CrO_4$$

     (c)   MM of $MgBr_2 = 24.3 \text{ g} + 2(79.9) \text{ g} = 184.1 \text{ g/mol}$

         250.0 mL solution = 0.2500 L solution

$$\frac{20.0 \text{ g } MgBr_2}{0.2500 \text{ L solution}} \times \frac{1 \text{ mol } MgBr_2}{184.1 \text{ g } MgBr_2} = 0.435 \text{ } M \text{ } MgBr_2$$

     (d)   MM of $Li_2CO_3 = 2(6.9) \text{ g} + 12.0 \text{ g} + 3(16.0) \text{ g} = 73.8 \text{ g/mol}$

         250.0 mL solution = 0.2500 L solution

$$\frac{20.0 \text{ g } Li_2CO_3}{0.2500 \text{ L solution}} \times \frac{1 \text{ mol } Li_2CO_3}{73.8 \text{ g } Li_2CO_3} = 1.08 \text{ } M \text{ } Li_2CO_3$$

56.   <u>Solution</u>   <u>Unit Factors</u>

(a)   0.150 M KBr

$$\frac{0.150 \text{ mol KBr}}{1 \text{ L solution}} \text{ and } \frac{1 \text{ L solution}}{0.150 \text{ mol KBr}}$$

$$\frac{0.150 \text{ mol KBr}}{1000 \text{ mL solution}} \text{ and } \frac{1000 \text{ mL solution}}{0.150 \text{ mol KBr}}$$

(b)   0.150 M Ca(NO$_3$)$_2$

$$\frac{0.150 \text{ mol Ca(NO}_3)_2}{1 \text{ L solution}} \text{ and } \frac{1 \text{ L solution}}{0.150 \text{ mol Ca(NO}_3)_2}$$

$$\frac{0.150 \text{ mol Ca(NO}_3)_2}{1000 \text{ mL solution}} \text{ and } \frac{1000 \text{ mL solution}}{0.150 \text{ mol Ca(NO}_3)_2}$$

(c)   0.333 M Sr(C$_2$H$_3$O$_2$)$_2$

$$\frac{0.333 \text{ mol Sr(C}_2\text{H}_3\text{O}_2)_2}{1 \text{ L solution}} \text{ and } \frac{1 \text{ L solution}}{0.333 \text{ mol Sr(C}_2\text{H}_3\text{O}_2)_2}$$

$$\frac{0.333 \text{ mol Sr(C}_2\text{H}_3\text{O}_2)_2}{1000 \text{ mL solution}} \text{ and } \frac{1000 \text{ mL solution}}{0.333 \text{ mol Sr(C}_2\text{H}_3\text{O}_2)_2}$$

(d)   0.333 M NH$_4$Cl

$$\frac{0.333 \text{ mol NH}_4\text{Cl}}{1 \text{ L solution}} \text{ and } \frac{1 \text{ L solution}}{0.333 \text{ mol NH}_4\text{Cl}}$$

$$\frac{0.333 \text{ mol NH}_4\text{Cl}}{1000 \text{ mL solution}} \text{ and } \frac{1000 \text{ mL solution}}{0.333 \text{ mol NH}_4\text{Cl}}$$

58.

(a)   MM of KNO$_3$ = 39.1 g + 14.0 g + 3(16.0) g = 101.1 g/mol

$$2.50 \text{ g KNO}_3 \times \frac{1 \text{ mol KNO}_3}{101.1 \text{ g KNO}_3} \times \frac{1 \text{ L solution}}{0.325 \text{ mol KNO}_3} = 0.0761 \text{ L solution}$$

(b)   MM of AlBr$_3$ = 27.0 g + 3(79.9) g = 266.7 g/mol

$$2.50 \text{ g AlBr}_3 \times \frac{1 \text{ mol AlBr}_3}{266.7 \text{ g AlBr}_3} \times \frac{1 \text{ L solution}}{0.325 \text{ mol AlBr}_3} = 0.0288 \text{ L solution}$$

(c)   MM of Co(C$_2$H$_3$O$_2$)$_2$ = 58.9 g + 4(12.0) g + 6(1.0) g + 4(16.0) g
                                 = 176.9 g/mol

$$2.50 \text{ g Co(C}_2\text{H}_3\text{O}_2)_2 \times \frac{1 \text{ mol Co(C}_2\text{H}_3\text{O}_2)_2}{176.9 \text{ g Co(C}_2\text{H}_3\text{O}_2)_2} \times$$
$$\frac{1 \text{ L solution}}{1.00 \text{ mol Co(C}_2\text{H}_3\text{O}_2)_2} = 0.0141 \text{ L solution}$$

(d)   MM of (NH$_4$)$_3$PO$_4$ = 3(14.0) g + 12(1.0) g + 31.0 g + 4(16.0) g
                                 = 149.0 g/mol

$$2.50 \text{ g (NH}_4)_3\text{PO}_4 \times \frac{1 \text{ mol (NH}_4)_3\text{PO}_4}{149.0 \text{ g (NH}_4)_3\text{PO}_4} \times \frac{1 \text{ L solution}}{1.00 \text{ mol (NH}_4)_3\text{PO}_4}$$
$$= 0.0168 \text{ L solution}$$

60.   (a)   MM of $FeCl_3$ = 55.8 g + 3(35.5) g = 162.3 g/mol

$$2.25 \text{ L solution} \times \frac{0.200 \text{ mol FeCl}_3}{1 \text{ L solution}} \times \frac{162.3 \text{ g FeCl}_3}{1 \text{ mol FeCl}_3} = 73.0 \text{ g FeCl}_3$$

(b)   MM of KIO_4 = 39.1 g + 126.9 g + 4(16.0) g = 230.0 g/mol

$$2.25 \text{ L solution} \times \frac{0.200 \text{ mol KIO}_4}{1 \text{ L solution}} \times \frac{230.0 \text{ g KIO}_4}{1 \text{ mol KIO}_4} = 104 \text{ g KIO}_4$$

(c)   MM of $ZnSO_4$ = 65.4 g + 32.1 g + 4(16.0) g = 161.5 g/mol

$$50.0 \text{ mL solution} \times \frac{0.295 \text{ mol ZnSO}_4}{1000 \text{ mL solution}} \times \frac{161.5 \text{ g ZnSO}_4}{1 \text{ mol ZnSO}_4} = 2.38 \text{ g ZnSO}_4$$

(d)   MM of $Ni(NO_3)_2$ = 58.7 g + 2(14.0) g + 6(16.0) g = 182.7 g/mol

$$50.0 \text{ mL solution} \times \frac{0.295 \text{ mol Ni(NO}_3)_2}{1000 \text{ mL solution}} \times \frac{182.7 \text{ g Ni(NO}_3)_2}{1 \text{ mol Ni(NO}_3)_2}$$
$$= 2.69 \text{ g Ni(NO}_3)_2$$

62.   MM of $Ca(OH)_2$ = 40.1 g + 2(16.0) g + 2(1.0) g = 74.1 g/mol
100 mL solution = 0.100 L solution
$$\frac{0.185 \text{ g Ca(OH)}_2}{0.100 \text{ L solution}} \times \frac{1 \text{ mol Ca(OH)}_2}{74.1 \text{ g Ca(OH)}_2} = 0.0250 \ M \text{ Ca(OH)}_2$$

64.   (a) $$\frac{0.453 \text{ g NaCl}}{50.320 \text{ g solution}} \times 100 = 0.900\%$$

(b)   MM of NaCl = 23.0 g + 35.5 g = 58.5 g/mol
50.0 mL solution = 0.0500 L solution
$$\frac{0.453 \text{ g NaCl}}{0.0500 \text{ L solution}} \times \frac{1 \text{ mol NaCl}}{58.5 \text{ g NaCl}} = 0.155 \ M \text{ NaCl}$$

Section 14.10 Molal Concentration and Colligative Properties

66.   (a)   MM of NH_4Cl = 14.0 g + 4(1.0) g + 35.5 g = 53.5 g/mol
$$\frac{55.0 \text{ g NH}_4\text{Cl}}{2.50 \text{ kg H}_2\text{O}} \times \frac{1 \text{ mol NH}_4\text{Cl}}{53.5 \text{ g NH}_4\text{Cl}} = 0.411 \ m \text{ NH}_4\text{Cl}$$

(b)   MM of $Ca(NO_3)_2$ = 40.1 g + 2(14.0) g + 6(16.0) g = 164.1 g/mol
375 g H_2O = 0.375 kg H_2O
$$\frac{55.5 \text{ g Ca(NO}_3)_2}{0.375 \text{ kg H}_2\text{O}} \times \frac{1 \text{ mol Ca(NO}_3)_2}{164.1 \text{ g Ca(NO}_3)_2} = 0.902 \ m \text{ Ca(NO}_3)_2$$

68.   MM of CH_3OH = 12.0 g + 4(1.0) g + 16.0 g = 32.0 g/mol
125 g H_2O = 0.125 kg H_2O
$$0.125 \text{ kg H}_2\text{O} \times \frac{0.500 \text{ mol CH}_3\text{OH}}{1 \text{ kg H}_2\text{O}} \times \frac{32.0 \text{ g CH}_3\text{OH}}{1 \text{ mol CH}_3\text{OH}} = 2.00 \text{ g CH}_3\text{OH}$$

70. $\Delta T_f = m\,K_f$

$m = \dfrac{125 \text{ g } \cancel{CH_3OH}}{1.15 \text{ kg ethyl alcohol}} \times \dfrac{1 \text{ mol } CH_3OH}{32.0 \text{ g } \cancel{CH_3OH}} = 3.40\ m$

$K_f = \dfrac{1.99\ ^\circ C}{m}$

$\Delta T_f = 3.40\ \cancel{m} \times \dfrac{1.99\ ^\circ C}{\cancel{m}} = 6.77\ ^\circ C$

Freezing point of solution $=$ normal freezing point $- \Delta T_f$

Freezing point of solution $= -117.3\ ^\circ C - 6.77\ ^\circ C = -124.1\ ^\circ C$

72. $m = \dfrac{\Delta T_f}{K_f}$

$\Delta T_f = (16.6\ ^\circ C - 12.2\ ^\circ C) = 4.4\ ^\circ C$

$K_f = \dfrac{3.90\ ^\circ C}{m}$

$m = 4.4\ \cancel{^\circ C} \times \dfrac{m}{3.90\ \cancel{^\circ C}} = 1.1\ m$

$75.0 \text{ g } HC_2H_3O_2 = 0.0750 \text{ kg } HC_2H_3O_2$

MM of unknown: $\dfrac{7.50 \text{ g unknown}}{0.0750 \text{ kg } \cancel{HC_2H_3O_2}} \times \dfrac{1 \text{ kg } \cancel{HC_2H_3O_2}}{1.1 \text{ mol unknown}} = 91 \text{ g/mol}$

74. $m = \dfrac{\Delta T_f}{K_f}$

$\Delta T_f = (5.5\ ^\circ C - 4.0\ ^\circ C) = 1.5\ ^\circ C$

$K_f = \dfrac{5.12\ ^\circ C}{m}$

$m = 1.5\ \cancel{^\circ C} \times \dfrac{m}{5.12\ \cancel{^\circ C}} = 0.29\ m$

$88.5 \text{ g benzene} = 0.0885 \text{ kg benzene}$

MM of unknown: $\dfrac{3.00 \text{ g unknown}}{0.0885 \text{ kg } \cancel{benzene}} \times \dfrac{1 \text{ kg } \cancel{benzene}}{0.29 \text{ mol unknown}} = 120 \text{ g/mol}$

Section 14.11 Colloids

76. In order for the Tyndall effect to occur, small, solid particles must be present in the air. The most likely source of these particles is either smoke or dust.

78.

	Observation	Classification
(a)	dispersed particles settle from solution	not a colloid
(b)	dispersed particles scatter light	colloid
(c)	dispersed particles pass separate with filter paper	not a colloid

General Exercises

80. A helium mixture is used because:
    (1) Helium is less soluble than nitrogen in blood.
    (2) Helium atoms escape blood more rapidly than nitrogen molecules allowing a faster return to the surface.

82. $500.0 \text{ mL solution} \times \dfrac{0.63 \text{ g Cl}_2}{100 \text{ mL solution}} = 3.2 \text{ g Cl}_2$

84. Even though amyl alcohol contains a polar group (–OH) that can form hydrogen bonds, it is only partially soluble in water because most of the molecule is nonpolar. The nonpolar characteristics of amyl alcohol result from the arrangement of the carbon and hydrogen atoms (C_5H_{11}–).

86.

	Household Substance	Better Solvent
(a)	grease	carbon tetrachloride
(b)	maple syrup	water
(c)	food coloring	water
(d)	gasoline	carbon tetrachloride

88. Grinding a solid solute causes the rate of dissolving to increase because more surface area of the solid becomes exposed to water. This greater area of contact with water means that the polar water molecules can attack the solute more effectively and faster.

90. MM of $HC_2H_3O_2$ = 4(1.0) g + 2(12.0) g + 2(16.0) g = 60.0 g/mol

    Solute: $5.25 \text{ g HC}_2\text{H}_3\text{O}_2 \times \dfrac{1 \text{ mol HC}_2\text{H}_3\text{O}_2}{60.0 \text{ g HC}_2\text{H}_3\text{O}_2} = 0.0875 \text{ mol HC}_2\text{H}_3\text{O}_2$

    Solution: $100 \text{ g vinegar} \times \dfrac{1 \text{ mL vinegar}}{1.01 \text{ g vinegar}} \times \dfrac{1 \text{ L vinegar}}{1000 \text{ mL vinegar}} =$
    $= 0.0990 \text{ L vinegar}$

    Molarity: $\dfrac{0.0875 \text{ mol HC}_2\text{H}_3\text{O}_2}{0.0990 \text{ L vinegar}} = 0.884 \text{ M HC}_2\text{H}_3\text{O}$

92. The three aqueous solutions have different freezing points because the three solutes vary. That is, sugar dissociates into single molecules when dissolved in water. On the other hand, sodium chloride dissociates into two ions and barium chloride dissociates into three ions when dissolved in water.

    The amount of freezing point depression is related to the number of particles dissolved in solution. Thus, the NaCl (Na^+ and Cl^-) solute depresses the freezing point two times that of sugar; the $BaCl_2$ (Ba^{2+} and 2 Cl^-) solute depresses the freezing point three times that of sugar.

CHAPTER 15

Acids and Bases

Section 15.1 Properties of Acids and Bases

2.   Three General Properties of Bases
   (1)   Bases have a bitter taste
   (2)   Bases have a pH > 7
   (3)   Bases turn red litmus paper blue

4.
	Solution	pH	Classification
(a)	0.1 M NaOH	13.0	strongly basic
(b)	0.1 M NaCl	7.0	neutral
(c)	0.1 M Na_2CO_3	11.7	weakly basic
(d)	0.1 M $NaHCO_3$	8.3	weakly basic
(e)	0.1 M H_2CO_3	3.7	weakly acidic
(f)	0.1 M HNO_3	1.0	strongly acidic

Section 15.2 Acid-Base Indicators

6.   (a)   yellow   (b)   blue

8.
pH	Methyl Red Color
5	orange (yellow + red)

10.
pH	Phenolphthalein Color
7	colorless

Section 15.3 Standard Solutions of Acids and Bases

12. $H_2SO_{4(aq)} + 2\,NaHCO_{3(s)} \rightarrow Na_2SO_{4(aq)} + 2\,H_2O_{(l)} + 2\,CO_{2(g)}$
MM of $NaHCO_3$ = 84.0 g/mol

$$0.750\ \text{g NaHCO}_3 \times \frac{1\ \text{mol NaHCO}_3}{84.0\ \text{g NaHCO}_3} \times \frac{1\ \text{mol H}_2\text{SO}_4}{2\ \text{mol NaHCO}_3}$$
$$= 0.00446\ \text{mol H}_2\text{SO}_4$$

12. $$\frac{0.00446 \text{ mol } H_2SO_4}{32.35 \text{ mL solution}} \times \frac{1000 \text{ mL solution}}{1 \text{ L solution}} = \frac{0.138 \text{ mol } H_2SO_4}{1 \text{ L solution}}$$

   Molarity of sulfuric acid: $0.138 \, M \, H_2SO_4$

14. $H_2C_2O_{4(s)} + NaOH_{(aq)} \rightarrow NaHC_2O_{4(aq)} + H_2O_{(l)}$
    MM of $H_2C_2O_4$ = 90.0 g/mol

   $$0.506 \text{ g } H_2C_2O_4 \times \frac{1 \text{ mol } H_2C_2O_4}{90.0 \text{ g } H_2C_2O_4} \times \frac{1 \text{ mol NaOH}}{1 \text{ mol } H_2C_2O_4} = 0.00562 \text{ mol NaOH}$$

   $$\frac{0.00562 \text{ mol NaOH}}{28.85 \text{ mL solution}} \times \frac{1000 \text{ mL solution}}{1 \text{ L solution}} = \frac{1.95 \text{ mol NaOH}}{1 \text{ L solution}}$$

   Molarity of sodium hydroxide: $1.95 \, M \, NaOH$

16. $2 \text{ KHP}_{(s)} + Ba(OH)_{2(aq)} \rightarrow K_2BaP_{2(aq)} + 2 \, H_2O_{(l)}$
    MM of KHP = 204.2 g/mol

   $$1.655 \text{ g KHP} \times \frac{1 \text{ mol KHP}}{204.2 \text{ g KHP}} \times \frac{1 \text{ mol } Ba(OH)_2}{2 \text{ mol KHP}} = 0.004052 \text{ mol } Ba(OH)_2$$

   $$\frac{0.004052 \text{ mol } Ba(OH)_2}{24.65 \text{ mL solution}} \times \frac{1000 \text{ mL solution}}{1 \text{ L solution}} = \frac{0.1644 \text{ mol } Ba(OH)_2}{1 \text{ L solution}}$$

   Molarity of barium hydroxide: $0.1644 \, M \, Ba(OH)_2$

18. $H_2Tart_{(s)} + 2 \, NaOH_{(aq)} \rightarrow Na_2Tart_{(aq)} + 2 \, H_2O_{(l)}$
   $$28.15 \text{ mL solution} \times \frac{0.295 \text{ mol NaOH}}{1000 \text{ mL solution}} = 0.00830 \text{ mol NaOH}$$

   $$0.00830 \text{ mol NaOH} \times \frac{1 \text{ mol } H_2Tart}{2 \text{ mol NaOH}} = 0.00415 \text{ mol } H_2Tart$$

   $$\text{MM of tartaric acid} = \frac{0.623 \text{ g } H_2Tart}{0.00415 \text{ mol } H_2Tart} = 150 \text{ g/mol}$$

20. $$21.35 \text{ mL solution} \times \frac{0.115 \text{ mol HCl}}{1000 \text{ mL solution}} = 0.00246 \text{ mol HCl}$$

   $$0.00246 \text{ mol HCl} \times \frac{1 \text{ mol THAM}}{1 \text{ mol HCl}} = 0.00246 \text{ mol THAM}$$

   $$\text{MM of THAM} = \frac{0.297 \text{ g THAM}}{0.00246 \text{ mol THAM}} = 121 \text{ g/mol}$$

Section 15.4 Acid-Base Titrations

22. $2 \text{ HClO}_{4(aq)} + Ca(OH)_{2(aq)} \rightarrow Ca(ClO_4)_{2(aq)} + 2 \, H_2O_{(l)}$
   $$34.45 \text{ mL solution} \times \frac{0.100 \text{ mol } HClO_4}{1000 \text{ mL solution}} = 0.00345 \text{ mol } HClO_4$$

22. $0.00345 \text{ mol HClO}_4 \times \dfrac{1 \text{ mol Ca(OH)}_2}{2 \text{ mol HClO}_4} = 0.00173 \text{ mol Ca(OH)}_2$

$\dfrac{0.00173 \text{ mol Ca(OH)}_2}{50.0 \text{ mL solution}} \times \dfrac{1000 \text{ mL solution}}{1 \text{ L solution}} = \dfrac{0.0346 \text{ mol Ca(OH)}_2}{1 \text{ L solution}}$

Molarity of calcium hydroxide: $0.0346 \, M$ Ca(OH)$_2$

24. $HNO_{3(aq)} + NH_4OH_{(aq)} \rightarrow NH_4NO_{3(aq)} + H_2O_{(l)}$

$25.0 \text{ mL solution} \times \dfrac{0.119 \text{ mol NH}_4\text{OH}}{1000 \text{ mL solution}} = 0.00298 \text{ mol NH}_4\text{OH}$

$0.00298 \text{ mol NH}_4\text{OH} \times \dfrac{1 \text{ mol HNO}_3}{1 \text{ mol NH}_4\text{OH}} = 0.00298 \text{ mol HNO}_3$

$0.00298 \text{ mol HNO}_3 \times \dfrac{1000 \text{ mL solution}}{0.175 \text{ mol HNO}_3} = 17.0 \text{ mL HNO}_3 \text{ solution}$

26. $2 \, HNO_{2(aq)} + Ba(OH)_{2(aq)} \rightarrow Ba(NO_2)_{2(aq)} + 2 \, H_2O_{(l)}$

$10.0 \text{ mL solution} \times \dfrac{0.225 \text{ mol HNO}_2}{1000 \text{ mL solution}} = 0.00225 \text{ mol HNO}_2$

$0.00225 \text{ mol HNO}_2 \times \dfrac{1 \text{ mol Ba(OH)}_2}{2 \text{ mol HNO}_2} = 0.00113 \text{ mol Ba(OH)}_2$

$0.00113 \text{ mol Ba(OH)}_2 \times \dfrac{1000 \text{ mL solution}}{0.100 \text{ mol Ba(OH)}_2} = 11.3 \text{ mL Ba(OH)}_2 \text{ solution}$

28. (a) MM of NaOH = 40.0 g/mol

$\dfrac{3.00 \text{ mol NaOH}}{1000 \text{ mL solution}} \times \dfrac{40.0 \text{ g NaOH}}{1 \text{ mol NaOH}} \times \dfrac{1 \text{ mL solution}}{1.12 \text{ g solution}} \times 100$
$= 10.7\% \text{ NaOH}$

(b) MM of KOH = 56.1 g/mol

$\dfrac{0.500 \text{ mol KOH}}{1000 \text{ mL solution}} \times \dfrac{56.1 \text{ g KOH}}{1 \text{ mol KOH}} \times \dfrac{1 \text{ mL solution}}{1.02 \text{ g solution}} \times 100$
$= 2.75\% \text{ KOH}$

(c) MM of NH$_3$ = 17.0 g/mol

$\dfrac{6.00 \text{ mol NH}_3}{1000 \text{ mL solution}} \times \dfrac{17.0 \text{ g NH}_3}{1 \text{ mol NH}_3} \times \dfrac{1 \text{ mL solution}}{0.954 \text{ g solution}} \times 100$
$= 10.7\% \text{ NH}_3$

(d) MM of Na$_2$CO$_3$ = 106.0 g/mol

$\dfrac{1.00 \text{ mol Na}_2\text{CO}_3}{1000 \text{ mL solution}} \times \dfrac{106.0 \text{ g Na}_2\text{CO}_3}{1 \text{ mol Na}_2\text{CO}_3} \times \dfrac{1 \text{ mL solution}}{1.10 \text{ g solution}} \times 100$
$= 9.64\% \text{ Na}_2\text{CO}_3$

(e) MM of K$_2$C$_2$O$_4$ = 166.2 g/mol

$\dfrac{0.250 \text{ mol K}_2\text{C}_2\text{O}_4}{1000 \text{ mL solution}} \times \dfrac{166.2 \text{ g K}_2\text{C}_2\text{O}_4}{1 \text{ mol K}_2\text{C}_2\text{O}_4} \times \dfrac{1 \text{ mL solution}}{1.03 \text{ g solution}} \times 100$
$= 4.03\% \text{ K}_2\text{C}_2\text{O}_4$

Section 15.5 Arrhenius Acid-Base Theory

30.

	Base	Degree of Ionization	Strength
(a)	$Zn(OH)_{2(s)}$	~ 1%	weak
(b)	$LiOH_{(aq)}$	~ 100%	strong
(c)	$Mn(OH)_{2(s)}$	~ 1%	weak
(d)	$Sr(OH)_{2(aq)}$	~ 100%	strong

32.

	Arrhenius Acid	Arrhenius Base	Salt
(a)	$HI_{(aq)}$	$NaOH_{(aq)}$	$NaI_{(aq)}$
(b)	$HC_2H_3O_{2(aq)}$	$LiOH_{(aq)}$	$LiC_2H_3O_{2(aq)}$
(c)	$HClO_{3(aq)}$	$Ba(OH)_{2(aq)}$	$Ba(ClO_3)_{2(aq)}$
(d)	$H_2SO_{4(aq)}$	$KOH_{(aq)}$	$K_2SO_{4(aq)}$

34.
(a) $HF_{(aq)} + NaOH_{(aq)} \rightarrow NaF_{(aq)} + H_2O_{(l)}$

(b) $2\ HI_{(aq)} + Mg(OH)_{2(s)} \rightarrow MgI_{2(aq)} + 2\ H_2O_{(l)}$

(c) $HNO_{2(aq)} + KOH_{(aq)} \rightarrow KNO_{2(aq)} + H_2O_{(l)}$

(d) $2\ HClO_{4(aq)} + Zn(OH)_{2(s)} \rightarrow Zn(ClO_4)_{2(aq)} + 2\ H_2O_{(l)}$

(e) $3\ H_2SO_{4(aq)} + 2\ Bi(OH)_{3(s)} \rightarrow Bi_2(SO_4)_{3(aq)} + 6\ H_2O_{(l)}$

(f) $HCHO_{2(aq)} + NaOH_{(aq)} \rightarrow NaCHO_{2(aq)} + H_2O_{(l)}$

Section 15.6 Brønsted-Lowry Acid-Base Theory

36.

	Acid	Base		Acid	Base
(a)	$HI_{(aq)}$	$H_2O_{(l)}$	(b)	$HC_2H_3O_{2(aq)}$	$HS^-_{(aq)}$
(c)	$HCO_3^-{}_{(aq)}$	$OH^-_{(aq)}$	(d)	$HClO_{4(aq)}$	$NO_2^-{}_{(aq)}$

38.

	Stronger Acid	Stronger Base		Stronger Acid	Stronger Base
(a)	$HNO_{2(aq)}$	$NaC_2H_3O_{2(aq)}$	(b)	$HF_{(aq)}$	$NaHS_{(aq)}$
(c)	$H_2PO_4^-{}_{(aq)}$	$HCO_3^-{}_{(aq)}$	(d)	$HCl_{(aq)}$	$SO_4^{2-}{}_{(aq)}$

Section 15.7 Ionization of Water

40. $[OH^-] = \dfrac{1.0 \times 10^{-14}}{[H^+]}$

(a) $[OH^-] = \dfrac{1.0 \times 10^{-14}}{2.5 \times 10^{-2}} = 4.0 \times 10^{-13}$

(b) $[OH^-] = \dfrac{1.0 \times 10^{-14}}{1.7 \times 10^{-5}} = 5.9 \times 10^{-10}$

(c) $[OH^-] = \dfrac{1.0 \times 10^{-14}}{6.2 \times 10^{-7}} = 1.6 \times 10^{-8}$

(d) $[OH^-] = \dfrac{1.0 \times 10^{-14}}{4.6 \times 10^{-12}} = 2.2 \times 10^{-3}$

42.

	Change	$[OH^-]$		Change	$[OH^-]$
(a)	increase $[H^+]$	decreases	(b)	decrease $[H^+]$	increases

Section 15.8 The pH Concept

44. $[H^+] = 10^{-pH}$
   (a) $[H^+] = 10^{-6} = 0.000\,001\ M$ $(1 \times 10^{-6}\ M)$
   (b) $[H^+] = 10^{-6} = 0.000\,001\ M$ $(1 \times 10^{-6}\ M)$
   (c) $[H^+] = 10^{-9} = 0.000\,000\,001\ M$ $(1 \times 10^{-9}\ M)$
   (d) $[H^+] = 10^{-11} = 0.000\,000\,000\,01 M$ $(1 \times 10^{-11}\ M)$

Section 15.9 Advanced pH and pOH Calculations

46. (a) $[H^+] = 10^{-1.80} = 10^{0.20} \times 10^{-2}$
        $[H^+] = 1.6 \times 10^{-2}\ M = 0.016\ M$
     (b) $[H^+] = 10^{-4.75} = 10^{0.25} \times 10^{-5}$
        $[H^+] = 1.8 \times 10^{-5}\ M = 0.000\,018\ M$
     (c) $[H^+] = 10^{-6.55} = 10^{0.45} \times 10^{-7}$
        $[H^+] = 2.8 \times 10^{-7}\ M = 0.000\,000\,28\ M$
     (d) $[H^+] = 10^{-7.50} = 10^{0.50} \times 10^{-8}$
        $[H^+] = 3.2 \times 10^{-8}\ M = 0.000\,000\,032\ M$

48. (a) $[OH^-] = 10^{-0.90} = 10^{0.10} \times 10^{-1}$
        $[OH^-] = 1.3 \times 10^{-1}\ M = 0.13\ M$
     (b) $[OH^-] = 10^{-1.62} = 10^{0.38} \times 10^{-2}$
        $[OH^-] = 2.4 \times 10^{-2}\ M = 0.024\ M$
     (c) $[OH^-] = 10^{-4.55} = 10^{0.45} \times 10^{-5}$
        $[OH^-] = 2.8 \times 10^{-5}\ M = 0.000\,028\ M$
     (d) $[OH^-] = 10^{-5.20} = 10^{0.80} \times 10^{-6}$
        $[OH^-] = 6.3 \times 10^{-6}\ M = 0.000\,0063\ M$

50. (a) $pH = 14.00 - 0.60 = 13.40$
     (b) $pH = 14.00 - 2.67 = 11.33$

Section 15.10 Strong and Weak Electrolytes

52.

	Solution	Number of Ions
(a)	strong acids	many
(b)	weak acids	few
(c)	strong bases	many
(d)	weak bases	few
(e)	soluble ionic compounds	many
(f)	slightly soluble ionic compounds	few

54.

	Solution	Electrolyte	Contains
(a)	$HCl_{(aq)}$	strong	$H^+_{(aq)}$ and $Cl^-_{(aq)}$
(b)	$HF_{(aq)}$	weak	$HF_{(aq)}$
(c)	$HClO_{(aq)}$	weak	$HClO_{(aq)}$
(d)	$HClO_{4(aq)}$	strong	$H^+_{(aq)}$ and $ClO_4^-_{(aq)}$
(e)	$Sr(OH)_{2(aq)}$	strong	$Sr^{2+}_{(aq)}$ and $2\,OH^-_{(aq)}$
(f)	$NH_4OH_{(aq)}$	weak	$NH_4OH_{(aq)}$
(g)	$CuSO_{4(aq)}$	strong	$Cu^{2+}_{(aq)}$ and $SO_4^{2-}_{(aq)}$
(h)	$BaSO_{4(s)}$	weak	$BaSO_{4(s)}$

Section 15.11 Net Ionic Equations

56. The ions that appear in the total ionic equation, but not in the net ionic equation are called spectator ions.

58. (a) molecular equation:

$$AgNO_{3(aq)} + KI_{(aq)} \rightarrow AgI_{(s)} + KNO_{3(aq)}$$

total ionic equation:

$$Ag^+_{(aq)} + \cancel{NO_3^-}_{(aq)} + \cancel{K^+}_{(aq)} + I^-_{(aq)} \rightarrow \cancel{K^+}_{(aq)} + \cancel{NO_3^-}_{(aq)} + AgI_{(s)}$$

net ionic equation:

$$Ag^+_{(aq)} + I^-_{(aq)} \rightarrow AgI_{(s)}$$

(b) molecular equation:

$$BaCl_{2(aq)} + K_2CrO_{4(aq)} \rightarrow BaCrO_{4(s)} + 2\,KCl_{(aq)}$$

total ionic equation:

$$Ba^{2+}_{(aq)} + \cancel{2\,Cl^-}_{(aq)} + \cancel{2\,K^+}_{(aq)} + CrO_4^{2-}_{(aq)} \rightarrow$$
$$BaCrO_{4(s)} + \cancel{2\,K^+}_{(aq)} + \cancel{2\,Cl^-}_{(aq)}$$

net ionic equation:

$$Ba^{2+}_{(aq)} + CrO_4^{2-}_{(aq)} \rightarrow BaCrO_{4(s)}$$

(c) molecular equation:

$$Zn(NO_3)_{2(aq)} + 2\,NaOH_{(aq)} \rightarrow Zn(OH)_{2(s)} + 2\,NaNO_{3(aq)}$$

total ionic equation:

$$Zn^{2+}_{(aq)} + \cancel{2\,NO_3^-}_{(aq)} + \cancel{2\,Na^+}_{(aq)} + 2\,OH^-_{(aq)} \rightarrow$$
$$Zn(OH)_{2(s)} + \cancel{2\,Na^+}_{(aq)} + \cancel{2\,NO_3^-}_{(aq)}$$

net ionic equation:

$$Zn^{2+}_{(aq)} + 2\,OH^-_{(aq)} \rightarrow Zn(OH)_{2(s)}$$

58.   (d)   molecular equation:
$$MgSO_{4(aq)} + 2\,NH_4OH_{(aq)} \rightarrow Mg(OH)_{2(s)} + (NH_4)_2SO_{4(aq)}$$

total ionic equation:
$$Mg^{2+}_{(aq)} + \cancel{SO_4^{2-}}_{(aq)} + 2\,NH_4OH_{(aq)} \rightarrow$$
$$Mg(OH)_{2(s)} + 2\,NH_4^+_{(aq)} + \cancel{SO_4^{2-}}_{(aq)}$$

net ionic equation:
$$Mg^{2+}_{(aq)} + 2\,NH_4OH_{(aq)} \rightarrow Mg(OH)_{2(s)} + 2\,NH_4^+_{(aq)}$$

(e)   molecular equation:
$$2\,HC_2H_3O_{2(aq)} + Sn_{(s)} \rightarrow Sn(C_2H_3O_2)_{2(aq)} + H_{2(g)}$$

total ionic equation:
$$2\,HC_2H_3O_{2(aq)} + Sn_{(s)} \rightarrow Sn^{2+}_{(aq)} + 2\,C_2H_3O_2^-_{(aq)} + H_{2(g)}$$

net ionic equation:
$$2\,HC_2H_3O_{2(aq)} + Sn_{(s)} \rightarrow Sn^{2+}_{(aq)} + 2\,C_2H_3O_2^-_{(aq)} + H_{2(g)}$$

General Exercises

60.   A pH of 4.6 is in the middle of the color change range for bromcresol green (3.8 to 5.4). Thus, the indicator will have equal amounts of yellow and blue, which give *green*.

62. $42.10 \cancel{\text{ mL solution}} \times \dfrac{0.100 \text{ mol Ba(OH)}_2}{1000 \cancel{\text{ mL solution}}} = 0.00421 \text{ mol Ba(OH)}_2$

$0.00421 \cancel{\text{ mol Ba(OH)}_2} \times \dfrac{2 \text{ mol cream of tartar}}{1 \cancel{\text{ mol Ba(OH)}_2}}$
$$= 0.00842 \text{ mol cream of tartar}$$

$\text{MM of cream of tartar} = \dfrac{1.585 \text{ g cream of tartar}}{0.00842 \text{ mol cream of tartar}} = 188 \text{ g/mol}$

64.   The species $H_2O_{(l)}$ is a proton acceptor in the first reaction and a proton donor in the second reaction. Thus, $H_2O_{(l)}$ is amphiprotic.

66.   Autoprotolysis of Water
$$H_2O_{(l)} + H_2O_{(l)} \rightleftarrows H_3O^+_{(aq)} + OH^-_{(aq)}$$

68.   pOH 3 = pH 11
pOH 5 = pH 9
Therefore, a solution of pOH = 3 is more basic than a solution of pOH = 5.

70. Molecular equation:

$$Fe(NO_3)_{2(aq)} + NiSO_{4(aq)} \rightarrow FeSO_{4(aq)} + Ni(NO_3)_{2(aq)}$$

Total ionic equation:

$$\cancel{Fe^{2+}}_{(aq)} + \cancel{2NO_3^-}_{(aq)} + \cancel{Ni^{2+}}_{(aq)} + \cancel{SO_4^{2-}}_{(aq)} \rightarrow$$
$$\cancel{Fe^{2+}}_{(aq)} + \cancel{SO_4^{2-}}_{(aq)} + \cancel{Ni^{2+}}_{(aq)} + \cancel{2NO_3^-}_{(aq)}$$

Net ionic:
None (All ions are spectators)

CHAPTER 16

Chemical Equilibrium

Section 16.1 Collision Theory of Reaction Rates

2. When temperature increases, the rate of effective collisions increases because:
   (1) collision frequency increases
   (2) collision energy increases

4. Ineffective Collision Geometry

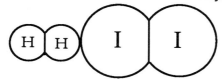

6. No, the catalyst speeds up the rate of producing ammonia, but does not increase the amount of ammonia produced.

8. The ultraviolet rays in sunlight serve as a catalyst to speed up the reaction between methane gas and chlorine gas.

Section 16.2 Energy Profiles of Chemical Reactions

10. $2 O_{3(g)} \rightarrow 3 O_{2(g)} + \text{heat}$

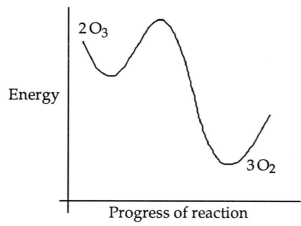

12. $H_{2(g)} + Cl_{2(g)} \rightarrow 2\,HCl_{(g)}$

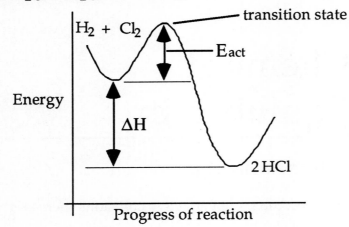

14.   The heat of reaction (ΔH) is independent from the effects of a catalyst.

16.   Since exothermic reactions produce energy, it takes energy to make a reversible, exothermic reaction to go in the reverse direction. Hence, the E_{act} is greater in the reverse direction.

Section 16.3 Rates of Reaction

(Note: If the rate of reaction doubles, the reaction time is halved.)

18.   For every 10°C decrease in temperature the time is doubled.
Since there are two 10°C decreases in temperature, the rate is
$2 \times 2 = 4$ times slower.

120 seconds $\times$ 4 = 480 seconds
Thus, at 0°C the reaction takes 480 seconds.

20.   rate = k $[NO_2]^2$
(a)   rate = k $\times$ 4 $[NO_2]^2$
       If $[NO_2]$ increases twofold, the rate quadruples.
       Since the rate quadruples, the amount of time decreases by a factor of 4.
       10.0 minutes/4 = 2.50 minutes

(b)   rate $= \dfrac{k\,[NO_2]^2}{4}$

       If $[NO_2]^2$ decreases twofold, then the rate decreases fourfold.
       Since the rate decreases fourfold, the amount of time quadruples.
       10.0 minutes $\times$ 4 = 40.0 minutes

20.   (c)   rate = k × 9 [NO$_2$]^2
       If [NO$_2$]^2 is tripled, the rate increases by a factor of 9.
       Since the rate increases by a factor of 9, the amount of time decreases
       by a factor of 9.
       10.0 minutes/9 = 1.11 minutes

       (d)   rate = $\dfrac{k \, [NO_2]^2}{16}$

       If [NO$_2$]^2 is quartered, the rate decreases by a factor of 16.
       Since the rate decreases by a factor of 16, the amount of time is
       increased by a factor of 16.
       10.0 minutes × 16 = 160.0 minutes

22.   rate = k [CHCl$_3$] [Cl$_2$]$^{1/2}$
       (a)   If [CHCl$_3$] increases from 0.100 M to 0.500 M, then [CHCl$_3$] increases
              by a factor of 0.500/0.100 and the rate increases by a factor of
              0.500/0.100. Thus, the rate increases 5.00 times.

       (b)   If [CHCl$_3$] decreases from 0.250 M to 0.100 M, then [CHCl$_3$] decreases
              by a factor of 0.100/0.250 and the rate decreases by a factor of
              0.100/0.250. Thus, the rate decreases 0.400 times.

       (c)   If [Cl$_2$] increases from 0.360 M to 0.480 M, then [Cl$_2$] increases by a
              factor of 0.480/0.360 and the rate increases by a factor of
              $(0.480/0.360)^{1/2}$. Thus, the rate increases 1.15 times.

              (Note: A square root key ($\sqrt{}$) can be used instead of raising the
              fraction to the one half power.)

       (d)   If [Cl$_2$] decreases from 0.200 M to 0.115 M, then [Cl$_2$] decreases by a
              factor of 0.115/0.200 and the rate decreases by a factor of
              $(0.115/0.200)^{1/2}$. Thus, the rate decreases 0.758 times.

Section 16.4 Law of Chemical Equilibrium

24.   A chemical system is said to be in chemical equilibrium if the forward rate
       of reaction (rate$_f$) is equal to the reverse rate of reaction (rate$_r$). Or in
       other words, chemical equilibrium occurs when: rate$_f$ = rate$_r$

26. Corrected Statements
    (a) The value of K_{eq} is *dependent upon* temperature.
    (b) The K_{eq} expression contains *all substances* participating in the equilibrium. However, a substance in a different state (such as a solid in solution) is assigned a concentration of [1], which simplifies the K_{eq} expression.

28.   Reaction   General Eq. Constant Expression

    (a) $3\,A \rightleftarrows 2\,C$ $K_{eq} = \dfrac{[C]^2}{[A]^3}$

    (b) $A + B \rightleftarrows 2\,C$ $K_{eq} = \dfrac{[C]^2}{[A]\,[B]}$

    (c) $3\,A + 5\,B \rightleftarrows C + 4\,D$ $K_{eq} = \dfrac{[C]\,[D]^4}{[A]^3\,[B]^5}$

Section 16.5 Concentration Equilibrium Constant, K_c

30. No; the amount of any liquid present has no effect on the equilibrium of a gaseous state reaction. Therefore, any substance in the liquid state will not appear in the equilibrium expression.

32.   Reaction   Eq. Constant Expression

    (a) $H_{2(g)} + Br_{2(g)} \rightleftarrows 2\,HBr_{(g)}$ $K_c = \dfrac{[HBr]^2}{[H_2]\,[Br_2]}$

    (b) $4\,HCl_{(g)} + O_{2(g)} \rightleftarrows 2\,Cl_{2(g)} + 2\,H_2O_{(g)}$ $K_c = \dfrac{[Cl_2]^2\,[H_2O]^2}{[HCl]^4\,[O_2]}$

    (c) $CO_{(g)} + 2\,H_{2(g)} \rightleftarrows CH_3OH_{(l)}$ $K_c = \dfrac{1}{[CO]\,[H_2]^2}$

34. $N_{2(g)} + 3\,H_{2(g)} \rightleftarrows 2\,NH_{3(g)}$
    $[N_2] = 0.400$
    $[H_2] = 1.20$
    $[NH_3] = 0.195$
    $$K_c = \frac{[NH_3]^2}{[N_2]\,[H_2]^3} = \frac{(0.195)^2}{(0.400)\,(1.20)^3} = 0.0550$$

Section 16.6 Gaseous State Equilibria Shifts

36. (a) As the temperature increases, the heat shifts the equilibrium to the left reducing the concentration of NH_3.
     (b) As pressure increases, the equilibrium shifts to the right to relieve the stress. As a result, the concentration of NH_3 increases.

38.

	Stress	Shift		Stress	Shift
(a)	[CH_4] increases	right	(b)	[CO] increases	left
(c)	[H_2O] decreases	left	(d)	[H_2] decreases	right
(e)	xenon gas is added	none	(f)	temperature decreases	left
(g)	pressure decreases	right	(h)	volume decreases	left

40.

	Stress	Shift		Stress	Shift
(a)	[C_2H_4] increases	right	(b)	[CH_2O] increases	left
(c)	[O_3] decreases	left	(d)	[O_2] decreases	right
(e)	temperature increases	left	(f)	pressure decreases	right
(g)	volume decreases	left	(h)	a catalyst is added	none

Section 16.7 Aqueous Solution Equilibria

42.   Drives a Reversible Reaction to Completion
     (b) formation of a weak acid
     (d) formation of a weak base
     (f) formation of an insoluble salt
     (g) formation of water
     (h) formation of a gas

44.

	Product	Classification	Effect on Equilibrium
(a)	$HNO_{3(aq)}$	strong electrolyte	no effect
(b)	$HNO_{2(aq)}$	weak electrolyte	drives reaction to completion
(c)	$H_2O_{(l)}$	weak electrolyte	drives reaction to completion
(d)	$H_2S_{(g)}$	gas	drives reaction to completion
(e)	$Na_2CO_{3(aq)}$	strong electrolyte	no effect
(f)	$MgCO_{3(s)}$	precipitate	drives reaction to completion

46.   Product(s) Responsible For Driving Reaction to Completion
     (a) $BaCO_{3(s)}$ (insoluble precipitate)
     (b) $NH_4OH_{(aq)}$ (weak electrolyte)
     (c) $BaSO_{4(s)}$ (insoluble precipitate) and $H_2O_{(l)}$ (weak electrolyte)

Section 16.8 Ionization Constant, K_i

48.   (a) $NH_2OH_{(aq)} + H_2O_{(l)} \rightleftharpoons NH_3OH^+_{(aq)} + OH^-_{(aq)}$

$$K_i = \frac{[NH_3OH^+][OH^-]}{[NH_2OH]}$$

      (b) $C_6H_5NH_{2(aq)} + H_2O_{(l)} \rightleftharpoons C_6H_5NH_3^+_{(aq)} + OH^-_{(aq)}$

$$K_i = \frac{[C_6H_5NH_3^+][OH^-]}{[C_6H_5NH_2]}$$

      (c) $(CH_3)_2NH_{(aq)} + H_2O_{(l)} \rightleftharpoons (CH_3)_2NH_2^+_{(aq)} + OH^-_{(aq)}$

$$K_i = \frac{[(CH_3)_2NH_2^+][OH^-]}{[(CH_3)_2NH]}$$

50. $NH_4OH_{(aq)} \rightleftharpoons NH_4^+_{(aq)} + OH^-_{(aq)}$

$[NH_4OH] = 0.245$

$[NH_4^+] = 2.1 \times 10^{-3}$

$[OH^-] = 2.1 \times 10^{-3}$

$$K_i = \frac{[NH_4^+][OH^-]}{[NH_4OH]} = \frac{(2.1 \times 10^{-3})(2.1 \times 10^{-3})}{(0.245)} = 1.8 \times 10^{-5}$$

52. $N_2H_{4(aq)} + H_2O_{(l)} \rightleftharpoons N_2H_5^+_{(aq)} + OH^-_{(aq)}$

$[N_2H_4] = 0.769$

$[OH^-] = 10^{-pOH} = 10^{-3.00} = 0.0010$

$[N_2H_5^+] = 0.0010$

$$K_i = \frac{[N_2H_5^+][OH^-]}{[N_2H_4]} = \frac{(0.0010)(0.0010)}{(0.769)} = 1.3 \times 10^{-6}$$

Section 16.9 Weak Acid-Base Equilibria Shifts

54.

	Stress	Shift		Stress	Shift
(a)	decrease $[HNO_2]$	left	(b)	decrease $[H^+]$	right
(c)	increase $[HNO_2]$	right	(d)	increase $[NO_2^-]$	left
(e)	add KNO_2 solid	left	(f)	add KCl solid	none
(g)	add KOH solid	right	(h)	increase pH	right

56.

	Stress	Shift		Stress	Shift
(a)	increase $[NH_4^+]$	left	(b)	decrease $[OH^-]$	right
(c)	increase $[NH_4OH]$	right	(d)	decrease pH	right
(e)	add NH_3 gas	right	(f)	add KCl solid	none
(g)	add KOH solid	left	(h)	add NH_4Cl solid	left

Section 16.10 Solubility Product Equilibrium Constant, K_{sp}

58.

Reaction	Solubility Product Expression
(a) $AuI_{3(s)} \rightleftarrows Au^{3+}_{(aq)} + 3\,I^-_{(aq)}$	$K_{sp} = [Au^{3+}]\,[I^-]^3$
(b) $Ag_2SO_{4(s)} \rightleftarrows 2\,Ag^+_{(aq)} + SO_4^{2-}_{(aq)}$	$K_{sp} = [Ag^+]^2\,[SO_4^{2-}]$
(c) $Co_3(PO_4)_{2(s)} \rightleftarrows 3\,Co^{2+}_{(aq)} + 2\,PO_4^{\,3-}_{(aq)}$	$K_{sp} = [Co^{2+}]^3\,[PO_4^{\,3-}]^2$

60. $MgF_{2(s)} \rightleftarrows Mg^{2+}_{(aq)} + 2\,F^-_{(aq)}$

$[F^-] = 2.3 \times 10^{-3}$

Since 2 F^- are produced for every Mg^{2+}, then

$[Mg^{2+}] = \dfrac{1}{2}[F^-] = \dfrac{1}{2}(2.3 \times 10^{-3}) = 1.2 \times 10^{-3}$

$K_{sp} = [Mg^{2+}]\,[F^-]^2 = (1.2 \times 10^{-3})(2.3 \times 10^{-3})^2 = 6.3 \times 10^{-9}$

62. $Fe(OH)_{3(s)} \rightleftarrows Fe^{3+}_{(aq)} + 3\,OH^-_{(aq)}$

$[OH^-] = 2.2 \times 10^{-10}$

Since 3 OH^- are produced for every Fe^{3+}, then

$[Fe^{3+}] = \dfrac{1}{3}[OH^-] = \dfrac{1}{3}(2.2 \times 10^{-10}) = 7.3 \times 10^{-11}$

$K_{sp} = [Fe^{3+}]\,[OH^-]^3 = (7.3 \times 10^{-11})(2.2 \times 10^{-10})^3 = 7.8 \times 10^{-40}$

64. Let S = solubility

$$MnCO_{3(s)} \rightleftarrows \underset{S}{Mn^{2+}_{(aq)}} + \underset{S}{CO_3^{2-}_{(aq)}}$$

$[Mn^{2+}]\,[CO_3^{2-}] = (S)(S) = K_{sp} = 1.8 \times 10^{-11}$

$S^2 = 1.8 \times 10^{-11}$

$S = \left(1.8 \times 10^{-11}\right)^{1/2} = 4.2 \times 10^{-6}$

Let S = solubility

$$Mn(OH)_{2(s)} \rightleftarrows \underset{S}{Mn^{2+}_{(aq)}} + \underset{2\,S}{2\,OH^-_{(aq)}}$$

$[Mn^{2+}]\,[OH^-]^2 = (S)(2\,S)^2 = K_{sp} = 4.6 \times 10^{-14}$

$4\,S^3 = 4.6 \times 10^{-14}$

$S = \left(4.6 \times 10^{-14}/4\right)^{1/3} = 2.3 \times 10^{-5}$

Since the solubility (S) of $Mn(OH)_2$ is greater, it is more soluble.

Section 16.11 Dissociation Equilibria Shifts

66.

Stress	Shift	Stress	Shift
(a) increase $[Cd^{2+}]$	left	(b) increase $[S^{2-}]$	left
(c) decrease $[Cd^{2+}]$	right	(d) decrease $[S^{2-}]$	right
(e) add solid $Cd(NO_3)_2$	left	(f) add solid $NaNO_3$	none

68.

	Stress	Shift		Stress	Shift
(a)	increase $[Sr^{2+}]$	left	(b)	increase $[CO_3^{2-}]$	left
(c)	decrease $[Sr^{2+}]$	right	(d)	decrease $[CO_3^{2-}]$	right
(e)	add solid $SrCO_3$	none	(f)	add solid $Sr(NO_3)_2$	left
(g)	add solid KNO_3	none	(h)	add Ca^{2+}	right

General Exercises

70. With regard to rate and concentration, a system at equilibrium has the following two characteristics:
 (1) The rate of the forward reaction is equal to the rate of the reverse reaction.
 (2) The concentrations of the reactants and products are not necessarily equal, but the concentrations of the products divided by the concentrations of the reactants, each raised to a coefficient power from the balanced equation, is a constant.

72.

	Change	Effect on Equilibrium
(a)	adding more liquid to a liquid-vapor equilibrium	no effect
(b)	adding helium to a gaseous state equilibrium	no effect
(c)	adding precipitate to a saturated solution	no effect

74. $N_2O_{4(g)} \rightleftarrows 2\, NO_{2(g)}$
$P_{N_2O_4} = 0.0014$
$P_{NO_2} = 0.092$
$$K_p = \frac{(P_{NO_2})^2}{P_{N_2O_4}} = \frac{(0.092)^2}{0.0014} = 6.0$$

76.

	Stress	Shift		Stress	Shift
(a)	increase $[H^+]$	left	(b)	increase $[OH^-]$	left
(c)	decrease $[H^+]$	right	(d)	decrease $[OH^-]$	right
(e)	add liquid H_2SO_4	left	(f)	add solid $Ba(OH)_2$	left
(g)	add gaseous HCl	left	(h)	add solid NaF	right
(i)	add solid $FeCl_3$	right	(j)	decrease pH	left

78. $Sn(OH)_{2(s)} \rightleftarrows Sn^{2+}_{(aq)} + 2\, OH^-_{(aq)}$
$[OH^-] = 10^{-pOH} = 10^{-8.47} = 10^{0.53} \times 10^{-9} = 3.4 \times 10^{-9}$
Since 2 OH^- are produced for every Sn^{2+}, then
$$[Sn^{2+}] = \frac{1}{2}[OH^-] = \frac{1}{2}(3.4 \times 10^{-9}) = 1.7 \times 10^{-9}$$
$$K_{sp} = [Sn^{2+}][OH^-]^2 = (1.7 \times 10^{-9})(3.4 \times 10^{-9})^2 = 2.0 \times 10^{-26}$$

17 Oxidation and Reduction

Section 17.1 Oxidation Numbers

2.

	Nonmetal	Oxidation Number			Nonmetal	Oxidation Number
(a)	H_2	0		(b)	He	0
(c)	P_4	0		(d)	I_2	0

4.

	Anion	Oxidation Number			Anion	Oxidation Number
(a)	F^-	-1		(b)	H^-	-1
(c)	P^{3-}	-3		(d)	Te^{2-}	-2

6.

	Compound	Oxidation Number of Nitrogen
(a)	NH_3	$(\text{ox no N}) + 3(\text{ox no H}) = 0$
		$(\text{ox no N}) + 3(+1) = 0$
		$(\text{ox no N}) + 3 = 0$
		$\text{ox no N} = -3$
(b)	N_2O_4	$2(\text{ox no N}) + 4(\text{ox no O}) = 0$
		$2(\text{ox no N}) + 4(-2) = 0$
		$2(\text{ox no N}) + (-8) = 0$
		$2(\text{ox no N}) = +8$
		$\text{ox no N} = +4$
(c)	Li_3N	$3(\text{ox no Li}) + (\text{ox no N}) = 0$
		$3(+1) + (\text{ox no N}) = 0$
		$\text{ox no N} = -3$
(d)	KNO_3	$(\text{ox no K}) + (\text{ox no N}) + 3(\text{ox no O}) = 0$
		$(+1) + (\text{ox no N}) + 3(-2) = 0$
		$(\text{ox no N}) + (-5) = 0$
		$\text{ox no N} = +5$

8.

	Ion	Oxidation Number of Sulfur
(a)	$SO_3{}^{2-}$	$(\text{ox no S}) + 3(\text{ox no O}) = -2$
		$(\text{ox no S}) + 3(-2) = -2$
		$(\text{ox no S}) + (-6) = -2$
		$\text{ox no S} = +4$

8.

Ion	Oxidation Number of Sulfur

(b) HSO_4^- (ox no H) + (ox no S) + 4(ox no O) $= -1$
$(+1)$ + (ox no S) + $4(-2) = -1$
$(+1)$ + (ox no S) + $(-8) = -1$
ox no S $= +6$

(c) $S_2O_3^{2-}$ 2(ox no S) + 3(ox no O) $= -2$
2(ox no S) + $3(-2) = -2$
2(ox no S) + $(-6) = -2$
2(ox no S) $= +4$
ox no S $= +2$

(d) $S_2O_8^{2-}$ 2(ox no S) + 8(ox no O) $= -2$
2(ox no S) + $8(-2) = -2$
2(ox no S) + $(-16) = -2$
2(ox no S) $= +14$
ox no S $= +7$

Section 17.2   Oxidation-Reduction Reactions

10.   (a)   the substance that loses electrons in a redox reaction: reducing agent

      (b)   the substance that gains electrons in a redox reaction: oxidizing agent

12.   (a)

$$\overset{0}{Mn}_{(s)} + \overset{0}{O}_{2(g)} \rightarrow \overset{+4\qquad -2}{MnO_2}_{(s)}$$

Oxidizing agent: O_2
Reducing agent: Mn

      (b)

$$\overset{0}{S}_{(s)} + \overset{0}{O}_{2(g)} \rightarrow \overset{+4\qquad -2}{SO_2}_{(g)}$$

Oxidizing agent: O_2
Reducing agent: S

      (c)

$$\overset{0}{Cd}_{(s)} + \overset{0}{F}_{2(g)} \rightarrow \overset{+2\qquad -1}{CdF_2}_{(s)}$$

Oxidizing agent: F_2
Reducing agent: Cd

12. (d)

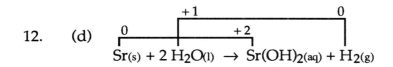

$$Sr_{(s)} + 2\,H_2O_{(l)} \rightarrow Sr(OH)_{2(aq)} + H_{2(g)}$$

Oxidizing agent: H_2O
Reducing agent: Sr

(e)

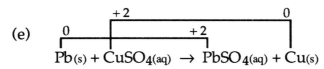

$$Pb_{(s)} + CuSO_{4(aq)} \rightarrow PbSO_{4(aq)} + Cu_{(s)}$$

Oxidizing agent: $CuSO_4$
Reducing agent: Pb

14. (a)

$$CuO_{(s)} + H_{2(g)} \rightarrow Cu_{(s)} + H_2O_{(l)}$$

Oxidizing agent: CuO
Reducing agent: H_2

(b)

$$Cl_{2(g)} + 2\,KBr_{(aq)} \rightarrow Br_{2(l)} + 2\,KCl_{(aq)}$$

Oxidizing agent: Cl_2
Reducing agent: KBr

(c)

$$Ca_{(s)} + 2\,H_2O_{(l)} \rightarrow Ca(OH)_{2(aq)} + H_{2(g)}$$

Oxidizing agent: H_2O
Reducing agent: Ca

(d)

$$Mg_{(s)} + 2\,HCl_{(aq)} \rightarrow MgCl_{2(aq)} + H_{2(g)}$$

Oxidizing agent: HCl
Reducing agent: Mg

14. (e)

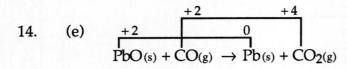

$$PbO_{(s)} + CO_{(g)} \rightarrow Pb_{(s)} + CO_{2(g)}$$

Oxidizing agent: PbO
Reducing agent: CO

16. (a)

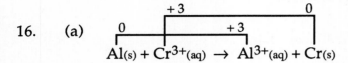

$$Al_{(s)} + Cr^{3+}_{(aq)} \rightarrow Al^{3+}_{(aq)} + Cr_{(s)}$$

Oxidizing agent: Cr^{3+}
Reducing agent: Al

(b)

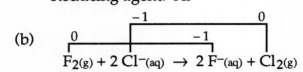

$$F_{2(g)} + 2\,Cl^-_{(aq)} \rightarrow 2\,F^-_{(aq)} + Cl_{2(g)}$$

Oxidizing agent: F_2
Reducing agent: Cl^-

(c)

$$H_2O_{(l)} + 2\,Fe^{3+}_{(aq)} + SO_3{}^{2-}_{(aq)} \rightarrow 2\,Fe^{2+}_{(aq)} + SO_4{}^{2-}_{(aq)} + 2\,H^+_{(aq)}$$

Oxidizing agent: Fe^{3+}
Reducing agent: $SO_3{}^{2-}$

(d)

$$Sn^{2+}_{(aq)} + 2\,Hg^{2+}_{(aq)} \rightarrow Sn^{4+}_{(aq)} + Hg_2{}^{2+}_{(aq)}$$

Oxidizing agent: Hg^{2+}
Reducing agent: Sn^{2+}

(e)

$$Cr^{2+}_{(aq)} + AgI_{(s)} \rightarrow Cr^{3+}_{(aq)} + Ag_{(s)} + I^-_{(aq)}$$

Oxidizing agent: AgI
Reducing agent: Cr^{2+}

18. (a)

$$\overset{-1}{2\ Br^-_{(aq)}} + \overset{+2}{Pt^{2+}_{(aq)}} \rightarrow \overset{0}{Br_{2(l)}} + \overset{0}{Pt_{(s)}}$$

Oxidizing agent: Pt^{2+}
Reducing agent: Br^-

(b)

$$\overset{+4}{TeO_{2(s)}} + 4\ H^+_{(aq)} + \overset{0}{Zr_{(s)}} \rightarrow \overset{0}{Te_{(s)}} + \overset{+4}{Zr^{4+}_{(aq)}} + 2\ H_2O_{(l)}$$

Oxidizing agent: TeO_2
Reducing agent: Zr

(c)

$$\overset{+4}{MnO_{2(s)}} + \overset{+4}{SO_{2(g)}} \rightarrow \overset{+2}{Mn^{2+}_{(aq)}} + \overset{+6}{SO_4^{2-}_{(aq)}}$$

Oxidizing agent: MnO_2
Reducing agent: SO_2

(d)

$$\overset{+4}{Pb^{4+}_{(aq)}} + \overset{-1}{H_2O_{2(aq)}} \rightarrow \overset{+2}{Pb^{2+}_{(aq)}} + \overset{0}{O_{2(g)}} + 2\ H^+_{(aq)}$$

Oxidizing agent: Pb^{4+}
Reducing agent: H_2O_2

(e)

$$H_2O_{(l)} + \overset{+4}{SO_3^{2-}_{(aq)}} + \overset{0}{I_{2(s)}} \rightarrow \overset{+6}{SO_4^{2-}_{(aq)}} + \overset{-1}{2\ I^-_{(aq)}} + 2\ H^+_{(aq)}$$

Oxidizing agent: I_2
Reducing agent: SO_3^{2-}

Section 17.3 Balancing Redox Equations: Oxidation Number Method

20. Yes, the total ionic charge on the reactant side always equals the total ionic charge on the product side of a balanced redox reaction.

22.   (a)

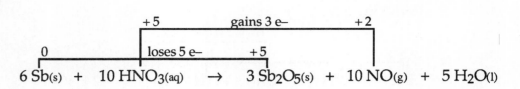

$$Cl_{2(g)} + 2\,KI_{(aq)} \rightarrow 2\,KCl_{(aq)} + I_{2(s)}$$

(b)

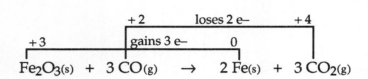

$$6\,Sb_{(s)} + 10\,HNO_{3(aq)} \rightarrow 3\,Sb_2O_{5(s)} + 10\,NO_{(g)} + 5\,H_2O_{(l)}$$

(c)

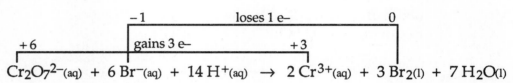

$$Fe_2O_{3(s)} + 3\,CO_{(g)} \rightarrow 2\,Fe_{(s)} + 3\,CO_{2(g)}$$

24.   (a)

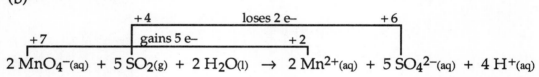

$$Cr_2O_7{}^{2-}{}_{(aq)} + 6\,Br^-{}_{(aq)} + 14\,H^+{}_{(aq)} \rightarrow 2\,Cr^{3+}{}_{(aq)} + 3\,Br_{2(l)} + 7\,H_2O_{(l)}$$

(b)

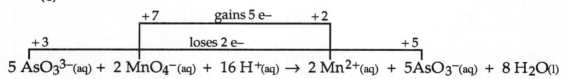

$$2\,MnO_4{}^-{}_{(aq)} + 5\,SO_{2(g)} + 2\,H_2O_{(l)} \rightarrow 2\,Mn^{2+}{}_{(aq)} + 5\,SO_4{}^{2-}{}_{(aq)} + 4\,H^+{}_{(aq)}$$

(c)

$$5\,AsO_3{}^{3-}{}_{(aq)} + 2\,MnO_4{}^-{}_{(aq)} + 16\,H^+{}_{(aq)} \rightarrow 2\,Mn^{2+}{}_{(aq)} + 5\,AsO_3{}^-{}_{(aq)} + 8\,H_2O_{(l)}$$

Section 17.4 Balancing Redox Equations: Ion-Electron Method

26.   (a) $ClO^-{}_{(aq)} + H_2O_{(l)} + 2\,e^- \rightarrow Cl^-{}_{(aq)} + 2\,OH^-{}_{(aq)}$

(b) $MnO_4{}^-{}_{(aq)} + 2\,H_2O_{(l)} + 3\,e^- \rightarrow MnO_{2(s)} + 4\,OH^-{}_{(aq)}$

(c) $Ni(OH)_{2(s)} + 2\,OH^-{}_{(aq)} \rightarrow NiO_{2(s)} + 2\,H_2O_{(l)} + 2\,e^-$

(d) $2\,NO_2{}^-{}_{(aq)} + 3\,H_2O_{(l)} + 4\,e^- \rightarrow N_2O_{(g)} + 6\,OH^-{}_{(aq)}$

(e) $NO_2{}^-{}_{(aq)} + 2\,OH^-{}_{(aq)} \rightarrow NO_3{}^-{}_{(aq)} + H_2O_{(l)} + 2\,e^-$

28. (a) Oxidation: $3 (S^{2-} \rightarrow S + 2\,e^-)$
    Reduction: $2 (MnO_4^- + 2\,H_2O + 3\,e^- \rightarrow MnO_2 + 4\,OH^-)$

    $3\,S^{2-}{}_{(aq)} + 2\,MnO_4^-{}_{(aq)} + 4\,H_2O_{(l)} \rightarrow 3\,S_{(s)} + 2\,MnO_2{}_{(s)} + 8\,OH^-{}_{(aq)}$

    (b) Oxidation: $Cu \rightarrow Cu^{2+} + 2\,e^-$
    Reduction: $ClO^- + H_2O + 2\,e^- \rightarrow Cl^- + 2\,OH^-$

    $Cu_{(s)} + ClO^-{}_{(aq)} + H_2O_{(l)} \rightarrow Cu^{2+}{}_{(aq)} + Cl^-{}_{(aq)} + 2\,OH^-{}_{(aq)}$

    (c) Oxidation: $BrO_2^- + 2\,OH^- \rightarrow BrO_3^- + H_2O + 2\,e^-$
    Reduction: $Cl_2 + 2\,e^- \rightarrow 2\,Cl^-$

    $BrO_2^-{}_{(aq)} + 2\,OH^-{}_{(aq)} + Cl_2{}_{(g)} \rightarrow BrO_3^-{}_{(aq)} + 2\,Cl^-{}_{(aq)} + H_2O_{(l)}$

    (d) Oxidation: $Mn^{2+} + 4\,OH^- \rightarrow MnO_2 + 2\,H_2O + 2\,e^-$
    Reduction: $H_2O_2 + 2\,e^- \rightarrow 2\,OH^-$

    $Mn^{2+}{}_{(aq)} + 2\,OH^-{}_{(aq)} + H_2O_2{}_{(aq)} \rightarrow MnO_2{}_{(s)} + 2\,H_2O_{(l)}$

    (e) Oxidation: $4(MnO_2 + 4\,OH^- \rightarrow MnO_4^- + 2\,H_2O + 3\,e^-)$
    Reduction: $3(O_2 + 2\,H_2O + 4\,e^- \rightarrow 4\,OH^-)$

    $4\,MnO_2{}_{(s)} + 4\,OH^-{}_{(aq)} + 3\,O_2{}_{(g)} \rightarrow 4\,MnO_4^-{}_{(aq)} + 2\,H_2O_{(l)}$

30. (a) Oxidation: $Cl_2 + 8\,OH^- \rightarrow 2\,ClO_2^- + 4\,H_2O + 6\,e^-$
    Reduction: $3 (Cl_2 + 2\,e^- \rightarrow 2\,Cl^-)$

    $4\,Cl_2{}_{(g)} + 8\,OH^-{}_{(aq)} \rightarrow 2\,ClO_2^-{}_{(aq)} + 6\,Cl^-{}_{(aq)} + 4\,H_2O_{(l)}$

    (b) Oxidation: $Br_2 + 12\,OH^- \rightarrow 2\,BrO_3^- + 6\,H_2O + 10\,e^-$
    Reduction: $5 (Br_2 + 2\,e^- \rightarrow 2\,Br^-)$

    $6\,Br_2{}_{(l)} + 12\,OH^-{}_{(aq)} \rightarrow 2\,BrO_3^-{}_{(aq)} + 6\,H_2O_{(l)} + 10\,Br^-{}_{(aq)}$

    (c) Oxidation: $S + 6\,OH^- \rightarrow SO_3^{2-} + 3\,H_2O + 4\,e^-$
    Reduction: $2 (S + 2\,e^- \rightarrow S^{2-})$

    $3\,S_{(s)} + 6\,OH^-{}_{(aq)} \rightarrow SO_3^{2-}{}_{(aq)} + 3\,H_2O_{(l)} + 2\,S^{2-}{}_{(aq)}$

Section 17.5 Predicting Spontaneous Redox Reactions

32.   <u>Substances</u>   <u>Most Likely to be Oxidized</u>
    - (a) $Na_{(s)}$ or $K_{(s)}$ $K_{(s)}$
    - (b) $Ag_{(s)}$ or $Hg_{(l)}$ $Ag_{(s)}$
    - (c) $Fe^{2+}_{(aq)}$ or $Fe_{(s)}$ $Fe_{(s)}$
    - (d) $Br^-_{(aq)}$ or $Cl^-_{(aq)}$ $Br^-_{(aq)}$

34.   <u>Substances</u>   <u>Stronger Reducing Agent</u>
    - (a) $Cu_{(s)}$ or $Hg_{(l)}$ $Cu_{(s)}$
    - (b) $H_{2(g)}$ or $Ba_{(s)}$ $Ba_{(s)}$
    - (c) $Al_{(s)}$ or $I^-_{(aq)}$ $Al_{(s)}$
    - (d) $Cl^-_{(aq)}$ or $H_{2(g)}$ $H_{2(g)}$

36.   (a)   nonspontaneous   (b)   nonspontaneous
        (c)   spontaneous   (d)   nonspontaneous
        (e)   spontaneous

38.   <u>Balanced Redox Reactions</u>
    - (a) $Br_{2(l)} + 2\,LiF_{(aq)} \rightarrow F_{2(g)} + 2\,LiBr_{(aq)}$
    - (b) $2\,Al(NO_3)_{3(aq)} + 3\,Co_{(s)} \rightarrow 3\,Co(NO_3)_{2(aq)} + 2\,Al_{(s)}$
    - (c) $2\,Cr_{(s)} + 3\,H_2SO_{4(aq)} \rightarrow Cr_2(SO_4)_{3(aq)} + 3\,H_{2(g)}$
    - (d) $2\,Au_{(s)} + 6\,HCl_{(aq)} \rightarrow 2\,AuCl_{3(aq)} + 3\,H_{2(g)}$
    - (e) $2\,FeCl_{3(aq)} + 2\,NaI_{(aq)} \rightarrow 2\,FeCl_{2(aq)} + 2\,NaCl_{(aq)} + I_{2(s)}$

Section 17.6 Voltaic Cells

40.

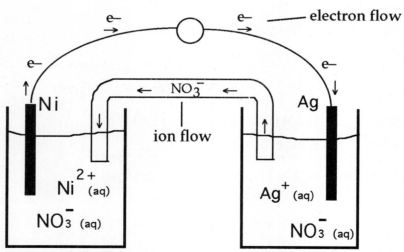

$$Ni_{(s)} + 2\,AgNO_{3(aq)} \rightarrow 2\,Ag_{(s)} + Ni(NO_3)_{2(aq)}$$

42.

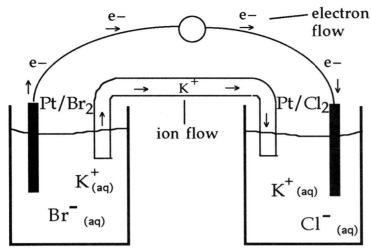

$$Cl_{2(g)} + 2\ KBr_{(aq)} \rightarrow 2\ KCl_{(aq)} + Br_{2(l)}$$

44. $Co_{(s)} + 2\ Fe^{3+}_{(aq)} \rightarrow Co^{2+}_{(aq)} + 2\ Fe^{2+}_{(aq)}$

    (a) oxidation half-cell reaction: $Co_{(s)} \rightarrow Co^{2+}_{(aq)} + 2\ e^-$

    (b) reduction half-cell reaction: $Fe^{3+}_{(aq)} + 1\ e^- \rightarrow Fe^{2+}_{(aq)}$

    (c) anode: Co electrode
            cathode: Fe electrode

    (d) direction of e^- flow: Co anode $\rightarrow$ Fe cathode

    (e) direction of Cl^- in the salt bridge: Fe half-cell $\rightarrow$ Co half-cell

46. $H_{2(g)} + I_{2(s)} \rightarrow 2\ H^+_{(aq)} + 2\ I^-_{(aq)}$

    (a) oxidation half-cell reaction: $H_{2(g)} \rightarrow 2\ H^+_{(aq)} + 2\ e^-$

    (b) reduction half-cell reaction: $I_{2(s)} + 2\ e^- \rightarrow 2\ I^-_{(aq)}$

    (c) anode: Pt (H_2) electrode
            cathode: Pt (I_2) electrode

    (d) direction of e^- flow: Pt (H_2) anode $\rightarrow$ Pt (I_2) cathode

    (e) direction of I^- in the salt bridge: I_2 half-cell $\rightarrow$ H_2 half-cell

Section 17.7 Electrolytic Cells

48.

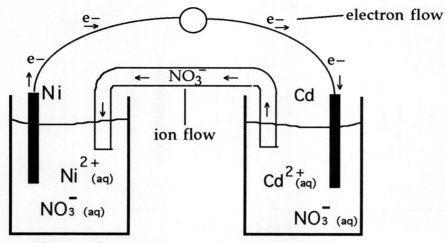

$$Ni_{(s)} + Cd(NO_3)_{2(aq)} \rightarrow Cd_{(s)} + Ni(NO_3)_{2(aq)}$$

50.

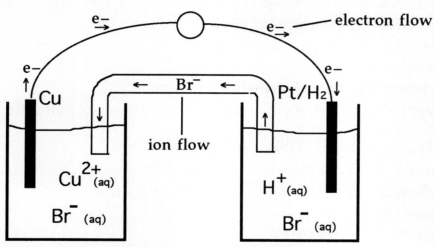

$$Cu_{(s)} + 2\,HBr_{(aq)} \rightarrow CuBr_{2(aq)} + H_{2(g)}$$

52. $Pb_{(s)} + Zn^{2+}_{(aq)} \rightarrow Zn_{(s)} + Pb^{2+}_{(aq)}$

   (a)   oxidation half-cell reaction: $Pb_{(s)} \rightarrow Pb^{2+}_{(aq)} + 2\,e^-$

   (b)   reduction half-cell reaction: $Zn^{2+}_{(aq)} + 2\,e^- \rightarrow Zn_{(s)}$

   (c)   anode: Pb electrode
         cathode: Zn electrode

   (d)   direction of e^- flow: Pb anode $\rightarrow$ Zn cathode

   (e)   direction of NO_3^- in the salt bridge: Zn half-cell $\rightarrow$ Pb half-cell

54. $Cl_{2(g)} + 2\,NaF_{(aq)} \rightarrow 2\,NaCl_{(aq)} + F_{2(g)}$

   (a)   oxidation half-cell reaction: $2\,F^-_{(aq)} \rightarrow F_{2(g)} + 2\,e^-$

   (b)   reduction half-cell reaction: $Cl_{2(g)} + 2\,e^- \rightarrow 2\,Cl^-_{(aq)}$

   (c)   anode: Pt (F^-) electrode
         cathode: Pt (Cl_2) electrode

   (d)   direction of e^- flow: Pt (F^-) anode $\rightarrow$ Pt (Cl_2) cathode

   (e)   direction of Na^+ is the salt bridge: Cl_2 half-cell $\rightarrow$ F^- half-cell

General Exercises

56.   Compound   Oxidation Number of Sulfur
       $S_4O_6^{2-}$ $4(\text{ox no S}) + 6(\text{ox no O}) = -2$
                             $4(\text{ox no S}) + 6(-2) = -2$
                             $4(\text{ox no S}) + (-12) = -2$
                             $4(\text{ox no S}) = +10$
                             $\text{ox no S} = +2.5$

   $\left(\text{Note:}\ \begin{array}{l}\text{Although oxidation numbers are usually whole numbers, in this}\\ \text{complex example the } \textit{average} \text{ oxidation number of sulfur is 2.5}\end{array}\right)$

58.   molecular equation: $Co_{(s)} + Hg(NO_2)_{2(aq)} \rightarrow Co(NO_2)_{2(aq)} + Hg_{(l)}$

       net ionic equation: $Co_{(s)} + Hg^{2+}_{(aq)} \rightarrow Co^{2+}_{(aq)} + Hg_{(l)}$

       oxidizing agent: Hg^{2+}

       reducing agent: Co

60.   molecular equation: $2\,K_{(s)} + 2\,H_2O_{(l)} \rightarrow 2\,KOH_{(aq)} + H_{2(g)}$

       net ionic equation: $2\,K_{(s)} + 2\,H_2O_{(l)} \rightarrow 2\,K^+_{(aq)} + 2\,OH^-_{(aq)} + H_{2(g)}$

       oxidizing agent: $H_2O\ (H^+)$

       reducing agent: K

62.   net ionic equation:
       $3\,C_2H_5OH_{(aq)} + 2\,Cr_2O_7^{2-}{}_{(aq)} + 16\,H^+_{(aq)} \rightarrow$
       $$3\,HC_2H_3O_{2(aq)} + 4\,Cr^{3+}_{(aq)} + 11\,H_2O_{(l)}$$

       oxidizing agent: $Cr_2O_7^{2-}$ reducing agent: C_2H_5OH

64.   The principal problem with obtaining energy from a hydrogen-oxygen
       fuel cell is in supplying the hydrogen, which doesn't occur naturally.
       However, the hydrogen can be produced by another primary source of
       energy such as fossil fuels, solar power, or nuclear power.

CHAPTER 18 | Advanced Chemical Calculations

Section 18.1 Advanced Problem Solving

2.   (a)   If the answer has compound units, then the given quantity has compound units also.

       (b)   A balanced chemical equation must be written before any stoichiometry problem can be solved.

       (c)   Given information that is not relevant to the solution of a problem can simply be ignored.

       (d)   Three common references that can be utilized to help solve a problem are:
           (1) The periodic table of the elements
           (2) Chemistry textbooks
           (3) The *Handbook of Chemistry and Physics* (CRC Press)

       (e)   Density and ideal gas law problems are more easily solved by an algebraic method than by the unit analysis method.

       (f)   Attempt to approximate the answer after setting up a problem, but before the starting the calculations. After calculating a numerical answer, check the approximations.

4.

	Physical Quantity	Common Unit
(a)	length	meter
(b)	mass	gram
(c)	volume	liter
(d)	time	second
(e)	temperature	degree Celsius
(f)	heat energy	calorie
(g)	density	grams per cubic centimeter, grams per milliliter, grams per liter
(h)	solution concentrations	grams solute per 100 grams solution

6. A possible concept map for the college administration:

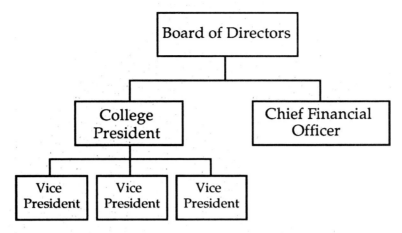

8. (a)

| mass CHCl$_3$ | — | moles CHCl$_3$ | — | molecules CHCl$_3$ |

(b)

| volume CO$_2$(aq) | — | moles CO$_2$ | — | mass CO$_2$ |

10. (a) Step 1: Compute molar mass of Cu.
    Step 2: Convert mass of Cu to moles of Cu using the molar mass.
    Step 3: Convert moles of Cu to atoms of Cu using Avogadro's number.

    (b) Step 1: Convert the volume of NaCl solution to moles of NaCl using the molarity.
    Step 2: Compute molar mass of NaCl.
    Step 3: Convert the moles of NaCl to mass of NaCl using the molar mass.

12. (a)

| volume of gaseous reactant | — | volume of gaseous product |

(Note: Assume the gases are at the same conditions)

    (b)

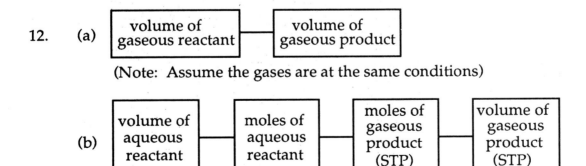

14. Consider the general equation: a A + b B   →   c C + d D
   (a)   Step 1:   Relate the volume of gaseous reactant to the volume of the gaseous product using the coefficients from the balanced chemical equation (assume constant conditions).
   (b)   Step 1:   Convert the volume of the aqueous solution reactant A to moles of A using molarity.
         Step 2:   Relate the moles of the reactant A to the moles of the gaseous product C using the balanced chemical equation.
         Step 3:   Convert the moles of the gaseous product C to the volume of C using molar volume (at STP).

16.   (a) $1.550 \; \cancel{g \; Cr_2O_3} \times \dfrac{1 \; \cancel{mol \; Cr_2O_3}}{152.0 \; \cancel{g \; Cr_2O_3}} \times \dfrac{2 \; \cancel{mol \; Cr}}{1 \; \cancel{mol \; Cr_2O_3}} \times \dfrac{52.0 \; g \; Cr}{1 \; \cancel{mol \; Cr}} = g \; Cr$

      Calculated answer: 1.06 g Cr

   (b) $42.0 \; \cancel{mL \; HNO_3} \times \dfrac{0.195 \; \cancel{mol \; HNO_3}}{1000 \; \cancel{mL \; HNO_3}} \times \dfrac{1 \; \cancel{mol \; Ba(OH)_2}}{2 \; \cancel{mol \; HNO_3}} \times$

      $\dfrac{1000 \; mL \; Ba(OH)_2}{0.105 \; \cancel{mol \; Ba(OH)_2}} = mL \; Ba(OH)_2$

      Calculated answer: 39.0 mL Ba(OH)$_2$

   (c) $21.5 \; \cancel{mL \; BiCl_3} \times \dfrac{0.115 \; \cancel{mol \; BiCl_3}}{1000 \; \cancel{mL \; BiCl_3}} \times \dfrac{3 \; \cancel{mol \; Hg_2Cl_2}}{2 \; \cancel{mol \; BiCl_3}} \times$

      $\dfrac{472.2 \; g \; Hg_2Cl_2}{1 \; \cancel{mol \; Hg_2Cl_2}} = g \; Hg_2Cl_2$

      Calculated answer: 1.75 g Hg$_2$Cl$_2$

Section 18.2 Chemical Formula Calculations

18.   (a) $0.0755 \; \cancel{mol \; NH_3} \times \dfrac{17.0 \; g \; NH_3}{1 \; \cancel{mol \; NH_3}} = 1.28 \; g \; NH_3$

   (b) $0.0755 \; \cancel{mol \; NH_3} \times \dfrac{22.4 \; L \; NH_3}{1 \; \cancel{mol \; NH_3}} = 1.69 \; L \; NH_3$

   (c) $0.0755 \; \cancel{mol \; NH_3} \times \dfrac{6.02 \times 10^{23} \; molecules \; NH_3}{1 \; \cancel{mol \; NH_3}}$

      $= 4.55 \times 10^{22} \; molecules \; NH_3$

   (d) $\dfrac{0.0755 \; mol \; NH_3}{0.155 \; L \; solution} = 0.487 \; M \; NH_3$

20.   (a) $2.00 \; \cancel{g \; N_2H_4} \times \dfrac{1 \; mL \; N_2H_4}{1.02 \; \cancel{g \; N_2H_4}} = 1.96 \; mL \; N_2H_4$

   (b) $2.00 \; \cancel{g \; N_2H_4} \times \dfrac{1 \; \cancel{mol \; N_2H_4}}{32.0 \; \cancel{g \; N_2H_4}} \times \dfrac{6.02 \times 10^{23} \; molecules \; N_2H_4}{1 \; \cancel{mol \; N_2H_4}}$

      $= 3.76 \times 10^{22} \; molecules \; N_2H_4$

   (c) $\dfrac{2.00 \; \cancel{g \; N_2H_4}}{0.250 \; L \; solution} \times \dfrac{1 \; mol \; N_2H_4}{32.0 \; \cancel{g \; N_2H_4}} = 0.250 \; M \; N_2H_4$

22.   (a) $555 \ \cancel{mL \ SO_2} \times \dfrac{1 \ \cancel{L \ SO_2}}{1000 \ \cancel{mL \ SO_2}} \times \dfrac{1 \ \cancel{mol \ SO_2}}{22.4 \ \cancel{L \ SO_2}} \times \dfrac{64.1 \ g \ SO_2}{1 \ \cancel{mol \ SO_2}}$

$$= 1.59 \ g \ SO_2$$

      (b) $555 \ \cancel{mL \ SO_2} \times \dfrac{1 \ \cancel{L \ SO_2}}{1000 \ \cancel{mL \ SO_2}} \times \dfrac{1 \ \cancel{mol \ SO_2}}{22.4 \ \cancel{L \ SO_2}} \times$

$$\dfrac{6.02 \times 10^{23} \ \text{molecules} \ SO_2}{1 \ \cancel{mol \ SO_2}} = 1.49 \times 10^{22} \ \text{molecules} \ SO_2$$

      (c) $\dfrac{555 \ \cancel{mL \ SO_2}}{0.250 \ L \ \text{solution}} \times \dfrac{1 \ \cancel{L \ SO_2}}{1000 \ \cancel{mL \ SO_2}} \times \dfrac{1 \ mol \ SO_2}{22.4 \ \cancel{L \ SO_2}} = 0.0991 \ M \ H_2SO_3$

24.   (a) $1.12 \times 10^{23} \ \cancel{\text{molecules} \ SO_3} \times \dfrac{1 \ \cancel{mol \ SO_3}}{6.02 \times 10^{23} \ \cancel{\text{molecules} \ SO_3}} \times$

$$\dfrac{22.4 \ L \ SO_3}{1 \ \cancel{mol \ SO_3}} = 4.17 \ L \ SO_3$$

      (b) $1.12 \times 10^{23} \ \cancel{\text{molecules} \ SO_3} \times \dfrac{1 \ \cancel{mol \ SO_3}}{6.02 \times 10^{23} \ \cancel{\text{molecules} \ SO_3}} \times$

$$\dfrac{80.1 \ g \ SO_3}{1 \ \cancel{mol \ SO_3}} = 14.9 \ g \ SO_3$$

      (c) $\dfrac{1.12 \times 10^{23} \ \cancel{\text{molecules} \ SO_3}}{0.325 \ L \ \text{solution}} \times \dfrac{1 \ mol \ SO_3}{6.02 \times 10^{23} \ \cancel{\text{molecules} \ SO_3}}$

$$= 0.572 \ M \ H_2SO_4$$

Section 18.3   Chemical Equation Calculations

26. $4 \ NH_{3(g)} + 5 \ O_{2(g)} \xrightarrow{\text{Pt}} 4 \ NO_{(g)} + 6 \ H_2O_{(l)}$

      (a) $25.0 \ \cancel{L \ NO} \times \dfrac{4 \ L \ NH_3}{4 \ \cancel{L \ NO}} = 25.0 \ L \ NH_3$

      (b) $25.0 \ \cancel{L \ NO} \times \dfrac{1 \ \cancel{mol \ NO}}{22.4 \ \cancel{L \ NO}} \times \dfrac{6 \ \cancel{mol \ H_2O}}{4 \ \cancel{mol \ NO}} \times \dfrac{18.0 \ g \ H_2O}{1 \ \cancel{mol \ H_2O}} = 30.1 \ g \ H_2O$

28. $2 \ KHCO_{3(s)} \rightarrow K_2CO_{3(s)} + H_2O_{(g)} + CO_{2(g)}$

      (a) $255 \ \cancel{mL \ CO_2} \times \dfrac{1 \ \cancel{L \ CO_2}}{1000 \ \cancel{mL \ CO_2}} \times \dfrac{1 \ \cancel{mol \ CO_2}}{22.4 \ \cancel{L \ CO_2}} \times \dfrac{2 \ \cancel{mol \ KHCO_3}}{1 \ \cancel{mol \ CO_2}} \times$

$$\dfrac{100.1 \ g \ KHCO_3}{1 \ \cancel{mol \ KHCO_3}} = 2.28 \ g \ KHCO_3$$

      (b) $255 \ \cancel{mL \ CO_2} \times \dfrac{1 \ \cancel{L \ CO_2}}{1000 \ \cancel{mL \ CO_2}} \times \dfrac{1 \ \cancel{mol \ CO_2}}{22.4 \ \cancel{L \ CO_2}} \times \dfrac{1 \ \cancel{mol \ K_2CO_3}}{1 \ \cancel{mol \ CO_2}} \times$

$$\dfrac{138.2 \ g \ K_2CO_3}{1 \ \cancel{mol \ K_2CO_3}} = 1.57 \ g \ K_2CO_3$$

30. $Hg(NO_3)_{2(aq)} + 2\ NaI_{(aq)} \rightarrow HgI_{2(s)} + 2\ NaNO_{3(aq)}$

(a) $24.0\ \cancel{mL\ NaI} \times \dfrac{0.170\ \cancel{mol\ NaI}}{1000\ \cancel{mL\ NaI}} \times \dfrac{1\ \cancel{mol\ Hg(NO_3)_2}}{2\ \cancel{mol\ NaI}} \times$

$$\dfrac{1000\ mL\ Hg(NO_3)_2}{0.209\ \cancel{mol\ Hg(NO_3)_2}} = 9.76\ mL\ Hg(NO_3)_2$$

(b) $24.0\ \cancel{mL\ NaI} \times \dfrac{0.170\ \cancel{mol\ NaI}}{1000\ \cancel{mL\ NaI}} \times \dfrac{1\ \cancel{mol\ HgI_2}}{2\ \cancel{mol\ NaI}} \times \dfrac{454.4\ g\ HgI_2}{1\ \cancel{mol\ HgI_2}}$

$$= 0.927\ g\ HgI_2$$

Section 18.4 Limiting Reactant Concept

32. $38,000\ \cancel{tires} \times \dfrac{1\ automobile}{4\ \cancel{tires}} = 9500$ automobiles can be shipped

Although there are 9555 automobile chassis, the number of tires limits the number of automobiles that can be shipped.

34. $N_{2(g)} + 2\ O_{2(g)} \rightarrow 2\ NO_{2(g)}$

$45.0\ \cancel{mL\ N_2} \times \dfrac{2\ mL\ NO_2}{1\ \cancel{mL\ N_2}} = 90.0\ mL\ NO_2$

$65.0\ \cancel{mL\ O_2} \times \dfrac{2\ mL\ NO_2}{2\ \cancel{mL\ O_2}} = 65.0\ mL\ NO_2$

(a) $65.0\ mL\ NO_2$

(b) O_2 is the limiting reactant

36. $Ca(C_2H_3O_2)_{2(aq)} + Na_2CO_{3(aq)} \rightarrow CaCO_{3(s)} + 2\ NaC_2H_3O_{2(aq)}$

$36.5\ \cancel{mL\ Ca(C_2H_3O_2)_2} \times \dfrac{0.266\ \cancel{mol\ Ca(C_2H_3O_2)_2}}{1000\ \cancel{mL\ Ca(C_2H_3O_2)_2}} \times \dfrac{1\ \cancel{mol\ CaCO_3}}{1\ \cancel{mol\ Ca(C_2H_3O_2)_2}} \times$

$$\dfrac{100.1\ g\ CaCO_3}{1\ \cancel{mol\ CaCO_3}} = 0.972\ g\ CaCO_3$$

$25.0\ \cancel{mL\ Na_2CO_3} \times \dfrac{0.385\ \cancel{mol\ Na_2CO_3}}{1000\ \cancel{mL\ Na_2CO_3}} \times \dfrac{1\ \cancel{mol\ CaCO_3}}{1\ \cancel{mol\ Na_2CO_3}} \times$

$$\dfrac{100.1\ g\ CaCO_3}{1\ \cancel{mol\ CaCO_3}} = 0.963\ g\ CaCO_3$$

(a) $0.963\ g\ CaCO_3$

(b) Na_2CO_3 is the limiting reactant

Section 18.5 Thermochemical Stoichiometry

38.   For exothermic reactions the ΔH value is negative because heat is lost.

40.   (a) $2\ H_2O_{(g)} + 115.6\ kcal \rightarrow 2\ H_{2(g)} + O_{2(g)}$

       (b) $P_{4(s)} + 5\ O_{2(g)} \rightarrow P_4O_{10(s)} + 696.4\ kcal$

42. $CaSO_{4(s)} + 96.4 \text{ kcal} \rightarrow CaO_{(s)} + SO_{3(g)}$

(a) $27.5 \,\cancel{\text{kcal}} \times \dfrac{1 \,\cancel{\text{mol CaO}}}{96.4 \,\cancel{\text{kcal}}} \times \dfrac{56.1 \text{ g CaO}}{1 \,\cancel{\text{mol CaO}}} = 16.0 \text{ g CaO}$

(b) $27.5 \,\cancel{\text{kcal}} \times \dfrac{1 \,\cancel{\text{mol SO}_3}}{96.4 \,\cancel{\text{kcal}}} \times \dfrac{22.4 \text{ L SO}_3}{1 \,\cancel{\text{mol SO}_3}} = 6.39 \text{ L SO}_3 \text{ at STP}$

Section 18.6 Multiple-Reaction Stoichiometry

44. $8 \, H_2S_{(aq)} + 8 \, Cl_{2(g)} \rightarrow 16 \, HCl_{(aq)} + S_{8(s)}$

$S_{8(s)} + 24 \, F_{2(g)} \rightarrow 8 \, SF_{6(g)}$

(a) $0.950 \,\cancel{\text{L Cl}_2} \times \dfrac{1 \,\cancel{\text{mol Cl}_2}}{22.4 \,\cancel{\text{L Cl}_2}} \times \dfrac{1 \,\cancel{\text{mol S}_8}}{8 \,\cancel{\text{mol Cl}_2}} \times \dfrac{8 \,\cancel{\text{mol SF}_6}}{1 \,\cancel{\text{mol S}_8}} \times \dfrac{146.1 \text{ g SF}_6}{1 \,\cancel{\text{mol SF}_6}}$

$$= 6.20 \text{ g SF}_6$$

(b) $0.950 \,\cancel{\text{L Cl}_2} \times \dfrac{1 \,\cancel{\text{L S}_8}}{8 \,\cancel{\text{L Cl}_2}} \times \dfrac{8 \text{ L SF}_6}{1 \,\cancel{\text{L S}_8}} = 0.950 \text{ L SF}_6$

(c) $0.950 \,\cancel{\text{L Cl}_2} \times \dfrac{1 \,\cancel{\text{mol Cl}_2}}{22.4 \,\cancel{\text{L Cl}_2}} \times \dfrac{8 \,\cancel{\text{mol H}_2\text{S}}}{8 \,\cancel{\text{mol Cl}_2}} \times \dfrac{1 \text{ L H}_2\text{S}}{0.0265 \,\cancel{\text{mol H}_2\text{S}}}$

$$= 1.60 \text{ L H}_2\text{S}$$

46. $3 \, Fe_2O_{3(s)} + CO_{(g)} \xrightarrow{\ 200°C\ } 2 \, Fe_3O_{4(s)} + CO_{2(g)}$

$Fe_3O_{4(s)} + CO_{(g)} \xrightarrow{\ 700°C\ } 3 \, FeO_{(s)} + CO_{2(g)}$

$FeO_{(g)} + CO_{(g)} \xrightarrow{\ 1200°C\ } Fe_{(l)} + CO_{2(g)}$

(a) $1.00 \,\cancel{\text{kg Fe}_2\text{O}_3} \times \dfrac{1000 \,\cancel{\text{g Fe}_2\text{O}_3}}{1 \,\cancel{\text{kg Fe}_2\text{O}_3}} \times \dfrac{1 \,\cancel{\text{mol Fe}_2\text{O}_3}}{159.6 \,\cancel{\text{g Fe}_2\text{O}_3}} \times \dfrac{2 \,\cancel{\text{mol Fe}_3\text{O}_4}}{3 \,\cancel{\text{mol Fe}_2\text{O}_3}} \times$

$\dfrac{3 \,\cancel{\text{mol FeO}}}{1 \,\cancel{\text{mol Fe}_3\text{O}_4}} \times \dfrac{71.8 \,\cancel{\text{g FeO}}}{1 \,\cancel{\text{mol FeO}}} \times \dfrac{1 \text{ kg FeO}}{1000 \,\cancel{\text{g FeO}}} = 0.900 \text{ kg FeO}$

(b) $1.00 \,\cancel{\text{kg Fe}_2\text{O}_3} \times \dfrac{1000 \,\cancel{\text{g Fe}_2\text{O}_3}}{1 \,\cancel{\text{kg Fe}_2\text{O}_3}} \times \dfrac{1 \,\cancel{\text{mol Fe}_2\text{O}_3}}{159.6 \,\cancel{\text{g Fe}_2\text{O}_3}} \times \dfrac{2 \,\cancel{\text{mol Fe}_3\text{O}_4}}{3 \,\cancel{\text{mol Fe}_2\text{O}_3}} \times$

$\dfrac{3 \,\cancel{\text{mol FeO}}}{1 \,\cancel{\text{mol Fe}_3\text{O}_4}} \times \dfrac{1 \,\cancel{\text{mol Fe}}}{1 \,\cancel{\text{mol FeO}}} \times \dfrac{55.8 \,\cancel{\text{g Fe}}}{1 \,\cancel{\text{mol Fe}}} \times \dfrac{1 \text{ kg Fe}}{1000 \,\cancel{\text{g Fe}}} = 0.699 \text{ kg Fe}$

(c) $1.00 \,\cancel{\text{kg Fe}_2\text{O}_3} \times \dfrac{1000 \,\cancel{\text{g Fe}_2\text{O}_3}}{1 \,\cancel{\text{kg Fe}_2\text{O}_3}} \times \dfrac{1 \,\cancel{\text{mol Fe}_2\text{O}_3}}{159.6 \,\cancel{\text{g Fe}_2\text{O}_3}} \times \dfrac{2 \,\cancel{\text{mol Fe}_3\text{O}_4}}{3 \,\cancel{\text{mol Fe}_2\text{O}_3}} \times$

$\dfrac{3 \,\cancel{\text{mol FeO}}}{1 \,\cancel{\text{mol Fe}_3\text{O}_4}} \times \dfrac{1 \,\cancel{\text{mol Fe}}}{1 \,\cancel{\text{mol FeO}}} \times \dfrac{55.8 \,\cancel{\text{g Fe}}}{1 \,\cancel{\text{mol Fe}}} \times \dfrac{1 \,\cancel{\text{kg Fe}}}{1000 \,\cancel{\text{g Fe}}} \times \dfrac{70.0 \text{ kg Fe}}{100.0 \,\cancel{\text{kg Fe}}}$

$$= 0.489 \text{ kg Fe}$$

48.　$C_3H_7OH_{(l)} + O_{2(g)} \rightarrow H_2O_{2(l)} + C_3H_6O_{(l)}$

　　　$2\,H_2O_{2(l)} + N_2H_{4(l)} \rightarrow N_{2(g)} + 4\,H_2O_{(g)}$

(a)　$50.0\ \text{mL}\ \cancel{C_3H_7OH} \times \dfrac{0.786\ \text{g}\ \cancel{C_3H_7OH}}{1\ \text{mL}\ \cancel{C_3H_7OH}} \times \dfrac{1\ \text{mol}\ \cancel{C_3H_7OH}}{60.0\ \text{g}\ \cancel{C_3H_7OH}} \times$

　　　$\dfrac{1\ \cancel{\text{mol}\ H_2O_2}}{1\ \cancel{\text{mol}\ C_3H_7OH}} \times \dfrac{1\ \cancel{\text{mol}\ N_2}}{2\ \cancel{\text{mol}\ H_2O_2}} \times \dfrac{28.0\ \text{g}\ N_2}{1\ \cancel{\text{mol}\ N_2}} = 9.17\ \text{g}\ N_2$

(b)　$50.0\ \text{mL}\ \cancel{C_3H_7OH} \times \dfrac{0.786\ \text{g}\ \cancel{C_3H_7OH}}{1\ \text{mL}\ \cancel{C_3H_7OH}} \times \dfrac{1\ \text{mol}\ \cancel{C_3H_7OH}}{60.0\ \text{g}\ \cancel{C_3H_7OH}} \times$

　　　$\dfrac{1\ \cancel{\text{mol}\ H_2O_2}}{1\ \cancel{\text{mol}\ C_3H_7OH}} \times \dfrac{1\ \cancel{\text{mol}\ N_2}}{2\ \cancel{\text{mol}\ H_2O_2}} \times \dfrac{22.4\ \text{L}\ N_2}{1\ \cancel{\text{mol}\ N_2}} = 7.34\ \text{L}\ N_2$

(c)　$50.0\ \text{mL}\ \cancel{C_3H_7OH} \times \dfrac{0.786\ \text{g}\ \cancel{C_3H_7OH}}{1\ \text{mL}\ \cancel{C_3H_7OH}} \times \dfrac{1\ \text{mol}\ \cancel{C_3H_7OH}}{60.0\ \text{g}\ \cancel{C_3H_7OH}} \times$

　　　$\dfrac{1\ \cancel{\text{mol}\ H_2O_2}}{1\ \cancel{\text{mol}\ C_3H_7OH}} \times \dfrac{4\ \cancel{\text{mol}\ H_2O}}{2\ \cancel{\text{mol}\ H_2O_2}} \times \dfrac{18.0\ \text{g}\ H_2O}{1\ \cancel{\text{mol}\ H_2O}} = 23.6\ \text{g}\ H_2O$

(d)　$50.0\ \text{mL}\ \cancel{C_3H_7OH} \times \dfrac{0.786\ \text{g}\ \cancel{C_3H_7OH}}{1\ \text{mL}\ \cancel{C_3H_7OH}} \times \dfrac{1\ \text{mol}\ \cancel{C_3H_7OH}}{60.0\ \text{g}\ \cancel{C_3H_7OH}} \times$

　　　$\dfrac{1\ \cancel{\text{mol}\ H_2O_2}}{1\ \cancel{\text{mol}\ C_3H_7OH}} \times \dfrac{4\ \cancel{\text{mol}\ H_2O}}{2\ \cancel{\text{mol}\ H_2O_2}} \times \dfrac{22.4\ \text{L}\ H_2O}{1\ \cancel{\text{mol}\ H_2O}} = 29.3\ \text{L}\ H_2O$

Section 18.7　Advanced Problem-Solving Examples

50.　$MM = \dfrac{g\,R\,T}{P\,V}$

　　　$g = 1.45\ \text{g}$

　　　$V = 1\ \text{L}$

　　　$P = 752\ \cancel{\text{mm Hg}} \times \dfrac{1.00\ \text{atm}}{760\ \cancel{\text{mm Hg}}} = 0.989\ \text{atm}$

　　　$T = 100\,°C + 273 = 373\ \text{K}$

　　　$MM = \dfrac{1.45\ \text{g} \times 373\ \cancel{K}}{0.989\ \cancel{\text{atm}} \times 1\ \cancel{L}} \times \dfrac{0.0821\ \cancel{\text{atm}} \cdot \cancel{L}}{1\ \text{mol} \cdot \cancel{K}} = 44.9\ \text{g/mol}$

52.　$100.0\ \cancel{\text{mL LiCl}} \times \dfrac{0.156\ \cancel{\text{mol LiCl}}}{1000\ \cancel{\text{mL LiCl}}} \times \dfrac{1\ \text{mol}\ Cl^-}{1\ \cancel{\text{mol LiCl}}} = 0.0156\ \text{mol}\ Cl^-$

　　　$150.0\ \cancel{\text{mL BaCl}_2} \times \dfrac{0.225\ \cancel{\text{mol BaCl}_2}}{1000\ \cancel{\text{mL BaCl}_2}} \times \dfrac{2\ \text{mol}\ Cl^-}{1\ \cancel{\text{mol BaCl}_2}} = 0.0675\ \text{mol}\ Cl^-$

　　　Molarity of Cl^-:　$\dfrac{(0.0156 + 0.0675)\ \text{mol}\ Cl^-}{(100.0 + 150.0)\ \cancel{\text{mL solution}}} \times \dfrac{1000\ \cancel{\text{mL solution}}}{1\ \text{L solution}}$

　　　　　　　　　　　　　　　　　　　　　　　　　$= 0.332\ M\ Cl^-$

54. $2 \, HCl_{(aq)} + Pb(NO_3)_{2(aq)} \rightarrow 2 \, HNO_{3(g)} + PbCl_{2(s)}$

$$1.88 \, \text{g PbCl}_2 \times \frac{1 \, \text{mol PbCl}_2}{278.2 \, \text{g PbCl}_2} \times \frac{2 \, \text{mol HCl}}{1 \, \text{mol PbCl}_2} \times \frac{1000 \, \text{mL HCl}}{0.150 \, \text{mol HCl}}$$
$$= 90.1 \, \text{mL HCl}$$

56. $V = \dfrac{n \, R \, T}{P}$

$n = 6.55 \, \text{g CO}_2 \times \dfrac{1 \, \text{mol CO}_2}{44 \, \text{g CO}_2} = 0.149 \, \text{mol CO}_2$

$T = 75°C + 273 = 348 \, K$

$P = 0.750 \, \text{atm}$

$V = \dfrac{0.149 \, \text{mol} \times 348 \, K}{0.750 \, \text{atm}} \times \dfrac{0.0821 \, \text{atm} \cdot L}{1 \, \text{mol} \cdot K} = 5.68 \, L \, CO_2$

$0.149 \, \text{mol CO}_2 \times \dfrac{6.02 \times 10^{23} \, \text{molecules CO}_2}{1 \, \text{mol CO}_2} = 8.97 \times 10^{22} \, \text{molecules CO}_2$

General Exercises

58. $12.0 \, \text{g Au} \times \dfrac{1 \, \text{mol Au}}{197.0 \, \text{g Au}} \times \dfrac{6.02 \times 10^{23} \, \text{atoms Au}}{1 \, \text{mol Au}} \times \dfrac{1 \, \text{mL seawater}}{1.22 \times 10^{10} \, \text{atoms Au}}$

$\times \dfrac{1.05 \, \text{g seawater}}{1 \, \text{mL seawater}} \times \dfrac{1 \, \text{kg seawater}}{1000 \, \text{g seawater}} = 3.16 \times 10^9 \, \text{kg seawater}$

60. $Cl_{2(g)} + 2 \, NaBr_{(aq)} \rightarrow Br_{2(l)} + 2 \, NaCl_{(aq)}$

$10.0 \, \text{g Cl}_2 \times \dfrac{1 \, \text{mol Cl}_2}{71.0 \, \text{g Cl}_2} \times \dfrac{1 \, \text{mol Br}_2}{1 \, \text{mol Cl}_2} \times \dfrac{159.8 \, \text{g Br}_2}{1 \, \text{mol Br}_2} \times \dfrac{1 \, \text{mL Br}_2}{3.12 \, \text{g Br}_2}$
$= 7.21 \, \text{mL Br}_2$

$10.0 \, \text{g NaBr} \times \dfrac{1 \, \text{mol NaBr}}{102.9 \, \text{g NaBr}} \times \dfrac{1 \, \text{mol Br}_2}{2 \, \text{mol NaBr}} \times \dfrac{159.8 \, \text{g Br}_2}{1 \, \text{mol Br}_2} \times \dfrac{1 \, \text{mL Br}_2}{3.12 \, \text{g Br}_2}$
$= 2.49 \, \text{mL Br}_2$

Since NaBr is the limiting reactant, 2.49 mL Br_2 are produced.

62. $2 \, KClO_{3(s)} \xrightarrow{\text{MnO}_2} 2 \, KCl_{(s)} + 3 \, O_{2(g)}$

$P_{total} = P_{oxygen} + P_{water \, vapor}$

$P_{oxygen} = P_{total} - P_{water \, vapor}$

$P_{oxygen} = 766 \, \text{mm Hg} - 21.1 \, \text{mm Hg} = 745 \, \text{mm Hg}$

$n = \dfrac{P \, V}{R \, T}$

$P = 745 \, \text{mm Hg} \times \dfrac{1.00 \, \text{atm}}{760 \, \text{mm Hg}} = 0.980 \, \text{atm}$

$V = 455 \, \text{mL} = 0.455 \, L$

$T = 23.0°C + 273 = 296 \, K$

62. $n = \dfrac{0.980\ \cancel{atm} \times 0.455\ \cancel{L}}{296\ \cancel{K}} \times \dfrac{1\ mol \cdot \cancel{K}}{0.0821\ \cancel{atm} \cdot \cancel{L}} = 0.0183\ mol\ O_2$

$0.0183\ \cancel{mol\ O_2} \times \dfrac{2\ \cancel{mol\ KClO_3}}{3\ \cancel{mol\ O_2}} \times \dfrac{122.6\ g\ KClO_3}{1\ \cancel{mol\ KClO_3}} = 1.50\ g\ KClO_3$

64.   (a) $\Delta H = \dfrac{90.3\ \cancel{kcal}}{mol\ NO} \times \dfrac{4.184\ kJ}{1\ \cancel{kcal}} = \dfrac{378\ kJ}{mol\ NO}$

     (b) $\Delta H = \dfrac{1209\ \cancel{kcal}}{mol\ SF_6} \times \dfrac{4.184\ kJ}{1\ \cancel{kcal}} = \dfrac{5058\ kJ}{mol\ SF_6}$

     (c) $\Delta H = \dfrac{-90.8\ \cancel{kcal}}{mol\ HgO} \times \dfrac{4.184\ kJ}{1\ \cancel{kcal}} = \dfrac{-380\ kJ}{mol\ HgO}$

     (d) $\Delta H = \dfrac{-124.4\ \cancel{kcal}}{mol\ AgNO_3} \times \dfrac{4.184\ kJ}{1\ \cancel{kcal}} = \dfrac{-520.5\ kJ}{mol\ AgNO_3}$

66. $BaCl_{2(s)} + 2\ AgNO_{3(aq)} \rightarrow 2\ AgCl_{(s)} + Ba(NO_3)_{2(aq)}$

    $2\ AgNO_{3(aq)} + K_2CrO_{4(aq)} \rightarrow Ag_2CrO_{4(s)} + KNO_{3(aq)}$

Total moles of $AgNO_3$:

$50.0\ \cancel{mL\ AgNO_3} \times \dfrac{0.100\ mol\ AgNO_3}{1000\ \cancel{mL\ AgNO_3}} = 0.00500\ mol\ AgNO_3$

Moles of $AgNO_3$ that reacted with K_2CrO_4:

$17.0\ \cancel{mL\ K_2CrO_4} \times \dfrac{0.125\ \cancel{mol\ K_2CrO_4}}{1000\ \cancel{mL\ K_2CrO_4}} \times \dfrac{2\ mol\ AgNO_3}{1\ \cancel{mol\ K_2CrO_4}}$

$= 0.00425\ mol\ AgNO_3$

Moles of $AgNO_3$ that reacted with $BaCl_2$:

$0.00500\ mol - 0.00425\ mol = 0.00075\ mol\ AgNO_3$

Mass of $BaCl_2$:

$0.00075\ \cancel{mol\ AgNO_3} \times \dfrac{1\ \cancel{mol\ BaCl_2}}{2\ \cancel{mol\ AgNO_3}} \times \dfrac{208.3\ g\ BaCl_2}{1\ \cancel{mol\ BaCl_2}} = 0.078\ g\ BaCl_2$

CHAPTER 19 Nuclear Chemistry

Section 19.1 Natural Radioactivity

2.
	Electrode	Radiation
(a)	positive	beta particles
(b)	negative	alpha particles

4. Gamma rays (γ) are a form of radiant light energy.

6. Gamma rays (γ) are not affected by an electric field.

8. Alpha particles (α) are emitted from the nucleus at ~ 10% the velocity of light.

10. Gamma rays (γ) require thick lead or concrete as minimum shielding and can pass through the human body.

12. Beta particles (β) require several centimeters of wood or aluminum as shielding and can penetrate about 1 cm of human flesh.

Section 19.2 Nuclear Equations

14.
	Particle	Approximate Mass	Relative Charge
(a)	γ	0	0
(b)	n°	1	0
(c)	β^-	0	-1
(d)	β^+	0	$+1$
(e)	α	4	$+2$
(f)	p^+	1	$+1$

16.
(a) $^{160}_{74}\text{W} \rightarrow \,^{156}_{72}\text{Hf} + \,^{4}_{2}\text{He}$

(b) $^{32}_{15}\text{P} \rightarrow \,^{32}_{16}\text{S} + \,^{0}_{-1}\text{e}$

(c) $^{15}_{8}\text{O} \rightarrow \,^{15}_{7}\text{N} + \,^{0}_{+1}\text{e}$

(d) $^{56}_{26}\text{Fe} + \,^{0}_{-1}\text{e} \rightarrow \,^{55}_{25}\text{Mn}$

18.

(a) $\quad ^{222}_{90}X \rightarrow \ ^{218}_{88}Ra + \ ^{4}_{2}He$

(b) $\quad ^{56}_{25}X \rightarrow \ ^{56}_{26}Fe + \ ^{0}_{-1}e$

(c) $\quad ^{73}_{36}X \rightarrow \ ^{73}_{35}Br + \ ^{0}_{+1}e$

(d) $\quad ^{133}_{56}X + \ ^{0}_{-1}e \rightarrow \ ^{133}_{55}Cs$

Answer

$^{222}_{90}X = \ ^{222}_{90}Th$

$^{56}_{25}X = \ ^{56}_{25}Mn$

$^{73}_{36}X = \ ^{73}_{36}Kr$

$^{133}_{56}X = \ ^{133}_{56}Ba$

Section 19.3 Radioactive Decay Series

20. $\quad ^{238}_{92}U \rightarrow \ ^{234}_{90}Th + \ ^{4}_{2}He$

$^{234}_{90}Th \rightarrow \ ^{234}_{91}Pa + \ ^{0}_{-1}e$

The isotope is: $^{234}_{91}Pa$

22. $\quad ^{235}_{92}U \rightarrow \ ^{231}_{90}Th + \ ^{4}_{2}He$

$^{231}_{90}Th \rightarrow \ ^{231}_{91}Pa + \ ^{0}_{-1}e$

The isotope is: $^{231}_{91}Pa$

24. $\quad ^{232}_{90}Th \rightarrow \ ^{228}_{88}Ra + \ ^{4}_{2}He$

$^{228}_{88}Ra \rightarrow \ ^{228}_{89}Ac + \ ^{0}_{-1}e$

The isotope is: $^{228}_{89}Ac$

26. $\quad$ <u>Decay Series for Neptunium-237</u>

$^{237}_{93}Np \xrightarrow{\ \alpha\ } \ ^{233}_{91}Pa \xrightarrow{\ \beta\ } \ ^{233}_{92}U$
$\qquad\qquad\qquad\qquad\qquad\qquad \downarrow \alpha$

$^{225}_{89}Ac \xleftarrow{\ \beta\ } \ ^{225}_{88}Ra \xleftarrow{\ \alpha\ } \ ^{229}_{90}Th$
$\alpha \downarrow$

$^{221}_{87}Fr \xrightarrow{\ \alpha\ } \ ^{217}_{85}At \xrightarrow{\ \alpha\ } \ ^{213}_{83}Bi$
$\qquad\qquad\qquad\qquad\qquad\qquad \downarrow \beta$

$^{209}_{83}Bi \xleftarrow{\ \beta\ } \ ^{209}_{82}Pb \xleftarrow{\ \alpha\ } \ ^{213}_{84}Po$

<u>Answers</u>

(a) $^{233}_{91}Pa$ (b) $^{233}_{92}U$

(c) $^{229}_{90}Th$ (d) $^{225}_{88}Ra$

(e) $^{225}_{89}Ac$ (f) α

(g) α (h) β

(i) α (j) β

Section 19.4 Radioactive Half-Life

28. $\quad$ Alpha, beta, and gamma radiation fog photographic film.

30. $\quad 100\% \times \dfrac{1}{2} \times \dfrac{1}{2} \times \dfrac{1}{2} = 12.5\%$

12.5% of a given radioactive isotope remains after three-lives.

32. $20\ t_{1/2} \times \dfrac{28.8\ \text{years}}{1\ t_{1/2}} = 576\ \text{years}$

34. | Activity(dpm) | Elapsed Time $(t_{1/2})$ |
     | --- | --- |
     | 240 | 0 |
     | 120 | 1 |
     | 60 | 2 |

$2\ t_{1/2} \times \dfrac{5730\ \text{years}}{1\ t_{1/2}} \approx 11{,}500\ \text{years old}$

36. $24\ \text{hours} \times \dfrac{1\ t_{1/2}}{6\ \text{hours}} = 4\ t_{1/2}$

$160\ \text{mg Tc-99} \times \dfrac{1}{2} \times \dfrac{1}{2} \times \dfrac{1}{2} \times \dfrac{1}{2} = 10\ \text{mg Tc-99}$

38. | Activity(dpm) | Elapsed Time $(t_{1/2})$ |
     | --- | --- |
     | 200 | 0 |
     | 100 | 1 |
     | 50 | 2 |
     | 25 | 3 |

$3\ t_{1/2} \times \dfrac{45\ \text{days}}{1\ t_{1/2}} = 135\ \text{days}$

40. | Activity(dpm) | Elapsed Time $(t_{1/2})$ |
     | --- | --- |
     | 2400 | 0 |
     | 1200 | 1 |
     | 600 | 2 |

$\text{half-life} \times 2\ t_{1/2} = 24.8\ \text{years}$

$\text{half-life} = \dfrac{24.8\ \text{years}}{2\ t_{1/2}} = \dfrac{12.4\ \text{years}}{1\ t_{1/2}}$

Section 19.5 Applications of Radioisotopes

42. It must be assumed that the amount of $^{14}CO_2$ has remained constant when using radiocarbon dating.

44. Both carbon-14 and hydrogen-3 can be used in research to trace the pathway in a series of chemical reactions.

46. The β-emitting radioisotope iron-59 can be used to diagnose anemia by attaching to a hemoglobin molecule.

48. The γ-emitting radioisotope xenon-131 can be used to diagnose the respiratory system and locate inactive lung tissue.

50. The γ-emitting radioisotope cobalt-60 can be used for radiation therapy. It is also used to sterilize male insects for agricultural pest control.

52. Radioimmunoassay (RIA) uses a radioisotope to selectively bind with a biologically active compound.

Section 19.6 Artificial Radioactivity

54. $^{6}_{3}\text{Li} + ^{1}_{0}\text{n} \rightarrow ^{3}_{1}\text{H} + ^{4}_{2}\text{He}$ The radioisotope is $^{3}_{1}\text{H}$

56. $^{23}_{11}\text{Na} + ^{1}_{1}\text{H} \rightarrow ^{23}_{12}\text{Mg} + ^{1}_{0}\text{n}$ The radioisotope is $^{23}_{12}\text{Mg}$

58. $^{81}_{35}\text{Br} + ^{0}_{0}\gamma \rightarrow ^{80}_{35}\text{Br} + ^{1}_{0}\text{n}$ The radioisotope is $^{80}_{35}\text{Br}$

60. $^{59}_{27}\text{Co} + ^{1}_{0}\text{n} \rightarrow ^{56}_{25}\text{Mn} + ^{4}_{2}\text{He}$ The target material is $^{59}_{27}\text{Co}$

62. $^{130}_{52}\text{Te} + ^{2}_{1}\text{H} \rightarrow ^{131}_{53}\text{I} + ^{1}_{0}\text{n}$ The target material is $^{130}_{52}\text{Te}$

64. $^{238}_{92}\text{U} + ^{2}_{1}\text{H} \rightarrow ^{238}_{94}\text{Pu} + ^{0}_{-1}\text{e} + 2\,^{1}_{0}\text{n}$ The target material is $^{238}_{92}\text{U}$

66. The Americans created $^{260}_{105}\text{Ha}$

68. $^{54}_{24}\text{Cr} + ^{209}_{83}\text{Bi} \rightarrow ^{1}_{0}\text{n} + ^{262}_{107}\text{Uns}$ The Germans created $^{262}_{107}\text{Uns}$

70. $^{200}_{80}\text{Hg} + ^{1}_{0}\text{n} \rightarrow ^{0}_{0}\gamma + ^{201}_{80}\text{Hg}$

Section 19.7 Nuclear Fission

72. $^{1}_{0}\text{n} \xrightarrow{\text{1st}} 3\,^{1}_{0}\text{n} \xrightarrow{\text{2nd}} 9\,^{1}_{0}\text{n} \xrightarrow{\text{3rd}} 27\,^{1}_{0}\text{n}$
    After the third step, 27 neutrons are produced.

74. Uranium must be enriched before it can be used in the fuel rods of a nuclear reactor because naturally occurring uranium contains only 0.7% fissionable U-235. Uranium-235 is necessary to obtain a chain reaction.

76. $^{235}_{92}\text{U} + ^{1}_{0}\text{n} \rightarrow ^{142}_{56}\text{Ba} + ^{91}_{36}\text{Kr} + 3\,^{1}_{0}\text{n}$
    This fission reaction produces three neutrons.

78. $^{239}_{94}\text{Pu} + ^{1}_{0}\text{n} \rightarrow ^{142}_{57}\text{La} + ^{94}_{37}\text{Rb} + 4\,^{1}_{0}\text{n}$

This fission reaction produces four neutrons.

80. $^{233}_{92}\text{U} + ^{1}_{0}\text{n} \rightarrow ^{142}_{54}\text{Xe} + ^{90}_{38}\text{Sr} + 2\,^{1}_{0}\text{n}$

Uranium-233 undergoes fission to give xenon-142, strontium-90, and two neutrons.

Section 19.8 Mass Defect and Binding Energy

82. Tritium has one proton and two neutrons

$1(1.0073 \text{ amu}) + 2(1.0087 \text{ amu}) = 3.0247 \text{ amu}$

Mass defect: $3.0247 \text{ amu} - 3.0155 \text{ amu} = 0.0092 \text{ amu}$

84. Lithium-6 has three protons and three neutrons

$3(1.0073 \text{ amu}) + 3(1.0087 \text{ amu}) = 6.0480 \text{ amu}$

Mass defect: $6.0480 \text{ amu} - 6.0151 \text{ amu} = 0.0329 \text{ amu}$

86. Beryllium-8 has four protons and four neutrons

$4(1.0073 \text{ amu}) + 4(1.0087 \text{ amu}) = 8.0640 \text{ amu}$

Mass defect: $8.0640 \text{ amu} - 8.0053 \text{ amu} = 0.0587 \text{ amu}$

Binding energy:

$E = mc^2$

$$E = \frac{0.0587 \text{ g}}{1 \text{ mol}} \times \frac{1 \text{ kg}}{1000 \text{ g}} \times \left(\frac{3.00 \times 10^8 \text{ m}}{\text{s}}\right)^2 = 5.28 \times 10^{12} \text{ J/mol}$$

88. Carbon-13 has six protons and seven neutrons

$6(1.0073 \text{ amu}) + 7(1.0087 \text{ amu}) = 13.1047 \text{ amu}$

Mass defect: $13.1047 \text{ amu} - 13.0034 \text{ amu} = 0.1013 \text{ amu}$

Binding energy:

$E = mc^2$

$$E = \frac{0.1013 \text{ g}}{1 \text{ mol}} \times \frac{1 \text{ kg}}{1000 \text{ g}} \times \left(\frac{3.00 \times 10^8 \text{ m}}{\text{s}}\right)^2 = 9.12 \times 10^{12} \text{ J/mol}$$

90. Oxygen-16 has eight protons and eight neutrons

$8(1.0073 \text{ amu}) + 8(1.0087 \text{ amu}) = 16.1280 \text{ amu}$

Mass defect: $16.1280 \text{ amu} - 15.9949 \text{ amu} = 0.1331 \text{ amu}$

Binding energy:

$E = mc^2$

$$E = \frac{0.1331 \text{ g}}{1 \text{ mol}} \times \frac{1 \text{ kg}}{1000 \text{ g}} \times \left(\frac{3.00 \times 10^8 \text{ m}}{\text{s}}\right)^2 = 1.20 \times 10^{13} \text{ J/mol}$$

92. Neon-20 has ten protons and ten neutrons
$$10(1.0073 \text{ amu}) + 10(1.0087 \text{ amu}) = 20.1600 \text{ amu}$$

Mass defect: $20.1600 \text{ amu} - 19.9924 \text{ amu} = 0.1676 \text{ amu}$

Binding energy:
$$E = mc^2$$
$$E = \frac{0.1676 \text{ g}}{1 \text{ mol}} \times \frac{1 \text{ kg}}{1000 \text{ g}} \times \left(\frac{3.00 \times 10^8 \text{ m}}{\text{s}}\right)^2 = 1.51 \times 10^{13} \text{ J/mol}$$

Section 19.9 Nuclear Fusion

94. $$^{2}_{1}\text{H} + ^{3}_{1}\text{X} \rightarrow ^{4}_{2}\text{He} + ^{1}_{0}\text{n}$$ Particle X $= ^{3}_{1}\text{H}$

96. $$^{3}_{2}\text{He} + ^{1}_{1}\text{X} \rightarrow ^{4}_{2}\text{He} + ^{0}_{+1}\text{e}$$ Particle X $= ^{1}_{1}\text{H}$

98. $$^{7}_{3}\text{Li} + ^{2}_{1}\text{X} \rightarrow 2\,^{4}_{2}\text{He} + ^{1}_{0}\text{n}$$ Particle X $= ^{2}_{1}\text{H}$

Section 19.10 Nuclear Reactors and Power Plants

100. Only 3% of the uranium in a fission reactor is U-235. In an atomic bomb, the percentage of U-235 is much higher.

102. In addition to absorbing heat, D_2O moderates the reaction in the core of heavy water reactors by slowing neutrons.

104. $$^{232}_{90}\text{Th} + ^{1}_{0}\text{n} \rightarrow ^{233}_{90}\text{Th}$$
$$^{233}_{90}\text{Th} \rightarrow ^{233}_{89}\text{Ac} + ^{0}_{-1}\text{e}$$
$$^{233}_{89}\text{Ac} \rightarrow ^{233}_{88}\text{Ra} + ^{0}_{-1}\text{e}$$ $^{233}_{88}\text{Ra}$ is the fissionable isotope.

106. Two possible types of environmental pollution from a nuclear power plant are:
    (1) Accidental releases of radiation
    (2) Highly radioactive spent fuel rods

General Exercises

108. $$^{137}_{53}\text{I} \rightarrow ^{0}_{-1}\text{e} + ^{1}_{0}\text{n} + ^{136}_{54}\text{Xe}$$

110. Since Pb-206 and U-238 are present in equal proportions, one half life has expired. Thus, the approximate age of the lunar rocks is 4.5 billion years old.

112. $^{241}_{95}\text{Am} \rightarrow ^{4}_{2}\text{He} + ^{237}_{93}\text{Np}$ 　　　　　　　　The radioisotope is $^{241}_{95}\text{Am}$

114. $^{238}_{92}\text{U} + 15\,^{1}_{0}\text{n} \rightarrow ^{253}_{99}\text{Es} + 7\,^{0}_{-1}\text{e}$
15 neutrons are needed to balance the reaction.

116. $^{253}_{99}\text{Es} + ^{4}_{2}\text{He} \rightarrow ^{1}_{0}\text{n} + ^{256}_{101}\text{Md}$ 　　The new isotope produced is $^{256}_{101}\text{Md}$

118. $^{198}_{78}\text{Pt} + ^{2}_{1}\text{H} \rightarrow ^{199}_{78}\text{Pt} + ^{1}_{1}\text{H}$
$^{199}_{78}\text{Pt} \rightarrow ^{0}_{-1}\text{e} + ^{199}_{79}\text{Au}$ 　　　　　The isotope that results is $^{199}_{79}\text{Au}$

120. $^{2}_{1}\text{H} + ^{3}_{1}\text{H} \rightarrow ^{4}_{2}\text{He} + ^{1}_{0}\text{X} + \text{energy}$ 　　　Particle X $= ^{1}_{0}\text{n}$

CHAPTER 20

Organic Chemistry

Section 20.1 Hydrocarbons

2.   Approximately 7 million organic compounds have been identified.

4.   A hydrocarbon contains only hydrogen and carbon atoms. On the other hand, a hydrocarbon derivative is a hydrocarbon in which one or more hydrogen atoms have been replaced by other atoms or groups of atoms.

6.
	Hydrocarbon	Bond Type
(a)	alkanes	single covalent
(b)	alkenes	double covalent
(c)	alkynes	triple covalent

Section 20.1 Alkanes

8.
	Number of H Atoms	Formula
(a)	H = 2(12) + 2 = 26	$C_{12}H_{26}$
(b)	H = 2(2) + 2 = 6	C_2H_6

10.
	Alkane	Condensed Structural Formula
(a)	pentane	$CH_3CH_2CH_2CH_2CH_3$
(b)	heptane	$CH_3CH_2CH_2CH_2CH_2CH_2CH_3$
(c)	propane	$CH_3CH_2CH_3$
(d)	nonane	$CH_3CH_2CH_2CH_2CH_2CH_2CH_2CH_2CH_3$

12. <u>Five Isomers of Hexane (C_6H_{14})</u>

$$CH_3 - CH_2 - CH_2 - CH_2 - CH_2 - CH_3$$

$$\begin{array}{c} \overset{\displaystyle CH_3}{|} \\ CH_3 - CH - CH_2 - CH_2 - CH_3 \end{array}$$

$$\begin{array}{c} \overset{\displaystyle CH_3}{|} \\ CH_3 - CH_2 - CH - CH_2 - CH_3 \end{array}$$

$$\begin{array}{c} \overset{\displaystyle CH_3}{|} \;\; \overset{\displaystyle CH_3}{|} \\ CH_3 - CH - CH - CH_3 \end{array}$$

$$\begin{array}{c} \overset{\displaystyle CH_3}{|} \\ CH_3 - C - CH_2 - CH_3 \\ \underset{\displaystyle CH_3}{|} \end{array}$$

14. <u>Four Isomers of Dibromopropane ($C_3H_6Br_2$)</u>

$$\begin{array}{c} \text{Br} \;\; \text{H} \;\; \text{H} \\ |\;\;\;\; |\;\;\;\; | \\ \text{H} - \text{C} - \text{C} - \text{C} - \text{H} \\ |\;\;\;\; |\;\;\;\; | \\ \text{Br} \;\; \text{H} \;\; \text{H} \end{array} \qquad \begin{array}{c} \text{H} \;\; \text{Br} \;\; \text{H} \\ |\;\;\;\; |\;\;\;\; | \\ \text{H} - \text{C} - \text{C} - \text{C} - \text{H} \\ |\;\;\;\; |\;\;\;\; | \\ \text{H} \;\; \text{Br} \;\; \text{H} \end{array}$$

$$\begin{array}{c} \text{Br} \;\; \text{Br} \;\; \text{H} \\ |\;\;\;\; |\;\;\;\; | \\ \text{H} - \text{C} - \text{C} - \text{C} - \text{H} \\ |\;\;\;\; |\;\;\;\; | \\ \text{H} \;\; \text{H} \;\; \text{H} \end{array} \qquad \begin{array}{c} \text{H} \;\; \text{H} \;\; \text{H} \\ |\;\;\;\; |\;\;\;\; | \\ \text{Br} - \text{C} - \text{C} - \text{C} - \text{Br} \\ |\;\;\;\; |\;\;\;\; | \\ \text{H} \;\; \text{H} \;\; \text{H} \end{array}$$

16. The shape of pentane is such that it has a longer continuous carbon chain than 2,2-dimethylpropane. The longer carbon chain causes the dispersion forces in pentane to be greater than the forces in 2,2-dimethylpropane. Thus, pentane has a higher boiling than 2,2-dimethylpropane.

18. (a) isopropyl

$$\begin{array}{c} CH_3 - \overset{\displaystyle |}{C} - CH_3 \\ \underset{\displaystyle H}{|} \end{array}$$

(b) phenyl

20. (a) 2-methylpropane

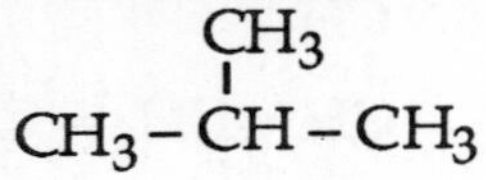

$$CH_3$$
$$|$$
$$CH_3 - CH - CH_3$$

(b) 2,2-dimethylbutane

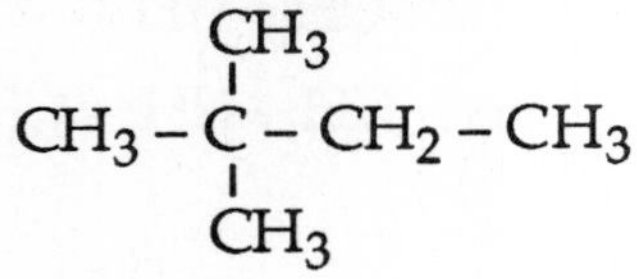

$$CH_3$$
$$|$$
$$CH_3 - C - CH_2 - CH_3$$
$$|$$
$$CH_3$$

(c) 3-ethylheptane

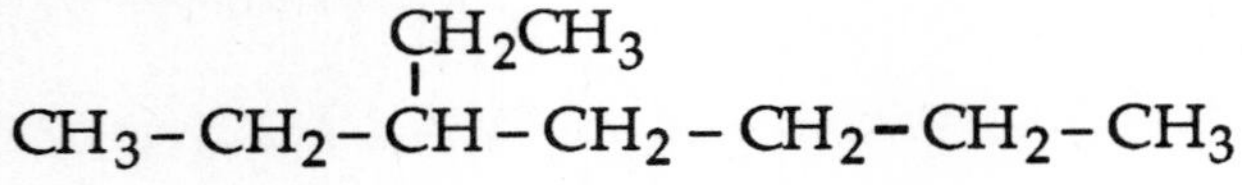

$$CH_2CH_3$$
$$|$$
$$CH_3 - CH_2 - CH - CH_2 - CH_2 - CH_2 - CH_3$$

(d) 3,3-diethylpentane

$$CH_2CH_3$$
$$|$$
$$CH_3 - CH_2 - C - CH_2 - CH_3$$
$$|$$
$$CH_2CH_3$$

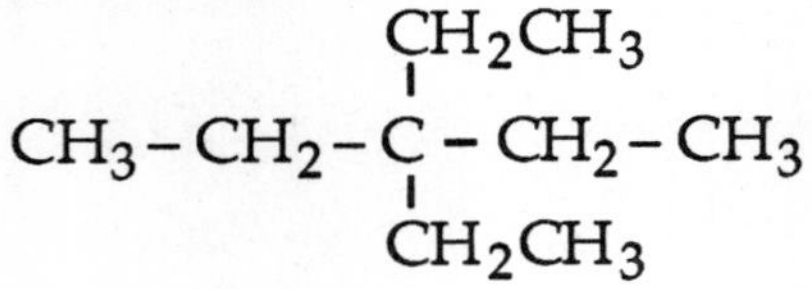

(e) 2-methyl-3-ethylhexane

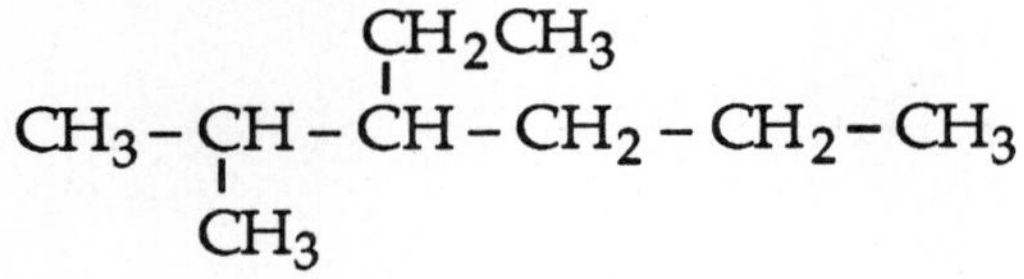

$$CH_2CH_3$$
$$|$$
$$CH_3 - CH - CH - CH_2 - CH_2 - CH_3$$
$$|$$
$$CH_3$$

(f) 2,4-dimethyl-3-ethylhexane

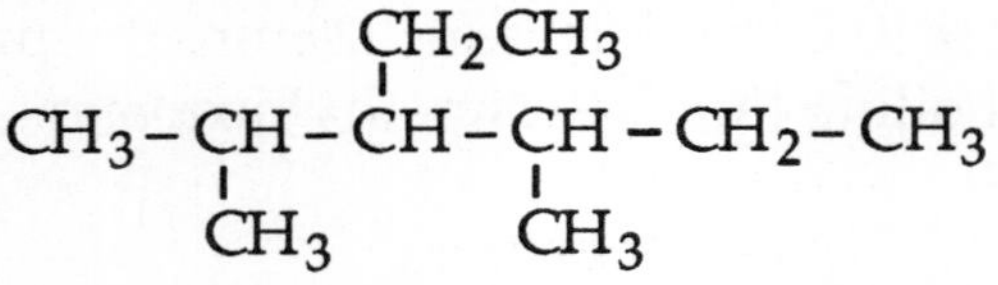

$$CH_2 CH_3$$
$$|$$
$$CH_3 - CH - CH - CH - CH_2 - CH_3$$
$$|\qquad\quad|$$
$$CH_3\qquad CH_3$$

22. When a hydrocarbon undergoes complete reaction with limited oxygen, the two principal products are CO and H_2O.

24. (a) $C_3H_8 + 5\,O_2 \rightarrow 3\,CO_2 + 4\,H_2O$

(b) $C_7H_{16} + 11\,O_2 \rightarrow 7\,CO_2 + 8\,H_2O$

(c) $2\,C_4H_{10} + 13\,O_2 \rightarrow 8\,CO_2 + 10\,H_2O$

(d) $2\,C_8H_{18} + 25\,O_2 \rightarrow 16\,CO_2 + 18\,H_2O$

26. UV light can initiate the halogenation of an alkane.

28. (a) $C_3H_8 + Cl_2 \xrightarrow{UV} C_3H_7Cl + HCl$

     (b) $C_4H_{10} + Cl_2 \xrightarrow{UV} C_4H_9Cl + HCl$

Section 20.3 Alkenes and Alkynes

30.
	Number of H Atoms	Formula
(a)	H = 2(12) = 24	$C_{12}H_{24}$
(b)	H = 2(20) = 40	$C_{20}H_{40}$

32.
	Alkene	Condensed Structural Formula
(a)	2-pentene	$CH_3CH{=}CHCH_2CH_3$
(b)	3-heptene	$CH_3CH_2CH{=}CHCH_2CH_2CH_3$
(c)	1-propene	$CH_2{=}CHCH_3$
(d)	4-nonene	$CH_3CH_2CH_2CH{=}CHCH_2CH_2CH_2CH_3$

34.
	Number of H Atoms	Formula
(a)	H = 2(12) – 2 = 22	$C_{12}H_{22}$
(b)	H = 2(20) – 2 = 38	$C_{20}H_{38}$

36.
	Alkyne	Condensed Structural Formula
(a)	1-propyne	$CH{\equiv}CCH_3$
(b)	4-octyne	$CH_3CH_2CH_2C{\equiv}CCH_2CH_2CH_3$
(c)	2-butyne	$CH_3C{\equiv}CCH_3$
(d)	3-decyne	$CH_3CH_2C{\equiv}CCH_2CH_2CH_2CH_2CH_2CH_3$

38. Two Structural Isomers of Difluoroethylene ($C_2H_2F_2$)
     $CHF{=}CHF$ and $CH_2{=}CF_2$

40. Two Geometric Isomers of Difluoroethylene ($C_2H_2F_2$)

cis   trans

42.
	Isomer	Chemical Properties
(a)	structural isomers	different
(b)	geometric isomers	different

44. (a) 2-methyl-1-propene

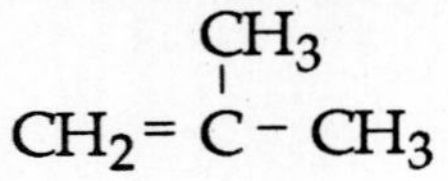

$$CH_2 = \overset{\overset{\textstyle CH_3}{|}}{C} - CH_3$$

(b) 3,3-dimethyl-1-butyne

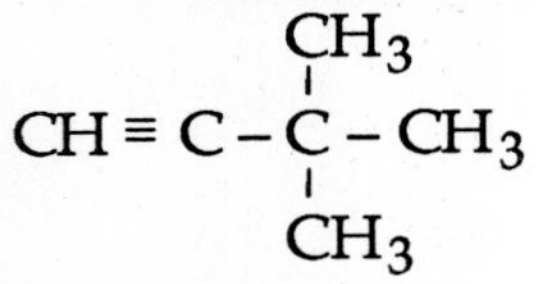

$$CH \equiv C - \overset{\overset{\textstyle CH_3}{|}}{\underset{\underset{\textstyle CH_3}{|}}{C}} - CH_3$$

(c) 3-ethyl-2-heptene

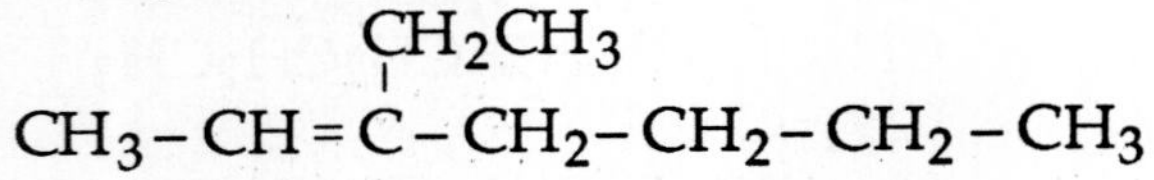

$$CH_3 - CH = \overset{\overset{\textstyle CH_2CH_3}{|}}{C} - CH_2 - CH_2 - CH_2 - CH_3$$

(d) 4,4-dimethyl-2-pentyne

$$CH_3 - C \equiv C - \overset{\overset{\textstyle CH_3}{|}}{\underset{\underset{\textstyle CH_3}{|}}{C}} - CH_3$$

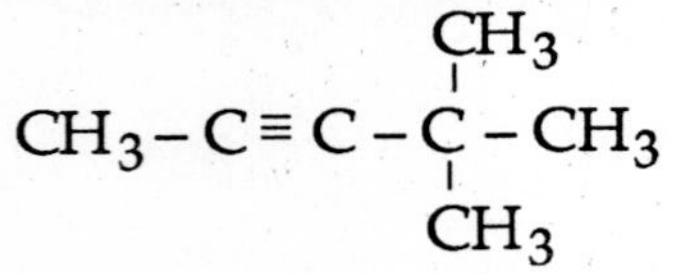

(e) 2-methyl-3-ethyl-2-hexene

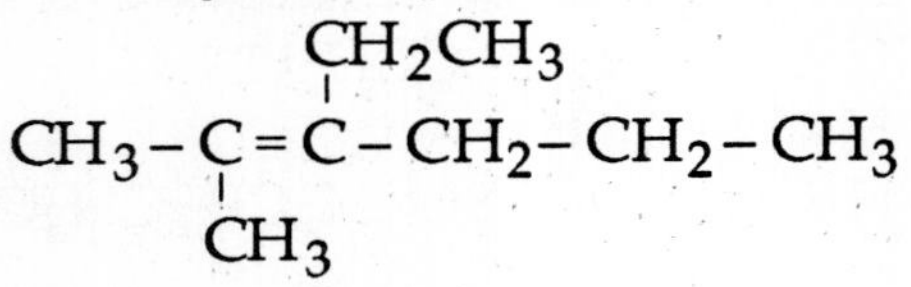

$$CH_3 - \overset{}{\underset{\underset{\textstyle CH_3}{|}}{C}} = \overset{\overset{\textstyle CH_2CH_3}{|}}{C} - CH_2 - CH_2 - CH_3$$

(f) 4-ethyl-5-methyl-2-hexyne

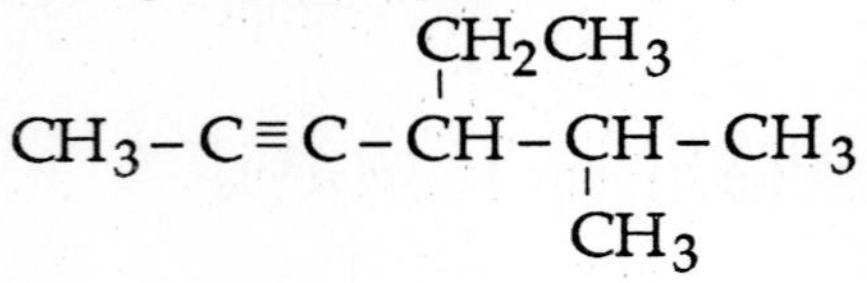

$$CH_3 - C \equiv C - CH - \overset{\overset{\textstyle CH_2CH_3}{|}}{\underset{\underset{\textstyle CH_3}{|}}{CH}} - CH_3$$

46. No, UV light is not necessary to initiate the halogenation of an alkene.

48. (a) $CH \equiv CCH_3 + 4 O_2 \rightarrow 3 CO_2 + 2 H_2O$

(b) $HC \equiv CCH_3 + 2 Cl_2 \rightarrow HCCl_2 - CCl_2CH_3$

(c) $CH_3C \equiv CCH_3 + 1 Br_2 \rightarrow CH_3BrC = CBrCH_3$

(d) $CH_3C \equiv CCH_3 + 2 Br_2 \rightarrow CH_3CBr_2 - CBr_2CH_3$

Section 20.4 Aromatic Hydrocarbons

50. Delocalized Structure of Benzene (C_6H_6)

52. Three Isomers of Xylene [$C_6H_4(CH_3)_2$]

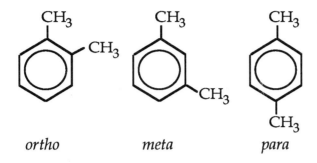

| *ortho* | *meta* | *para* |

Section 20.5 Hydrocarbon Derivatives

54.

General Formula	Derivative
(a) $R-\overset{\overset{\text{O}}{\|}}{C}-OH$	carboxylic acid
(b) $R-\overset{\overset{\text{O}}{\|}}{C}-H$	aldehyde
(c) $R-\overset{\overset{\text{O}}{\|}}{C}-R'$	ketone
(d) $R-\overset{\overset{\text{O}}{\|}}{C}-NH_2$	amide
(e) $R-\overset{\overset{\text{O}}{\|}}{C}-O-R'$	ester

56.

Compound	Class
(a) CH_3-OH	alcohol
(b) $CH_3CH_2-O-CH_2CH_3$	ether
(c) $CH_3-\overset{\overset{\text{O}}{\|}}{C}-NH_2$	amide

56.

Compound	Class
(d) $CH_3-\overset{\overset{\displaystyle O}{\|\|}}{C}-CH_2CH_3$	ketone
(e) $CH_3-\overset{\overset{\displaystyle O}{\|\|}}{C}-O-$ ◯	ester
(f) CH_3- ◯ $-OH$	phenol
(g) ◯ $-Cl$	organic halide
(h) ◯ $-CH_2-OH$	alcohol

Section 20.6 Organic Halides

58.

Organic Halide	IUPAC Name
(a) CH_2I_2	diiodomethane
(b) CH_3CHBr_2	1,1-dibromoethane
(c) $CH_3CH_2CF_3$	1,1,1-trifluoropropane
(d) $(CH_3)_2CHCl$	2-chloropropane

60.

Organic Halide	Structure
(a) dichloromethane	CH_2Cl_2
(b) iodoethane	CH_3-CH_2-I
(c) propyl fluoride	$CH_3-CH_2-CH_2-F$
(d) isopropyl bromide	$CH_3-\overset{\overset{\displaystyle Br}{\|}}{CH}-CH_3$

62. trichloroethylene

$$\overset{Cl}{\underset{H}{}}C=C\overset{Cl}{\underset{Cl}{}}$$

64.   <u>Boiling Points of Organic Halides Compared With:</u>
   (a)   alcohols: lower than
   (b)   hydrocarbons: similar to

Section 20.7 Alcohols, Phenols, and Ethers

66.   <u>Alcohol</u>   <u>Structure</u>
   (a)   ethyl alcohol $CH_3 - CH_2 - OH$
   (b)   isopropyl alcohol $CH_3 - CH(OH) - CH_3$
   (c)   butyl alcohol $CH_3 - CH_2 - CH_2 - CH_2 - OH$

   (d)   phenyl methyl alcohol $- CH_2 - OH$

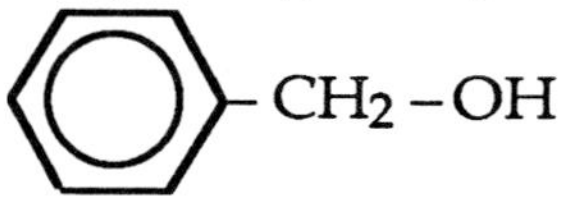

68.   <u>Phenol</u>   <u>Structure</u>

   (a)   *ortho*-chlorophenol

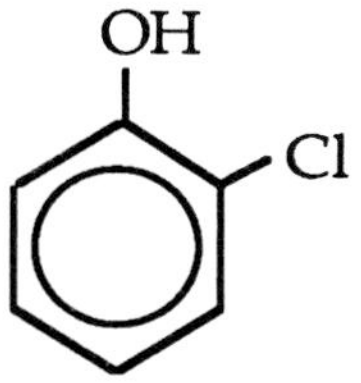

   (b)   *meta*-ethylphenol

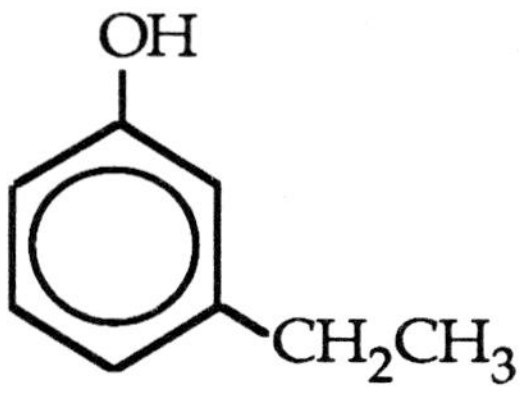

70.   <u>Ether</u>   <u>Structure</u>
   (a)   diisopropyl ether

   (b)   ethyl propyl ether $CH_3 - CH_2 - O - CH_2 - CH_2 - CH_3$

   (c)   diphenyl ether

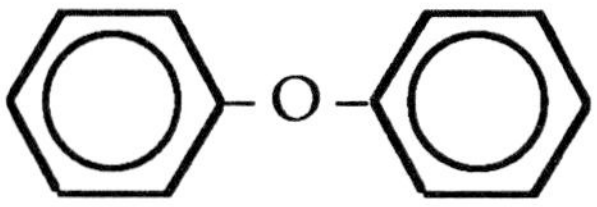

   (d)   methyl phenyl ether $CH_3 - O -$

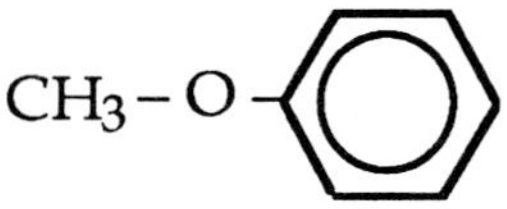

72.   Ethyl alcohol has a higher boiling point than dimethyl ether, even though
      they have the same molecular weight, because the alcohol has stronger
      intermolecular forces resulting from hydrogen bonding.

74. Butanol is only slightly soluble in water because the nonpolar C_xH_y–portion of the molecule is significantly larger than the polar –OH portion.

76. <u>Ether</u> (C_3H_8O)   <u>Alcohol</u> (C_3H_8O)   <u>Alcohol</u> (C_3H_8O)

$$CH_3-CH_2-O-CH_3$$

$$\underset{\underset{OH}{|}}{CH_3-CH-CH_3}$$

$$CH_3-CH_2-CH_2-OH$$

78. $2\,CH_3-OH_{(g)} + 3\,O_{2(g)} \rightarrow 2\,CO_{2(g)} + 4\,H_2O_{(g)}$

80. $2\,CH_3-OH \xrightarrow{\text{Acid}} CH_3-O-CH_3 + H_2O$

Section 20.8 Amines

82.
Amine		Structure
(a)	methyl amine	CH_3-NH_2

(b) isopropyl amine $\underset{\underset{CH_3-CH-CH_3}{}}{\overset{\overset{NH_2}{|}}{}}$

(c) triethylamine $(CH_3CH_2)_3N$

(d) phenyl methyl amine   —NH– CH_3

84. Ethyl amine has a higher boiling point than propane, even though they have approximately the same molecular weight, because ethyl amine molecules have higher intermolecular forces due to hydrogen bonding.

86. $C_6H_5NH_{2(l)} + HCl_{(aq)} \rightarrow C_6H_5NH_3^+{}_{(aq)} + Cl^-{}_{(aq)}$
Aniline is an organic base that is insoluble in water because it is mostly nonpolar. It is soluble in aqueous acid solutions because it undergoes neutralization to form an ionic salt that readily dissolves.

Section 20.9 Aldehydes and Ketones

88.
Aldehyde		Structure

(a) acetaldehyde $\overset{\overset{O}{\parallel}}{CH_3-C}-H$

(b) propionaldehyde $\overset{\overset{O}{\parallel}}{CH_3CH_2-C}-H$

88.   Aldehyde   Structure

    (c)   formaldehyde

$$\overset{\displaystyle O}{\overset{\|}{H-C-H}}$$

    (d)   benzaldehyde

$$\bigcirc\!\!\!\!\bigcirc - \overset{\displaystyle O}{\overset{\|}{C}}-H$$

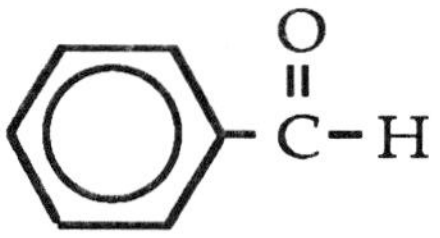

90.   Ketone   Structure

    (a)   methyl ethyl ketone

$$CH_3 - \overset{\displaystyle O}{\overset{\|}{C}} - CH_2CH_3$$

    (b)   diethyl ketone

$$CH_3CH_2 - \overset{\displaystyle O}{\overset{\|}{C}} - CH_2CH_3$$

    (c)   methyl phenyl ketone

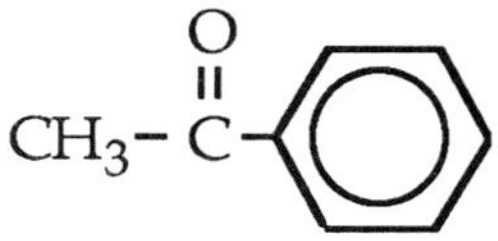

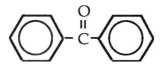

    (d)   diphenyl ketone

$$\bigcirc\!\!\!\!\bigcirc - \overset{\displaystyle O}{\overset{\|}{C}} - \bigcirc\!\!\!\!\bigcirc$$

92.   Solubility in Water
    (a)   aldehydes   insoluble (or slightly soluble)
    (b)   ketones   insoluble (or slightly soluble)

94.   Ketone ($C_6H_5 - C_2H_3O$)   Aldehyde ($C_6H_5 - C_2H_3O$)

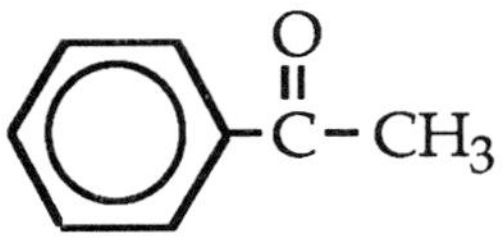

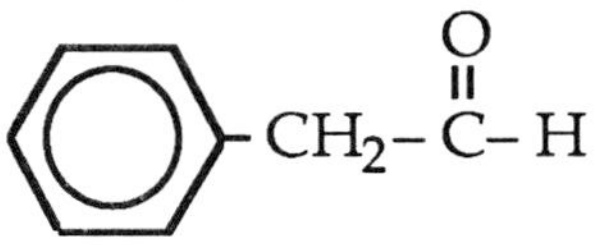

$$\bigcirc\!\!\!\!\bigcirc - \overset{\displaystyle O}{\overset{\|}{C}} - CH_3 \qquad \bigcirc\!\!\!\!\bigcirc - CH_2 - \overset{\displaystyle O}{\overset{\|}{C}} - H$$

Section 20.10 Carboxylic Acids, Esters, and Amides

96.   Carboxylic Acid   Structure

    (a)   acetic acid

$$CH_3 - \overset{\displaystyle O}{\overset{\|}{C}} - OH$$

    (b)   propionic acid

$$CH_3CH_2 - \overset{\displaystyle O}{\overset{\|}{C}} - OH$$

96.   <u>Carboxylic Acid</u>   <u>Structure</u>

   (c)   formic acid

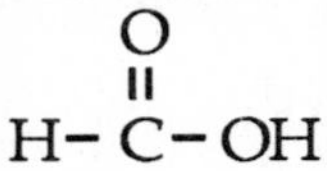

$$H-\overset{\overset{\displaystyle O}{\|}}{C}-OH$$

   (d)   benzoic acid

$$\text{(benzene ring)}-\overset{\overset{\displaystyle O}{\|}}{C}-OH$$

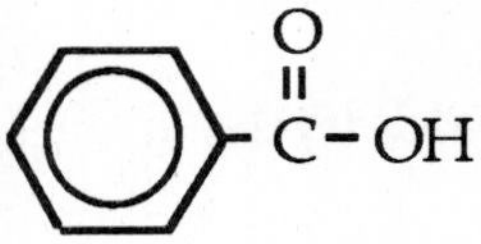

98.   <u>Ester</u>   <u>Structure</u>

   (a)   propyl formate

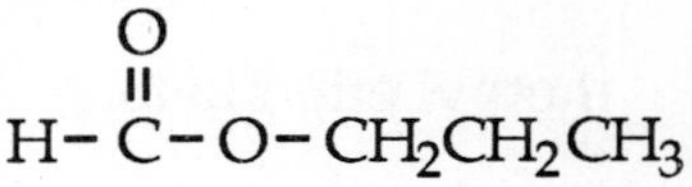

$$H-\overset{\overset{\displaystyle O}{\|}}{C}-O-CH_2CH_2CH_3$$

   (b)   methyl acetate

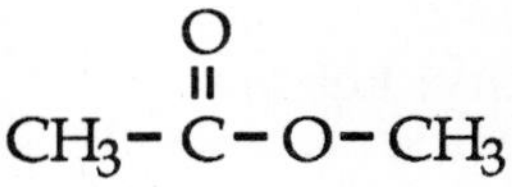

$$CH_3-\overset{\overset{\displaystyle O}{\|}}{C}-O-CH_3$$

   (c)   phenyl propionate

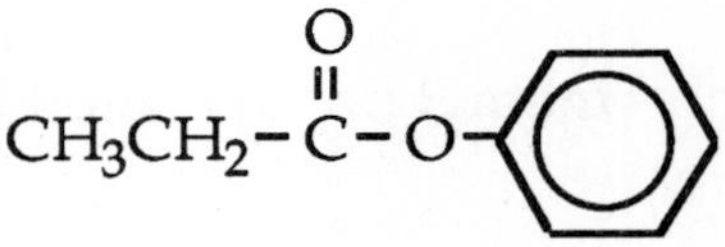

$$CH_3CH_2-\overset{\overset{\displaystyle O}{\|}}{C}-O-\text{(benzene ring)}$$

   (d)   ethyl benzoate

$$\text{(benzene ring)}-\overset{\overset{\displaystyle O}{\|}}{C}-O-CH_2CH_3$$

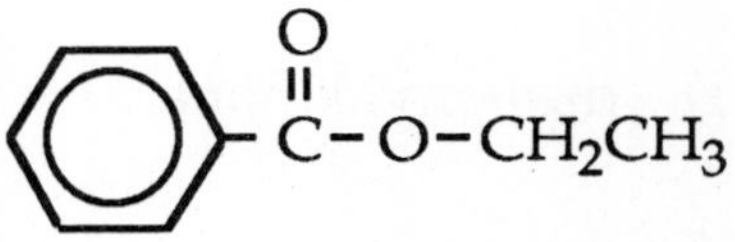

100.   <u>Amide</u>   <u>Structure</u>

   (a)   acetamide

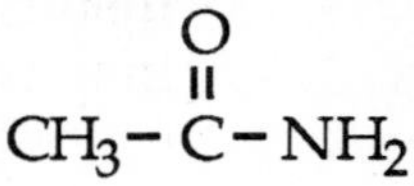

$$CH_3-\overset{\overset{\displaystyle O}{\|}}{C}-NH_2$$

   (b)   methyl acetamide

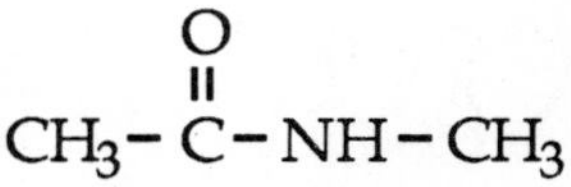

$$CH_3-\overset{\overset{\displaystyle O}{\|}}{C}-NH-CH_3$$

   (c)   dimethyl acetamide

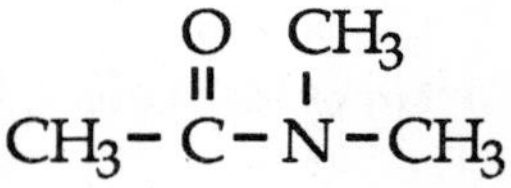

$$CH_3-\overset{\overset{\displaystyle O}{\|}}{C}-\overset{\overset{\displaystyle CH_3}{|}}{N}-CH_3$$

   (d)   phenyl acetamide

$$CH_3-\overset{\overset{\displaystyle O}{\|}}{C}-NH-\text{(benzene ring)}$$

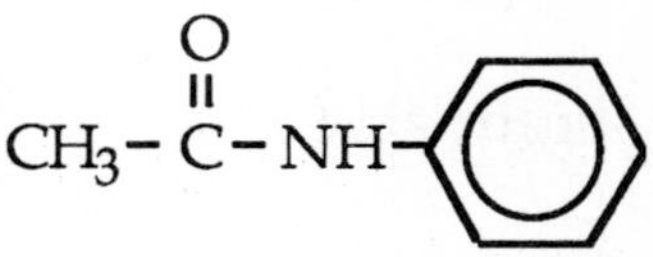

102.   Because esters cannot hydrogen bond, they are generally insoluble in
        water and have lower boiling points than carboxylic acids and amides.

104. <u>Carboxylic Acid</u> ($C_3H_6O_2$) <u>Ester</u> ($C_3H_6O_2$)   <u>Ester</u> ($C_3H_6O_2$)

$$CH_3CH_2-\overset{\displaystyle O}{\overset{\|}{C}}-OH \qquad CH_3-\overset{\displaystyle O}{\overset{\|}{C}}-O-CH_3 \qquad H-\overset{\displaystyle O}{\overset{\|}{C}}-O-CH_2CH_3$$

106. $HCHO + [O] \rightarrow HCOOH$

108. (a)

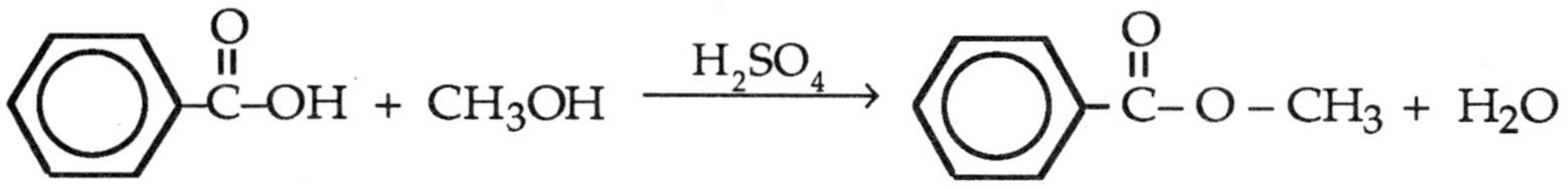

(b)

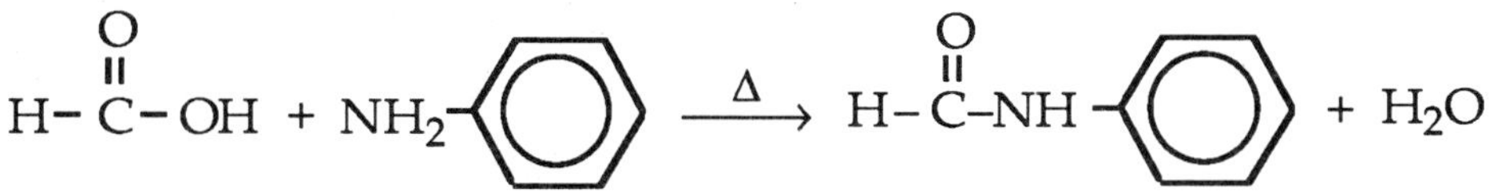

110. (a)
$$CH_3-\overset{\displaystyle O}{\overset{\|}{C}}-OH + HO-CH_3 \rightarrow CH_3-\overset{\displaystyle O}{\overset{\|}{C}}-O-CH_3 + H_2O$$
   acetic acid   methyl alcohol   methyl acetate

(b)
$$H-\overset{\displaystyle O}{\overset{\|}{C}}-OH + HO-CH_2CH_3 \rightarrow H-\overset{\displaystyle O}{\overset{\|}{C}}-O-CH_2CH_3 + H_2O$$
   formic acid   ethyl alcohol   ethyl formate

112. (a)
$$CH_3-\overset{\displaystyle O}{\overset{\|}{C}}-OH + NH_3 \rightarrow CH_3-\overset{\displaystyle O}{\overset{\|}{C}}-NH_2 + H_2O$$
   acetic acid   ammonia   acetamide

(b)

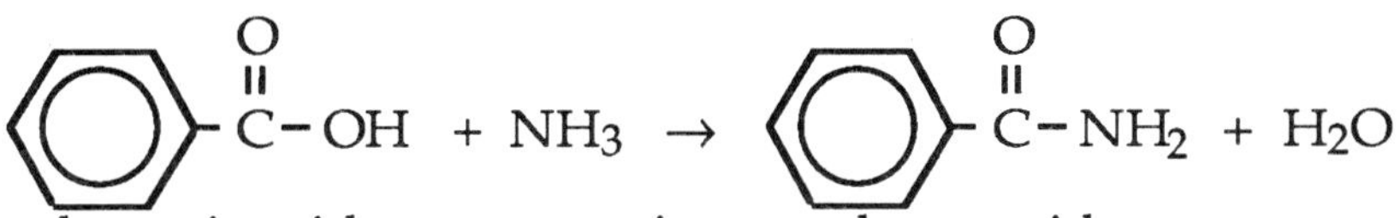

   benzoic acid   ammonia   benzamide

General Exercises

114. The three types of fossil fuels are:
    (1) petroleum
    (2) coal
    (3) natural gas

116. | Hydrocarbon (Incorrectly Named) | IUPAC Name |
|---|---|
| (a) isopropylmethane | 2-methylpropane |
| (b) 2-ethylbutane | 3-methylpentane |

118. | Compounds | Higher Boiling Point |
|---|---|
| (a) $CH_3CH_2CH_2CH_3$ or $CH_3CH_2CH_2OH$ | $CH_3CH_2CH_2OH$ |
| (b) $CH_3CH_2CH_2F$ or $CH_3CH_2CH_2OH$ | $CH_3CH_2CH_2OH$ |
| (c) CH_3-O-CH_3 or CH_3CH_2OH | CH_3CH_2OH |
| (d) $CH_3CH_2CH_3$ or $CH_3CH_2NH_2$ | $CH_3CH_2NH_2$ |
| (e) CH_3COOH or $HCOOCH_3$ | CH_3COOH |
| (f) $CH_3CH_2CONH_2$ or CH_3COOCH_3 | $CH_3CH_2CONH_2$ |

(Note: In each of the above pairs, the compound with the higher boiling point has an $-OH$ or $-NH_2$ group and can hydrogen bond. Hydrogen bonds increase the effective molar mass of the compound and therefore the compound requires more energy—a higher temperature—to escape the liquid state and attain the gaseous state.)

120. | Compound | Classification |
|---|---|
| (a) **chlor**dane | organic halide |
| (b) cortis**one** | ketone |
| (c) acetylsalicyl**ic acid** | carboxylic acid |
| (d) sulfanil**amide** | amide |
| (e) nicot**ine** | amine |
| (f) cres**ol** | phenol (or alcohol) |
| (g) pentyl acet**ate** | ester |
| (h) vinyl **ether** | ether |
| (i) chlor**al** hydrate | aldehyde |
| (j) eth**ynyl** estradi**ol** | alkyne and alcohol |

Chemistry:
Concepts & Connections

Sample Final Examination

Name _____
(LAST,   FIRST,   MI)

Section _____

1. Which of the following instruments is capable of providing an exact measurement?
    (a) electronic balance
    (b) digital stopwatch
    (c) micropipet
    (d) ruby laser
    (e) No instrument is capable of an exact measurement.

2. What is the number of significant digits in 0.0610 liter?
    (a) 1
    (b) 2
    (c) 3
    (d) 4
    (e) 5

3. Add 7.77 g to 11.666 g and round off the sum to the correct significant digits.
    (a) 19.0 g
    (b) 19.4 g
    (c) 19.43 g
    (d) 19.44 g
    (e) 19.436 g

4. Multiply 2.505 cm by 1.75 cm by 1.0 cm and round off the product to the correct significant digits.
    (a) 4 cm^3
    (b) 4.0 cm^3
    (c) 4.4 cm^3
    (d) 4.38 cm^3
    (e) 4.384 cm^3

5. If the radius of a sodium atom is 0.000 000 000 186 meter, what is the atomic radius expressed in scientific notation?
    (a) 1.86×10^{-11} m
    (b) 1.86×10^{-10} m
    (c) 1.86×10^{-9} m
    (d) 1.86×10^{9} m
    (e) 1.86×10^{10} m

6. According to the metric system, 1 m = 10^9 _____.
    (a) dm
    (b) Mm
    (c) km
    (d) nm
    (e) μm

7. If a pair of skis is 175 cm long, what is the length in decimeters?
    (a) 1.75 dm
    (b) 17.5 dm
    (c) 175 dm
    (d) 1750 dm
    (e) 17,500 dm

8. If 6.02×10^{23} atoms of gold have a mass of 197 g, what is the mass of gold in pounds? (1 lb = 454 g)
    (a) 0.208 lb
    (b) 0.434 lb
    (c) 197 lb
    (d) 89,400 lb
    (e) 186,000 lb

9. A glass cylinder contains four separate liquid layers: mercury (d = 13.6 g/mL), chloroform (d = 1.49 g/mL), water (d = 1.00 g/mL), and ether (d = 0.708 g/mL). If a rubber stopper (d = 1.3 g/mL) is dropped into the glass cylinder, where does it come to rest?
    (a) on the bottom of the cylinder
    (b) on top of the mercury layer
    (c) on top of the chloroform layer
    (d) on top of the water layer
    (e) on top of the ether layer

10. If liquid nitrogen boils at –196°C, what is the boiling point on the Kelvin scale?
    (a) –469 K
    (b) –196 K
    (c) –77 K
    (d) 77 K
    (e) 196 K

11. Which of the following elements is **not** one of the ten most abundant in the earth's crust, oceans, and atmosphere?
    (a) carbon
    (b) oxygen
    (c) aluminum
    (d) iron
    (e) silicon

12. Which of the following is **not** a general property of a metallic element?
    (a) malleable and ductile
    (b) conductor of heat and electricity
    (c) high melting point and high density
    (d) reacts by gaining electrons
    (e) reacts with nonmetallic elements

13. Which of the following elements is an example of a semimetal?
    (a) H
    (b) C
    (c) Fe
    (d) Sn
    (e) Te

14. How many atoms are in one molecule of vitamin C, $C_3H_4OH(COOH)_3$?
    (a) 10
    (b) 12
    (c) 15
    (d) 21
    (e) 39

15. Which of the following is a physical change and **not** a chemical change?
    (a) Sugar charring to a black residue.
    (b) Dry Ice sublimating to carbon dioxide gas.
    (c) Gasoline burning to give carbon dioxide and water.
    (d) Silver precipitating from an aqueous silver nitrate solution.
    (e) A mixture of hydrogen and oxygen gases exploding to give water vapor.

16. What scientist established the nuclear model of the atom by discovering that alpha particles were scattered by a thin gold foil?
    (a) James Chadwick
    (b) William Crookes
    (c) John Dalton
    (d) Ernest Rutherford
    (e) J.J. Thomson

17. How many neutrons are in an isotope of gold–197?
    (a) 79
    (b) 118
    (c) 197
    (d) 276
    (e) none of the above

18. Which of the following isotopes is deflected more than carbon–12 in the magnetic field of a mass spectrometer?
    (a) $^{4}_{2}He$
    (b) $^{16}_{8}O$
    (c) $^{20}_{10}Ne$
    (d) $^{55}_{26}Fe$
    (e) $^{238}_{92}U$

19. What atomic event is responsible for the emission line spectra of the elements?
    (a) atoms of the same element reacting
    (b) atoms of different elements reacting
    (c) electrons dropping to lower quantum levels
    (d) electrons jumping to higher quantum levels
    (e) electrons being captured by the nucleus

20. Which element is described by the following electron configuration:
$$1s^2\ 2s^2\ 2p^6\ 3s^2\ 3p^6\ 4s^2\ 3d^5\ 4p^6\ 5s^2\ 4d^{10}\ 5^6\ 6s^2\ 5d^1?$$
    (a) Th
    (b) Y
    (c) Ce
    (d) La
    (e) none of the above

21. Which of the following elements is the alkaline earth metal with the smallest atomic radius?
    (a) H
    (b) Li
    (c) Be
    (d) Fr
    (e) Ra

22. Predict the formula for gallium oxide, given the following chemical formulas: Na_2O, MgO, Al_2O_3.
    (a) GaO
    (b) Ga_2O
    (c) Ga_2O_3
    (d) GaO_3
    (e) Ga_3O_2

23. Which energy sublevel is being filled by the elements Th through Lr?
    (a) $6d$
    (b) $7d$
    (c) $4f$
    (d) $5f$
    (e) $6f$

24. Predict the number of valence electrons for an atom of sulfur by referring to the periodic table.
    (a) 2
    (b) 6
    (c) 8
    (d) 16
    (e) 32

25. Predict which group of elements in the periodic table has the highest ionization energy.
    (a) IA/1
    (b) IIA/2
    (c) IIIA/13
    (d) VIIA/17
    (e) VIIIA/18

26. What is the formula for aluminum bromide, a binary ionic compound?
    (a) $AlBr$
    (b) $AlBr_2$
    (c) $AlBr_3$
    (d) Al_3Br_2
    (e) Al_2Br_3

27. What is the Stock system name for Cu_3N_2 according to IUPAC nomenclature?
    (a) copper(I) nitride
    (b) copper(I) nitrite
    (c) copper(II) nitride
    (d) copper(II) nitrite
    (e) copper(III) nitride

28. What is the formula for ferrous sulfate, a ternary ionic compound?
    (a) $FeSO_3$
    (b) $FeSO_4$
    (c) $Fe(SO_3)_2$
    (d) $Fe(SO_4)_2$
    (e) $Fe_3(SO_4)_2$

29. What is the systematic name for the binary molecular compound P_2O_5?
    (a) phosphorus pentaoxide
    (b) diphosphorus oxide
    (c) diphosphorus pentaoxide
    (d) diphosphorus dioxide
    (e) pentaphosphorus dioxide

30. What is the formula for aqueous sulfuric acid (battery acid)?
    (a) $H_2S(aq)$
    (b) $HSO_3(aq)$
    (c) $HSO_4(aq)$
    (d) $H_2SO_3(aq)$
    (e) $H_2SO_4(aq)$

31. What is the mass of 3.30×10^{23} atoms of silver?
     (a)   1.97 g
     (b)   5.91 g
     (c)   59.1 g
     (d)   197 g
     (e)   356 g

32. The first noble gas compound, $XePtF_6$, was synthesized in 1962 at the University of British Columbia. What was the percentage of fluorine in the compound?
     (a)   4.31%
     (b)   5.50%
     (c)   25.9%
     (d)   29.8%
     (e)   44.3%

33. What is the volume of 4.80×10^{22} molecules of methane gas, CH_4, at STP?
     (a)   1.79 L
     (b)   2.81 L
     (c)   17.9 L
     (d)   179 L
     (e)   281 L

34. What is the density of nitrogen gas, N_2, at STP?
     (a)   0.510 g/L
     (b)   0.800 g/L
     (c)   1.00 g/L
     (d)   1.25 g/L
     (e)   2.24 g/L

35. If 1.00 liter of Freon–12 gas at STP has a mass of 5.40 grams, what is the molar mass of the compound?
     (a)   4.15 g/mol
     (b)   5.40 g/mol
     (c)   22.4 g/mol
     (d)   64.8 g/mol
     (e)   121 g/mol

36. What is the formula of the product obtained from heating magnesium metal in the presence of oxygen gas?
     (a) MgO
     (b) Mg_2O
     (c) MgO_2
     (d) Mg_2O_3
     (e) Mg_3O_2

37. What are the formulas of the products obtained from the reaction of acetic acid and aqueous sodium hydroxide?
    (a) $NaC_2H_3O_2(aq)$ and $H_2O(l)$
    (b) $Na_2C_2H_3O_2(aq)$ and $H_2O(l)$
    (c) $Na(C_2H_3O_2)_2(aq)$ and $H_2O(l)$
    (d) $NaHCO_3(aq)$ and $H_2O(l)$
    (e) $Na_2CO_3(aq)$ and $H_2O(l)$

38. Which of the following metals reacts with aqueous aluminum nitrate?
    Partial activity series: $Mg > Al > Zn > Co > Ag$
    (a) Mg
    (b) Al
    (c) Zn
    (d) Mg and Zn
    (e) Zn, Co, and Ag

39. After balancing the following equation, what is the coefficient of oxygen?

$$\_\_\_C_2H_6(g) + \_\_\_O_2(g) \rightarrow \_\_\_CO_2(g) + \_\_\_H_2O(g)$$

    (a) 1
    (b) 3
    (c) 5
    (d) 7
    (e) 10

40. After balancing the following equation, what is the coefficient of hydrogen?

$$\_\_\_Ca(s) + \_\_\_H_2O(l) \rightarrow \_\_\_Ca(OH)_2(aq) + \_\_\_H_2(g)$$

    (a) 0
    (b) 1
    (c) 2
    (d) 3
    (e) 6

41. According to the following equation, how many moles of oxygen gas react with 10.0 moles of propane gas, C_3H_8?

$$\_\_\_C_3H_8(g) + \_\_\_O_2(g) \rightarrow \_\_\_CO_2(g) + \_\_\_H_2O(g)$$

    (a) 2.00 mol
    (b) 10.0 mol
    (c) 30.0 mol
    (d) 40.0 mol
    (e) 50.0 mol

42. According to the following equation, how many moles of carbon dioxide are produced from the combustion of 2.50 moles of pentane, C_5H_{12}?

$$\_\_\_C_5H_{12}(g) \; + \; \_\_\_O_2(g) \;\; \rightarrow \;\; \_\_\_CO_2(g) \; + \; \_\_\_H_2O(g)$$

(a) 0.500 mol
(b) 0.833 mol
(c) 2.50 mol
(d) 7.50 mol
(e) 12.5 mol

43. If 0.170 g of silver nitrate (169.9 g/mol) reacts with aqueous calcium bromide, what is the mass of insoluble silver bromide (187.8 g/mol)?

$$\_\_\_AgNO_3(s) \; + \_\_\_CaBr_2(aq) \;\; \rightarrow \;\; \_\_\_AgBr(s) \; + \_\_\_Ca(NO_3)_2(aq)$$

(a) 0.0939 g
(b) 0.108 g
(c) 0.170 g
(d) 0.188 g
(e) 0.376 g

44. How many liters of hydrogen gas is produced at STP from the reaction of 2.70 g of aluminum and excess hydrochloric acid?

$$\_\_\_Al(s) \; + \_\_\_HCl(aq) \;\; \rightarrow \;\; \_\_\_AlCl_3(aq) \; + \_\_\_H_2(g)$$

(a) 1.12 L
(b) 1.49 L
(c) 2.24 L
(d) 3.36 L
(e) 6.72 L

45. If 20.0 L of oxygen gas react with excess ammonia gas, what is the volume of nitrogen monoxide gas produced? (Assume constant conditions.)

$$\_\_\_NH_3(g) \; + \_\_\_O_2(g) \;\; \rightarrow \;\; \_\_\_NO(g) \; + \_\_\_H_2O(l)$$

(a) 16.0 L
(b) 20.0 L
(c) 22.4 L
(d) 25.0 L
(e) 40.0 L

46. According to quantum theory, how many quanta are emitted when a single electron drops from the 5th to the 1st quantum level?
    (a) 1
    (b) 2
    (c) 3
    (d) 4
    (e) 6.02×10^{23}

47. In the quantum mechanical model of the atom, how many subshells can exist within the fourth shell?
    (a) 2
    (b) 3
    (c) 4
    (d) 5
    (e) 10

48. How many orbitals can exist within the 4*d* subshell?
    (a) 2
    (b) 3
    (c) 4
    (d) 5
    (e) 10

49. What is the maximum number of electrons that can be found in a 4*d* orbital?
    (a) 2
    (b) 3
    (c) 4
    (d) 5
    (e) 10

50. What is the shape of a 4*s* orbital?
    (a) circle
    (b) sphere
    (c) dumbbell
    (d) wave
    (e) none of the above

51. Which of the following statements is **not** correct regarding the formation of an ionic bond from potassium and fluorine?
    (a) Potassium loses valence electrons and fluorine gains valence electrons.
    (b) The potassium atom is larger in radius than the potassium ion.
    (c) The fluorine atom is smaller in radius than the fluoride ion.
    (d) Potassium and potassium fluoride have similar properties.
    (e) The bond formation from potassium and fluoride ions releases energy.

52. Which of the following does **not** occur naturally as a diatomic gas molecule?
    (a) argon
    (b) chlorine
    (c) fluorine
    (d hydrogen
    (e) oxygen

53. Using delta notation which of the following illustrates the bond polarity in a molecule of carbon monoxide, CO?
    (a) δ^+ C—O δ^+
    (b) δ^+ C—O δ^-
    (c) δ^- C—O δ^+
    (d) δ^- C—O δ^-
    (e) none of the above

54. What is the number of nonbonding electrons in an ammonia, NH_3, molecule?
    (a) 0
    (b) 1
    (c) 2
    (d) 4
    (e) 8

55. What is the number of bonding electron pairs in a nitrogen, N_2, molecule?
    (a) 1
    (b) 2
    (c) 3
    (d) 5
    (e) 7

56. Which one of the following is responsible for the liquid rising when you drink through a straw?
    (a) atmospheric pressure
    (b) kinetic energy
    (c) suction
    (d) vacuum
    (e) vapor pressure

57. The vapor pressure of mercury is 1 mm Hg at 126°C; 10 mm Hg at 184°C; 400 mm Hg at 323°C; 100 mm Hg at 262°C; 760 mm Hg at 357°C. What is the normal boiling point temperature for mercury?
    (a) 126°C
    (b) 184°C
    (c) 262°C
    (d) 323°C
    (e) 357°C

58. A sample of argon gas at STP has a volume of 1.00 L. What is the new pressure if the volume and Kelvin temperature are each doubled?
    (a) 0.250 atm
    (b) 0.500 atm
    (c) 1.00 atm
    (d   2.00 atm
    (e) 4.00 atm

59. If a sample of helium gas occupies a volume of 5.00 L at 500 K and 5.00 atm, how many moles of helium are in the sample? ($R = 0.0821$ atm $\cdot$ L/mol $\cdot$ K)
    (a) 0.609 mol
    (b) 1.64 mol
    (c) 5.00 mol
    (d) 25.0 mol
    (e) 6090 mol

60. Which of the following is **not true** of an ideal gas according to the kinetic theory of gases?
    (a) gas molecules occupy a negligible volume
    (b) gas molecules move randomly in straight line paths
    (c) gas molecules are not attracted to one another
    (d) gas molecules at the same temperature have the same kinetic energy
    (e) gas molecules lose energy when they collide

61. Which of the following is the strongest force of attraction between molecules in the liquid state?
    (a) dispersion forces
    (b) dipole forces
    (c) hydrogen bonds
    (d) London forces
    (e) all intermolecular forces are the same

62. Which of the following are types of crystalline solids?
    (a) ionic
    (b) molecular
    (c) metallic
    (d) all of the above
    (e) none of the above

63. What is the term for the heat required to convert a substance from the solid state to the liquid state at its melting point?
    (a) heat of fusion
    (b) heat of solidification
    (c) heat of vaporization
    (d) heat of condensation
    (e) specific heat

64. What are the products from the reaction of sodium metal and water?
    (a) $Na_2O + H_2$
    (b) $Na_2O + H_2O_2$
    (c) $NaOH + H_2$
    (d) $NaOH + H_2O$
    (e) $NaOH + H_2O_2$

65. Which of the following metal ions is found in soft water?
    (a) calcium ion
    (b) iron ion
    (c) magnesium ion
    (d) mercury ion
    (e) sodium ion

66. Soft drinks are carbonated by injection with carbon dioxide gas. What conditions favor the greatest amount of carbonation in the soft drink?
    (a) high temperature, high pressure
    (b) low temperature, low pressure
    (c) low temperature, high pressure
    (d) high temperature, low pressure
    (e) low temperature, pressure is not a factor

67. Predict which of the following liquids is **immiscible** with water by using the *like dissolves like* rule?
    (a) heptane, C_7H_{16}
    (b) acetic acid, CH_3–$COOH$
    (c) acetone, CH_3–CO–CH_3
    (d) ethanol, CH_3–CH_2–OH
    (e) isopropyl alcohol, C_3H_7OH

68. Which of the following **increases** the rate of dissolving for a solid substance in water?
    (a) grinding the solute
    (b) heating the solution
    (c) stirring the solution
    (d) all of the above
    (e) none of the above

69. A solution of sodium hydroxide is prepared using 10.0 g of NaOH solute. If the concentration of the solution is 12.5% NaOH, what is the mass of the solution?
    (a) 1.25 g
    (b) 8.00 g
    (c) 70.0 g
    (d) 80.0 g
    (e) 125 g

70. A 100.0 mL sample of normal saline solution was evaporated to dryness and the NaCl residue weighed 0.900 g. Find the molarity of the saline solution.
    (a) 0.154 M
    (b) 0.527 M
    (c) 1.54 M
    (d) 1.90 M
    (e) 5.27 M

71. Which of the following is **not** a general property of an acid?
    (a) tastes sour
    (b) feels soapy or slippery
    (c) turns blue litmus paper red
    (d) reacts with bases to produce water
    (e) reacts with metals to produce hydrogen gas

72. Which of the following is an example of an Arrhenius acid?
    (a) H_2CO_3(aq)
    (b) $NaC_2H_3O_2$(aq)
    (c) $NaNO_3$aq)
    (d) NaOH(aq)
    (e) H_2O(l)

73. Which of the following best explains why water is neutral?
    (a) Water reacts with acids and bases.
    (b) Water has no ions.
    (c) Water has no hydrogen ions.
    (d) Water has no hydroxide ions.
    (e) Water has an equal concentration of hydrogen and hydroxide ions.

74. What is the pH of a sample having a 0.0001 M hydrogen ion concentration?
    (a) 0
    (b) 1
    (c) 3
    (d) 4
    (e) 10

75. If an ammonia solution is observed to be a weak conductor of electricity, what can you conclude?
    (a) The solution is highly ionized.
    (b) The solution is slightly ionized.
    (c) The solution is highly reactive.
    (d) The solution is slightly reactive.
    (e) The solution does not contain any ions.

76. Which of the following is a factor that influences the rate of a reaction?
    (a) reactivity of reactants
    (b) concentration of reactants
    (c) temperature
    (d) catalyst
    (e) all of the above

77. Which of the following is true for a chemical reaction if the activation energy is lowered?
    (a) The rate of reaction increases.
    (b) The rate of reaction decreases.
    (c) The heat of reaction increases.
    (d) The heat of reaction decreases.
    (e) The amount of product increases.

78. What is the equilibrium constant expression, K_{eq}, for the following reaction?

$$N_2(g) + 3 H_2(g) \leftrightarrow 2 NH_3(g) + heat$$

    (a) $K_{eq} = [NH_3] / [N_2] [H_2]$
    (b) $K_{eq} = [NH_3]^2 / [N_2] [H_2]$
    (c) $K_{eq} = [NH_3]^2 / [N_2] [H_2]^3$
    (d) $K_{eq} = [NH_3] / [N_2] [H_2]^3$
    (e) $K_{eq} = [NH_3]^2 / [N_2]^2 [H_2]^3$

79. Which of the changes listed below for the following reaction would shift the gaseous equilibrium to the right?

$$H_2(g) + I_2(g) + heat \leftrightarrow 2 HI(g)$$

    (a) adding argon atoms
    (b) increasing temperature
    (c) increasing the volume of the reaction vessel
    (d) increasing HI concentration
    (e) adding a catalyst

80. The hydrogen ion concentration of a 0.100 M $HC_2H_3O_2$ solution is 0.00133 M. Calculate the ionization constant for acetic acid.
    (a) $K_i = 1.33 \times 10^{-2}$
    (b) $K_i = 1.33 \times 10^{-4}$
    (c) $K_i = 1.77 \times 10^{-4}$
    (d) $K_i = 1.77 \times 10^{-5}$
    (e) $K_i = 1.77 \times 10^{-6}$

81. Calculate the oxidation number for carbon in sodium oxalate, $Na_2C_2O_4$.
    (a) −2
    (b) +2
    (c) +3
    (d) −4
    (e) +4

82. After balancing the following redox equation, what is the coefficient of water?

$$\_H^+(aq) + \_Ag(s) + \_NO_3^-(aq) \rightarrow \_Ag^+(aq) + \_NO(aq) + \_H_2O(l)$$

    (a) 1
    (b) 2
    (c) 3
    (d) 4
    (e) 6

83. In question #82, which species is oxidized?
    (a) H^+
    (b) Ag
    (c) Ag^+
    (d) NO
    (e) NO_3^-

84. In question #82, which species is the oxidizing agent?
    (a) H^+
    (b) Ag
    (c) Ag^+
    (d) NO
    (e) NO_3^-

85. Given that the following redox reactions go essentially to completion, which metal is placed highest in the activity series?

$$Fe + Ni^{2+} \rightarrow Ni + Fe^{2+}$$
$$Sn + Cu^{2+} \rightarrow Cu + Sn^{2+}$$
$$Zn + Fe^{2+} \rightarrow Fe + Zn^{2+}$$
$$Ni + Sn^{2+} \rightarrow Sn + Ni^{2+}$$

    (a) Ni
    (b) Sn
    (c) Zn
    (d) Fe
    (e) Cu

86. A combustion analysis of acetylene gave the following elemental composition: 92.3% carbon and 7.7% hydrogen. Find the empirical formula for acetylene.
    (a) CH
    (b) CH_2
    (c) CH_8
    (d) C_8H_8
    (e) $C_{12}H$

87. The amino acid lysine has the empirical formula C_3H_7NO. Calculate the molecular formula of lysine if the molar mass is approximately 146 g/mol.
    (a) $C_3H_7N_1O$
    (b) $C_3H_7NO_2$
    (c) $C_6H_{14}NO_2$
    (d) $C_6H_{14}N_2O_2$
    (e) $C_6H_{14}N_2O_4$

88. If 3.00 L of sulfur dioxide is allowed to react with 3.00 L of oxygen gas, what is the volume of sulfur trioxide produced? (Assume conditions are constant.)

$$\_\_SO_2(g) \ + \ \_\_O_2(g) \ \xrightarrow{\Delta} \ \_\_SO_3(g)$$

    (a) 2.00 L
    (b) 3.00 L
    (c) 4.00 L
    (d) 5.00 L
    (e) 6.00 L

89. If 25.0 mL of 0.100 M sodium chloride is added to 50.0 mL of 0.100 M calcium chloride, what is the resulting chloride ion concentration?
    (a) 0.0667 M
    (b) 0.0833 M
    (c) 0.100 M
    (d) 0.167 M
    (e) 0.333 M

90. What is the molar mass of an unknown gas if 5.45 g occupies a volume of 4.75 L at 1500 K and 5.00 atm pressure? (R = 0.0821 atm · L/mol · K)
    (a) 21.5 g/mol
    (b) 23.8 g/mol
    (c) 28.3 g/mol
    (d) 141 g/mol
    (e) 344 g/mol

91. What type of nuclear radiation has a negative charge, a velocity which is 90% the speed of light and can penetrate heavy clothing?
    (a) alpha
    (b) beta
    (c) gamma
    (d) neutron
    (e) positron

92. If iron–59 has a half-life of 45 days, how long will it take for a sample of Fe–59 to drop from 240 to 30 disintegrations per minute?
    (a) 45 days
    (b) 90 days
    (c) 135 days
    (d) 210 days
    (e) 360 days

93. Which of the following particles is emitted when fluorine–20 radioactively decays into neon–20?
    (a) an alpha particle
    (b) a beta particle
    (c) a deuteron
    (d) a neutron
    (e) a positron

94. In 1982, German physicists smashed an iron–58 nucleus into a single atom of bismuth–209. A computer confirmed that an atom of a new element (X) had been synthesized but existed only 5 milliseconds. According to the equation for the reaction, what was the new element?

$$^{209}_{83}Bi \ + \ ^{58}_{26}Fe \ \rightarrow \ X \ + \ ^{1}_{0}n$$

    (a) element 106
    (b) element 107
    (c) element 108
    (d) element 109
    (e) element 110

95. If the fusion reaction of two deuterium atoms, $^{2}_{1}H$, produces a neutron and another particle, what is the other particle?
    (a) $^{1}_{1}H$
    (b) $^{2}_{1}H$
    (c) $^{3}_{1}H$
    (d) $^{3}_{2}He$
    (e) $^{4}_{2}He$

96. Which of the following molecular formulas corresponds to nonane?
   (a) C_5H_{12}
   (b) C_6H_{14}
   (c) C_7H_{16}
   (d) C_8H_{18}
   (e) C_9H_{20}

97. How many different structural isomers have the molecular formula C_5H_{12}?
   (a) 2
   (b) 3
   (c) 4
   (d) 5
   (e) 6

98. What is the IUPAC systematic name for $CH_3–CH_2–CH = CH_2$?
   (a) 1–butene
   (b) 3–butene
   (c) 1–butane
   (d) 3–butane
   (e) 1–butyne

99. Which functional group listed below is present in the following structure?

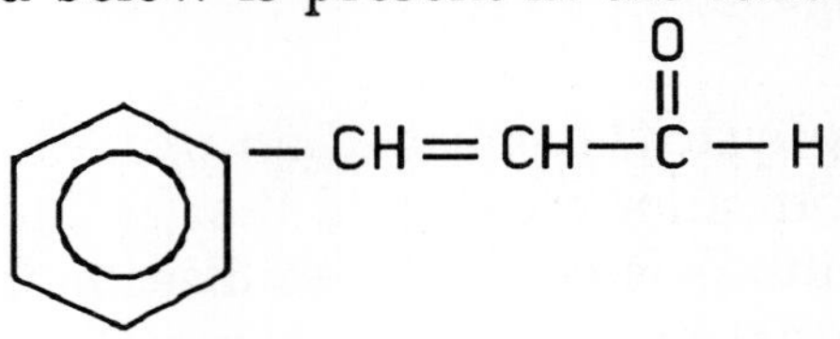

   (a) alcohol
   (b) aldehyde
   (c) amine
   (d) ester
   (e) ketone

100. Which functional group listed below is **not** present in the following structure that represents thyroxine (thyroid hormone)?

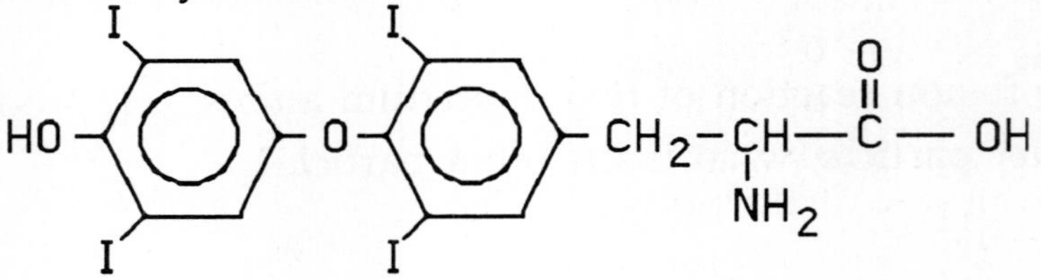

   (a) amide
   (b) carboxylic acid
   (c) ether
   (d) organic halide
   (e) phenol

101. (optional) Which of the following scientists established the conservation of mass law and is generally considered to be the founder of modern chemistry?
    (a) Svante Arrhenius
    (b) Robert Boyle
    (c) Antoine Lavoisier
    (d) G. N. Lewis
    (e) Dmitri Mendeleev

102. (optional) Which of the following ions in drinking water prevents tooth decay?
    (a) chloride ion
    (b) fluoride ion
    (c) hydrogen ion
    (d) hydroxide ion
    (e) sodium ion

103. (optional) Which of the following gases in the upper atmosphere shields the earth from high-energy ultraviolet radiation?
    (a) CO_2
    (b) NO_2
    (c) N_2O_4
    (d) SO_2
    (e) O_3

104. (optional) The *greenhouse effect* refers to a gradual increase in the earth's temperature as a result of trapping heat energy from the sun. Which of the following gases is most responsible for global warming?
    (a) CO_2
    (b) NO_2
    (c) N_2O_4
    (d) SO_2
    (e) O_3

105. (optional) Which of the following atmospheric pollutants contributes to acid rain?
    (a) oxides of carbon
    (b) oxides of nitrogen
    (c) oxides of sulfur
    (d) all of the above
    (e) none of the above

Answers to Final Examination

1. (e)	2. (c)	3. (d)	4. (c)	5. (b)
6. (d)	7. (b)	8. (b)	9. (c)	10. (d)
11. (a)	12. (d)	13. (e)	14. (d)	15. (b)
16. (d)	17. (b)	18. (a)	19. (c)	20. (d)
21. (c)	22. (c)	23. (d)	24. (b)	25. (e)
26. (c)	27. (c)	28. (b)	29. (c)	30. (e)
31. (c)	32. (c)	33. (a)	34. (d)	35. (e)
36. (a)	37. (a)	38. (a)	39. (d)	40. (b)
41. (e)	42. (e)	43. (d)	44. (d)	45. (a)
46. (a)	47. (c)	48. (d)	49. (a)	50. (b)
51. (d)	52. (a)	53. (b)	54. (c)	55. (c)
56. (a)	57. (e)	58. (c)	59. (a)	60. (e)
61. (c)	62. (d)	63. (a)	64. (c)	65. (e)
66. (c)	67. (a)	68. (d)	69. (d)	70. (c)
71. (b)	72. (a)	73. (e)	74. (d)	75. (b)
76. (e)	77. (a)	78. (c)	79. (b)	80. (d)
81. (c)	82. (b)	83. (b)	84. (e)	85. (c)
86. (a)	87. (d)	88. (b)	89. (d)	90. (c)
91. (b)	92. (c)	93. (b)	94. (d)	95. (d)
96. (e)	97. (b)	98. (a)	99. (b)	100. (a)
101. (c)	102. (b)	103. (e)	104. (a)	105. (d)